Ledbury

people and parish

before the Reformation

To James,
Thank you for your
help and advice,

Best wishes,

Sylvia Pick

28 iv 2010

An England's Past for Everyone paperback

Other titles in this series:

Bristol: Ethnic Minorities and the City 1000-2001

Bolsover: Castle, Town and Colliery

Burford: Buildings and People in a Cotswold Town

Codford: Wool and War in Wiltshire

Cornwall and the Coast: Mousehole and Newlyn

Cornwall and the Cross: Christianity 500-1560

Exmoor: The Making of an English Upland

Hardwick: A Great House and its Estate

Henley-on-Thames: Town, Trade and River

Ledbury: A Market Town and its Tudor Heritage

The Medway Valley: A Kent Landscape Transformed

Parham: An Elizabethan House and its Restoration

Sunderland and its Origins: Monks to Mariners

Sunderland: Building a City

Ledbury

people and parish
before the Reformation

SYLVIA PINCHES

with contributions from
Nigel Baker, Janet Cooper and Keith Ray

Phillimore

First published 2010

A Victoria County History publication
Published by Phillimore & Co. Ltd, Madam Green Farm Business Centre,
Oving, Chichester, West Sussex, England in association with the Institute of
Historical Research at the University of London.
www.phillimore.co.uk

ISBN 978-1-86077-614-4

British Library Cataloguing in Publication Data. A cataloguing record for this
book is available from the British Library.

Typeset in Humanist 521 and Minion

We wish particularly to thank the following EPE and VCH staff for their efforts
during the production of this volume:

John Beckett – Director of the Victoria County History
Matthew Bristow – Historic Environment Research Manager
Sarah Byrne – Production Assistant
Catherine Cavanagh – Project Manager
Jessica Davies – Publications Manager
Skye Dillon – Education and Skills Manager
Nafisa Gaffar – Finance and Contracts Officer
Mel Hackett – Communications Manager
Nick Hall – Administrator
Dmitri Nemchenko – Web Manager
Alan Thacker – Executive Editor of the Victoria County History
Elizabeth Williamson – Architectural Editor of the Victoria County History

Printed and bound in Great Britain
Manufacturing managed by Jellyfish Solutions Ltd

Front Cover: This view from the top of the church tower illustrates many of the
key topics covered in this book. Looking westwards over the productive Leadon
valley, one sees the Marcle Ridge on the horizon. In the middle distance on the
right an Iron-Age hillfort nestles in the woods of Wall Hills. The core of medieval
Ledbury is in the foreground, the narrow Church Lane linking churchyard and
market place. The timber-framed building at bottom left is the former vicarage
house. Image courtesy of English Heritage (Mike Hesketh Roberts).

Back Cover: Hugh Foliot, bishop of Hereford and founder of St Katherine's
Hospital, Ledbury in 1232. This late 16th-century imagined portrait once hung
in the parlour of the Master's house. It was lost for many years and is now on
display in the chapel of the Hospital (University of London).

Contents

Foreword   vi
Preface   viii

1. **Introducing Leadon Land**   1

2. **Settlement to AD600**   5

3. **Church and Parish to 1300**   29

4. **Growth of the Borough**   49

5. **Town Life, 1200-1500**   73

6. **Woods and Fields**   93

7. **Spiritual Life**   115

8. **A Time of Change**   137

   Abbreviations used in the Endnotes   155
   Endnotes   155
   Bibliography   171
   Index   175
   Picture Credits   182

Foreword

Ledbury: People and Parish Before the Reformation contributes to
the history of Herefordshire, which is itself valuable because the
county's past is not as thoroughly researched or as well known as
it deserves. We think of it now as a quiet rural county, which lacks
major industry and commerce. It was once a bulwark on England's
western frontier, and it was rich because it produced much wheat
and cattle, and some of the best wool in Europe. New ideas and
technologies came from Herefordshire, notably in horticulture,
in the early modern centuries. In the middle ages it had eleven
urban centres, and Hereford itself ranked near to the twentieth
place in the league tables of English towns measured by their size
and wealth.

This is a book about one of England's 600 medieval small
towns. Ledbury can be compared with many other similar places
scattered across the country. It has a number of typical features:
before it became a town, it was a settlement at the centre of
a landed estate, and from the eighth to the 11th century the
inhabitants were served by a rich minster church. Its streets
were planned by the bishop of Hereford (who was lord of the
manor) in the 12th century, and it grew by about 1300 to have a
population of a thousand. Among these people were many traders
and craftsmen, who pursued a variety of occupations. It was
provided with a Booth Hall, a hospital, and a grammar school, and
people from the surrounding countryside were attracted by the
market, entertainment, religious ceremonial and opportunities for
education and employment.

Every town is different, however, and Ledbury has some unusual
features. Now visitors walk up from the still busy market place
along Church Lane and find themselves in the apparently separate
world of the church and its surrounding buildings and spaces.
This site on the edge of the town has been compared to a cathedral
close, and here was the church itself, with its detached tower,
residences for the clergy, their gardens, ponds and other amenities,
and nearby (probably) the bishop's house. This ecclesiastical island
contained a group of clergy, including two 'portionaries' who
shared the income which would in most churches have rewarded
a single rector. Briefly in the 1320s a recluse, Katherine de Audley,
took up residence and has stimulated a rich vein of modern
legend. Throughout the middle ages this clerical enclave was not

really cut off from the town, but tied to it through many contacts and interactions.

Readers both from Herefordshire and elsewhere are informed by Dr Pinches and her collaborators about the various methods of research, which ought to stimulate others to employ similar techniques elsewhere. Ledbury has some important and useful written records, but they are not very abundant, and many valuable insights have come from the material evidence. The original boundaries and street pattern have been reconstructed from later maps, and the dimensions of the modern properties have been measured to reveal the plots laid out by 12th-century surveyors. The church building has been the subject of stone-by-stone recording in the expectation of revealing phases of construction. The results of various small excavations carried out by professional archaeologists in the course of the planning process have been supplemented by the digging of test pits (now known as community archaeology) to provide a distribution map of dated medieval pottery in the town. The tree rings of building timbers have been analysed to date houses. Out in the country aerial photographs throw light on early settlement. Woods have been surveyed to reveal boundary banks, and woodland management has been investigated. The lavish illustrations of this book are not being reproduced merely as decoration, but as visual evidence to enhance the meaning of the text.

The book's explanation of the street plan and buildings means that the town which is now visible and familiar can be connected with its past, going back more than 800 years. Anyone who knows the town will see it with a new understanding, and visitors will want to trace on the ground the town which has been analysed so lucidly by Dr Pinches and her team.

Christopher Dyer

Preface

Four years is merely the blink of an eye in the long history of Ledbury. Time spent on the England's Past for Everyone project has flown by, yet a wealth of history has been uncovered. The compilers of the first Herefordshire Victoria County History volume, on whose broad shoulders successive generations stand, recorded much, but new sources come to light, new methods of research are developed and new questions framed. The collaborative nature of the project, bringing together experts in many fields with local people, each with their own knowledge and expertise, has meant that the research has been wide-ranging and innovative. This book is the result of a happy collaboration, as was its companion volume on the later history of the town (published 2009).

I am particularly grateful to my fellow contributors, Nigel Baker (Senior Projects Archaeologist – Urban Archaeology with Herefordshire Archaeology), Janet Cooper (formerly County Editor for the Victoria County History of Essex and currently Chairman of the Victoria County History Trust for Herefordshire), and Keith Ray (County Archaeologist for Herefordshire). Not only have they written excellent chapters, but have also given me much advice and encouragement with my own. Chapter 1 is substantially the work of Keith Ray, and in chapter 2 he continues by charting human activity in the district from the time the first humans moved across the frozen landscape of what would become Herefordshire to the arrival of Anglo-Saxon settlers. Janet Cooper takes up the story in chapter 3, discussing the importance of the church as an institution and the influence of the church building on the development of Ledbury. In chapter 4 Nigel Baker gives a detailed examination of the medieval town, with a contribution from Chris Atkinson about the community archaeology project. I am grateful to many people who have shared their knowledge with me or read and commented on early drafts of chapters. These include Chris Dyer of Leicester University, John Freeman of the English Place-Name Society, Moira Jenkins of the Herefordshire and Worcestershire Earth Heritage Trust, Sylvia Gill, David Whitehead and Ann Workman. I am especially grateful to J.P. Toomey for allowing me to quote from his translation of the Duke of York's Household Accounts in chapter 5, which he also read and commented upon.

None of us could research and write without the work of archivists, librarians and museum curators. Herefordshire Heritage

Services have supported the project in many practical ways, as well as through the work of individual members of staff at the Hereford Museum Resource Centre. Members of Herefordshire Archaeology have offered stalwart support, not only in the chapters written by two of them here, but also in help with maps and aerial photographs. Christopher Atkinson led two projects with our volunteers, surveying sites in the ancient woodland of Frith Wood and conducting a series of test pit excavations in the town. Rebecca Lane, a buildings archaeologist, supervised the volunteers in surveying the parish church. I am very grateful to the staff of the Herefordshire Record Office and the Hereford Cathedral Library for their unfailing helpfulness and interest in this project. The Record Office is particularly to be thanked for allowing us to photograph the *Red Book* of the Bishops of Hereford. This meant that the volunteers, under the skilful and patient tutelage of Janet Cooper, could produce a full translation of the Ledbury entries from this important 13th-century rental.

Keith Ray would like to express his gratitude to colleagues who have contributed information to his chapter. They include: David Mullin of Gloucestershire County Council, Neil Shurety of Border Archaeology, Peter Reavill, Finds Liaison Officer for Herefordshire and Shropshire with the Portable Antiquities Scheme and Judy Stevenson of Hereford Museum. Christopher Atkinson, Community Archaeologist with Herefordshire Archaeology researched those collections, sourced aerial photographs and prepared a number of the illustrations, as did his colleague, Tim Hoverd. Neil Rimmington, Historic Environment Countryside Adviser with Herefordshire Archaeology shared helpful insights on the interpretation of sites visible on aerial photographs, while Nigel Baker commented helpfully on thoughts on the origins of the settlement at Ledbury. Bruce Coplestone-Crow provided valuable discussion of place-name data (but should not be held in any way responsible for Keith Ray's use of them), and Valerie Goodbury kindly assisted with the location of the H.H. Lines plan of Wall Hills Camp.

The work of the volunteers, whether transcribing documents, measuring burgage plots or digging holes has made a great contribution to the research. Even greater has been their cheerful encouragement and their obvious enthusiasm for and love of the history of their town and its surrounding area. It is a love that I have come to share.

Sylvia Pinches

Introducing Leadon Land

Then, hey for covert and woodland, and ash and elm and oak,
Tewkesbury inns, and Malvern roofs, and Worcester
chimney smoke,
The red-felled Hereford cattle a-lowing from field and byre,
And Bradlow Knoll, and Killibury Camp, and Ledbury
Church's spire …
So hey for the road, the west road, by mill and forge and fold,
Scent of the fern and song of the lark by brook, and field,
and wold,
To the comely folk at the hearth-stone and the ale beside the fire,
In the hearty land, the home land, my land of heart's desire.

From John Masefield, 'London Town'[1]

The land of Masefield's 'heart's desire' lay in the upper Leadon valley around Ledbury, the town of his birth. This excerpt from one of his poems evokes his memories of growing up there in the late 19th century, but it also conjures up features of a far more ancient world, to which he was always sensitive. Bradlow Knoll, a short walk from his family home, is probably a Bronze-Age burial mound; Kilbury (his Killibury) was long thought to be an Iron-Age fort; Ledbury church dates back a thousand years. This book sets out to explore that landscape and to chart the human history which has left traces to be discerned on its features, unearthed by archaeology or recovered from old documents.

A Topographical Sketch

The land of the upper Leadon stretches from the eastern flanks of the Marcle Ridge to the west-facing slopes of the Malvern Hills, rising to as much as 700 feet (213 metres) above the vale. Immediately to the west of the Malverns is the valley of the Cradley Brook, draining northwards to the river Teme, and covering the central areas of the parishes of Colwall and Mathon. Between the Cradley Brook and the river Leadon to the west, a chain of hills runs from Haffield (two miles south of Ledbury) to Oyster Hill in Coddington parish (four miles to the north). Part way along, Ledbury nestles between the hills and the Leadon, which flows quietly through the landscape. On its western bank, the plateau of Wall Hills is the only interruption of the valley before the Marcle Ridge is reached. The Leadon itself rises to the north-east, amid hills bordering the Frome valley, bubbling from a number of small streams in Bosbury.

Geology   This landscape has been formed by millennia of geological change. Some 750,000 to 500,000 years ago a river, dubbed the Mathon by geologists, flowed from north to south along the western flank of the Malverns. The Mathon River catchment area was much greater than that of the modern Leadon. It was contemporary with the Bytham River complex that flowed eastwards into the North Sea Basin and that has produced the earliest evidence of proto-human activity in Britain. The climate at this time was considerably warmer than today. We should envisage warm temperate grasslands here with our ancestral people hunting

Figure 2   A map of the upper Leadon valley showing key places mentioned in the book.

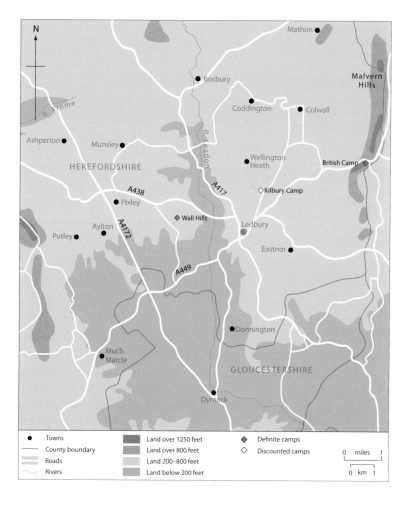

Figure 3 Herefordshire Beacon (British Camp), a large and prominent Iron-Age fort standing 1,114 feet (340 metres) above sea level on the Malvern Hills ridge, seen from Haysebrook, a mile to the west. The Mathon River flowed through here half a million years ago, and it was later the site of a naturally dammed glacial lake.

and camping along the banks of a river, similar in size to the Wye. The climate then turned cooler, and great ice-sheets formed, spreading outwards from Earth's polar regions. This process of glaciation happened several times during the Pleistocene. Over the last half a million years, there have been two episodes of extreme cold that affected Herefordshire. During the earliest of these, known as the Anglian glaciation of around 480,000 to 424,000 years ago, a lobe of the central Wales ice-sheet extended as far as the Malvern Hills. The Devensian glaciation, which reached a peak between 20,000 and 18,000 years ago, did not extend so far. During this period the drainage was transformed into today's patterns, and the Leadon and the Glynch Brook are the only south-flowing vestiges of the once-mighty Mathon River.[2]

A Farmed Landscape   John Duncumb, writing in the early
19th century, placed the western part of the Ledbury area firmly
within the premier wheat-growing zone of the county, sharing
as it does the rich Deep Argillaceous Loams of north-central,
west-central, and east-central Herefordshire. Today most of the
fields are either arable or improved pasture and wheat remains
popular, though now alongside potato and soft fruits as cash crops.
While hopfields and orchards still feature, especially to the north
and west, they are nowhere near as prominent as they were even
fifty years ago. Meanwhile, almost all the steeper hillsides are today
heavily wooded, although this has not always been so.[3]

The Town in its Setting

The human settlements of this landscape have ranged from
transient encampments, through individual farmsteads and
cottages clustered in hamlets, to the small market town of Ledbury.
In chapter 2 Keith Ray discusses the human activity in the vicinity
of what became Ledbury from the earliest times. Possible reasons
for the settlement pattern of the area in the post-Roman period
are weighed up, as is the significance of the Iron-Age forts which
ring the present town. In chapter 3 Janet Cooper addresses
the emergence of the church as the focus of settlement in the
area. Its importance both as a building and as an institution is
obvious. Even today the church building dominates the town
and its influence is taken up again in chapter 7. Both these
chapters include sections on the foundation and development of
St Katherine's Hospital and the impact it had on the townscape
and the life of the people. The factors which shaped the layout of
the town, not much altered at its core even today, are the subject
of detailed analysis by Nigel Baker in chapter 4. The ways in which
the people of the town earned their living and led their daily lives
is discussed in chapter 5. For all its urban characteristics, Ledbury
was, as it still is, a rural market town, and the way in which the
surrounding area was managed and farmed is explored in chapter
6. Chapter 2 covers the great sweep of time, largely without
written record, up until about AD600, while chapters 3 to 7 cover
the next 900 years or so. Chapter 8 reviews the town in the early
16th century, on the verge of a series of changes that would have
a major impact on Ledbury. Those changes are the subject of the
companion volume already published.[4]

Chapter 2

Settlement to AD600

INTRODUCTION

Men have forgotten how the dance began.
But once, up in the wind, atop the Down,
Beyond the ditch that made the huts a town,
This fancy fired in the soul of Man:
That, if they sacrificed with wine and bread,
And power spilled all day, in rhythm, at speed,
The god, who governs having, giving heed,
Might give again and let the tribe be fed.

From John Masefield, 'The Morris Dancers'[5]

Masefield was a poet with a keen awareness of the echoes of the past in the present. In this piece he envisaged the Morris dancers he had seen as a boy in the streets of Ledbury unknowingly re-enacting the ritual dances of the Iron-Age tribes-people who built the hillfort known as British Camp. This is an appropriate opening for this chapter, since the focus here is upon how Ledbury is the lineal successor to places at or near the centre of the upper Leadon valley, a district that has had a coherent identity over several millennia.

The shape of the hills and valleys of the district today is a legacy of the last Ice Age, ending around twelve thousand years ago. In the centuries following this, people gradually penetrated the sometimes dense woodlands that had developed after the glaciers had retreated, and their small flint tools occur in several places close to Ledbury. Their remote ancestors also left traces in the area, an example being a 300,000-year-old hand axe found in 1970 in a ploughed field at Hoe Farm, near Mathon. The axe still had sharp edges, so had not moved far from where it was buried. Those who made and used the axe lived in a warm period between glacial episodes, and while we do not know exactly what the landscape looked like then, it was probably significantly different from now. Recent geological study has, for instance, shown that around 500,000 years ago a large river flowed southwards along the western flank of the Malvern Hills.[6]

THE UPPER LEADON VALLEY BEFORE THE FIRST FIELDS

People of the Woodlands

In a fold of the hills overlooking the Leadon north of Ledbury, many flints characteristic of the period 6000-4000BC have been found near Frith Farm. The people who worked the flint to make these tools lived by hunting and gathering, and they set fires and created clearings in the then extensive woodland and heath-lands of the district. They did this to encourage new growth and attract animals, in effect managing the herds of red deer that were significant prey for them. The small family groups would have moved, season by season, around a territory probably covering the whole of the land between the Marcle Ridge in the west and the Malvern Hills in the east. The Frith Farm locality was typical of the places where they stayed periodically, sometimes building sophisticated shelters. Their cooking fires may have been the reason why some of the flints had clearly been burnt.

Figure 4 Two of the worked flints from Frith Farm, Ledbury. These blades are assigned to the late Mesolithic period. Made for cutting and processing animal hides and other domestic tasks, they were used alongside wooden, leather and fibre vessels before pottery began to be made in the succeeding Neolithic period. Length: 2in (5cm).

Not far from Frith Farm, but just to the south-west across the Leadon, very similar worked flints have been found in scatters around and also within the later Iron-Age hillfort at Wall Hills. One of these groups of flints, from Grovesend, included eight blades and flakes, and such tool types continued in use in the following centuries (into the early Neolithic period). More flints characteristic of the same period are known from other locations in the area, for instance from land north of Eastnor Park.[7]

Early Hill-Top Enclosures and Settlement

It may be significant that flint tools have been found at Wall Hills, because such finds have been made at other hillforts in Herefordshire, suggesting that there may be earlier sites, possibly simple enclosures, beneath them. For example, 46 worked flints and a polished stone-axe fragment made from stone quarried in North Wales were found during excavations within Midsummer Hill Iron-Age fort on the Malvern Hills at Eastnor. Both the flints and the axe fragment are indicative of activity in the fourth millennium BC, and it was in the period between 3500BC and 3300BC that places encircled by modest banks and ditches (mostly hill-top enclosures) were being built and used in this part of Britain.[8]

This possibility of early hill-top enclosures at Wall Hills and Midsummer Hill can be compared with discoveries elsewhere in the county. For example, excavations at Dorstone Hill in the Golden Valley produced large numbers of Neolithic flints and other finds within an enclosure occupied also in the Iron Age. Meanwhile excavations in 2006 on a hill-top overlooking Bodenham on the river Lugg between Leominster and Hereford produced secure radiocarbon dating evidence for an early enclosure. Flint blades, pieces of plain bowl pottery, animal and human bone, and a hammer-stone used for working flint were recovered from where they had been deliberately placed at the base of the rounded end of a ditch flanking an entrance to the enclosure. This initial activity was dated to the period around 3500BC, when the enclosure appears (from the shells of shade-loving land snails found in the same deposit) to have been built in a clearing in woodland. People used the site again around 3300BC.[9]

Human remains have been encountered in excavations of long barrows (elongated stone and earth burial mounds) both in the Cotswolds to the east and south of Ledbury across the River Severn, and around the Black Mountains to the west across the River Wye. Human bones of Neolithic date have also been found placed in the limestone caves and fissures of the Wye gorges south of Ross-on-Wye. However, so far no long barrows are known in the upper Leadon valley and no human bones have been found in crevices in the rocks of the Malvern Hills.

Finds of stone axes do not always signal the presence of enclosures, and examples that were either thrown away or

Figure 5 Completely polished axes made from honey-coloured flint like this one recently discovered at Haffield, near Ledbury, may have come from Dorset or East Yorkshire, or even from Belgium or southern Scandinavia. Such fine axes were often reworked or chopped up before being deposited in a variety of places in the landscape, and this axe shows signs of both re-polishing and subsequent flake removal.

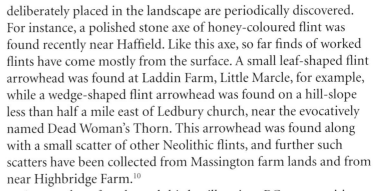

Figure 6   A Scandinavian
square-butted flint axe
found near Colwall Stone
in 1931 and now in
Hereford Museum.

deliberately placed in the landscape are periodically discovered.
For instance, a polished stone axe of honey-coloured flint was
found recently near Haffield. Like this axe, so far finds of worked
flints have come mostly from the surface. A small leaf-shaped flint
arrowhead was found at Laddin Farm, Little Marcle, for example,
while a wedge-shaped flint arrowhead was found on a hill-slope
less than half a mile east of Ledbury church, near the evocatively
named Dead Woman's Thorn. This arrowhead was found along
with a small scatter of other Neolithic flints, and further such
scatters have been collected from Massington farm lands and from
near Highbridge Farm.[10]

Among these fourth- and third-millennium BC communities,
arable farming was small scale and shifting, with cattle herding of
greater importance, along with the keeping of sheep and pigs. For
these mobile family groups, enclosures were places for occasional
gatherings, feasting and exchanges. In the later Neolithic, around
the middle of the third millennium BC, more elaborate ceremonial
structures and locations were created for gatherings. Some locations
would have been appropriate for the placing of particularly fine
objects in the ground. A rare and distinctive Scandinavian flint axe
found near the railway tunnel above Colwall Stone may derive from
such a context (Figs 6 and 7).[11]

Bronze-Age Communities

Figure 7   The Colwall
Stone. This block of
limestone is thought
by some to be part
of a standing stone of
prehistoric date. It may
not be coincidental that
the flint axe featured in
Fig. 6 was found near
the place from which the
stone came.

No Neolithic or Bronze-Age settlements have yet been found in
the Ledbury area. During the Early Bronze Age, however, between
2200 and 1600BC, circular burial mounds, often termed round
barrows, were built, and some of these survive as earthworks. For
instance, a damaged mound crowning Bradlow Knoll in Frith
Wood to the north-east of Ledbury town is a likely, if unproven,
round barrow. Another possible barrow with a diameter of nine
metres stands on a ridge overlooking the Glynch Brook at Eastnor.
Aerial photography has revealed the circular ditch surrounding a

levelled mound at New Mills by the Leadon on the western edge of
Ledbury, and others have been recorded at Great Heath south of
Haffield. Sherds of Early Bronze-Age 'Beaker' pottery (distinctive
drinking beaker-shaped vessels found right across Europe)
were found on Hollybush Hill, indicating either a settlement or
another former round barrow. A tanged flint arrowhead of a type
sometimes found in graves with Beaker pottery was found not far
away, at Sheep Hill, Eastnor.[12]

Besides individual barrows, some cemeteries existed, as is
suggested by discoveries at former sand quarries in the Mathon
area. From one site, a collared urn containing ashes was found
associated with a perforated stone axe (Fig. 8). Other urns were
seen nearby, one close to a small enclosure. At South End farm,
Mathon, up to 45 distinct cremation deposits were found. These
were accompanied by Late Bronze-Age urn fragments dated
to 1000BC, in some cases located within stone settings. Some

Figure 8   Pottery urn
from South End farm,
Mathon. The decoration
and form of this pot
places it in the Collared
Urn tradition, dated
within the period
2200-1400BC. It was
found with cremated
bone from a funeral
pyre, and a perforated
stone axe.

funerary pyres had contained gifts for the departed and two
bronze spearhead fragments were found amid the masses of
cremated material.[13]

Traces of early land divisions comprising simple if massive
earthwork banks aligned north-south along the tops of ridges are
evident throughout the area. These include one along the crest
of the Malvern Hills that in its early phase continued underneath
Midsummer Hill fort. Another, in Frith Wood, clearly runs up to
and around the Bradlow Knoll mound showing that the mound
already existed when the bank was constructed. A whole landscape
of (as yet undated) ancient enclosures can be traced in parts of
the district, as in the area between the Leadon at Donnington and
Great Heath south of Haffield, and their earliest elements may date
to the Bronze Age.

THE ERA OF HILLFORTS

Iron-Age Field Systems and Farms

At some point in the first millennium BC, people in the Ledbury
area started to live in more permanent settlements. It seems likely
that, as elsewhere in southern Britain, they did so among the fields
that were beginning to be created within the larger territorial
divisions marked by the major linear banks described above. Crop
marks in Donnington parish for instance reveal sets of associated
boundaries in an organised rectangular pattern characteristic
of both Iron-Age and Romano-British field systems (Fig. 9).
Individual circular marks near Haffield perhaps represent the
locations of houses sited among these fields, and since excavated
circular huts are dated to the Iron Age, they are presumed to be of
this date.[14]

The sites of individual early farmsteads have also been identified
by crop marks seen from the air in several places in the Ledbury
area. Under favourable conditions, dark lines indicate the position
of the now buried ditches that, with small banks next to them,
provided protection and definition to the homes of small family
groups. These enclosures are often rectangular in plan and
usually less than a hectare in size. They were similar in scale to the
19th-century farms of the district. Such sites have been noted in
the vicinity of Putley to the west, near Staplow a mile to the north
of Ledbury, close to the river Leadon at Donnington (Fig. 16),
and in two locations on the northern edge of Wellington Heath.
At the Ridgeway, Cradley, four miles to the north of Ledbury,
a simple cropmark measuring 260 feet by 200 feet (80 metres
by 60 metres) was also found by aerial photography, and was

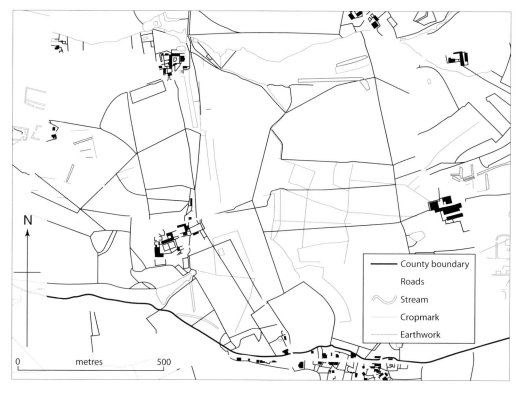

County boundary
Roads
Stream
Cropmark
Earthwork

0   metres   500

Figure 9   Early field boundaries identified from the air in the Donnington-Bromsberrow Heath area at Broom's Green and Great Heath. The mapped elements appear to be part of a continuous system spread over at least a mile (1.6km) from west to east. Parts of this system share a basic north-south orientation with present-day field boundaries, suggesting that they set a pattern followed by later fields.

initially interpreted as a small Roman fort. Test excavation by Herefordshire Archaeology staff in 2000 revealed that the site was a farmstead occupied only during the later Iron Age (200BC–AD50). The working area that had been created in the ditch after the enclosure bank had been levelled produced important evidence for metalworking.[15]

Low banks defining early fields attached to the western side of the ridge-top bank in Frith Wood, Ledbury, were noted during a woodland survey in 1999, together with two small groups of platforms. These platforms were triangular, with their long sides tucked into the hill slope. This is similar to several of the terraces recorded in recent surveys of hillfort sites such as Midsummer Hill, and it is therefore possible that these groups represent unenclosed settlements of the Iron Age, located among the early fields. One of these groups was recorded by measured survey by EPE volunteers as part of a project undertaken in 2008 at Frith Wood (panel 4).[16]

The Origins and Development of Hillforts

Hillforts must in some ways also have involved an organisation of the landscape, since numbers of people must have come together to

Hillforts: What were they for?

Figure A   *British Camp, Colwall, from the south. This dramatically sited and scarped hillfort echoes sites such as Hambledon Hill in Dorset where a series of steep embankments crowns a high hillside now under turf. Then as now, this presents an image of impregnability.*

The sites that archaeologists today refer to as hillforts are embanked and ditched enclosures, often occupying hill-summits, and sometimes with multiple and very dramatic defences. The diversity of form evident in all the sizeable hillforts in southern Britain may well represent a corresponding variety of purpose and complexity of history. The accumulating evidence from excavations at hillfort sites suggests that some were in near-permanent occupation, while others witnessed only sporadic encampment. Such contrasts might also relate to different phases of use. Judging by the exaggeration of scarps and the elaboration of entrances, an obvious purpose was to impress. At Midsummer Hill fort, on the Malvern Hills, for instance, stone was deliberately selected for facing the rampart, to make the defences stand out prominently within the landscape.

There is a danger at sites like British Camp and Midsummer Hill, where the interiors are so full of closely-packed terraces and platforms, that we simply assume that they were permanently occupied places. In practice, their occupation may have been either seasonal, or linked to specific periodic events. The key to establishing the actual nature of occupation may lie in a better understanding of the four-post structures found within the forts as both granaries and store-houses. So if the hillforts did serve as strong places in the landscape, we could envisage that they were places not only of refuge from foes, but also where the non-living moveable wealth of the tribe was stored. Such storage may have included sufficient foodstuffs to sustain large numbers of people gathered together for relatively short periods. Moreover, excavations elsewhere in southern Britain have shown that the structures recorded on the terraces within the forts were often very lightly constructed using less durable materials, and that many terraces were not built upon at all.

Talk of 'the tribe' introduces the question of who it was that occupied the forts. Beyond the idea that extended family groups (comprising multiple families allied by marriage) owned each site, we cannot be sure whether these were élite sites, or places where everyone could assemble. It seems likely that not only were many of the sites long-lived, but that they were places of legendary, symbolic and/or sacred importance from the sometimes distant past. This, rather than their strategic value, may have determined where the sites were located.

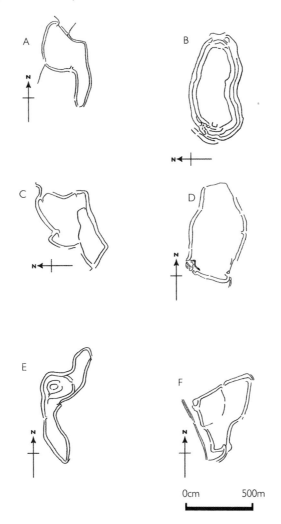

Figure B   *Simplified comparative plans of hillforts: a) Midsummer Hill Camp, b) Maiden Castle (Dorchester, Dorset), c) Wall Hills Camp, d) Credenhill Fort (Hereford), e) British Camp (Herefordshire Beacon), and f) Ivington Camp (Leominster). The Malvern Hills forts are very striking in the landscape, and Wall Hills dominates the Leadon valley. Ivington makes an interesting comparison with Wall Hills. The massive, regionally focal, sites close to the county towns of Herefordshire and Dorset, respectively, are, however, more closely comparable with one another.*

begin building them, and since, in Herefordshire at least, so many existed. Debate continues about whether these forts were places of occupation, or were simply meeting places and focal points for the communities concerned (panel 1). Whether the first fields in the Ledbury area were laid out in some cases earlier than the forts, or contemporary with them, or even after they had been abandoned, is still unknown.

An early enclosure was recognised as long ago as 1953 as preceding the developed earthworks of British Camp hillfort. Recent survey of the fort at Midsummer Hill has also traced an earlier enclosure. The arrangement at Wall Hills suggests a developmental sequence starting from an early core area (panel 2). Excavations at Midsummer Hill in the late 1960s indicated a possible start to the main hillfort entrance at around 470BC However, not enough dates were obtained from the site to be certain that this was when the fort was first built. The origin of these earliest enclosures is therefore far from proven, and they may not of course all have begun at the same time.

Across southern Britain, many of the early hillforts were deliberately made more complex from around 400BC, by the elaboration of entrances, deepening of ditches, and addition of new circuits of bank and ditch. The developed phase of British Camp covers around 13.5 hectares and has four entrances. The defences themselves are ranged across nearly a kilometre of the summit of the central part of the Malvern Hills. They comprise ramparts that

Figure 10 British Camp, Colwall, looking north over the northern defences from just to the west of the surviving earlier ramparts.

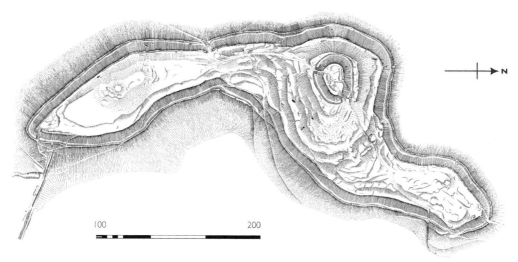

N

100

200

Figure 11 Survey plan of British Camp. Note the line of the early phase of defences, which survived later remodelling of the much-extended developed hillfort. The central circle of earthworks crowning the hilltop is a Norman earthen castle of the 11th century.

in themselves were slight, but were rendered massive-looking by ingenious use of the natural slopes above the ditches which even today (in their partially in-filled condition) lay as much as 38 feet (11.6 metres) below the rampart top.

Within the fort, around 118 circular or near circular terraces were scarped into the sides of the 'hog's back' shaped ridge (Fig. 11). One thing common to almost all these terraces or platforms upon which structures could have been built is that they enjoyed very wide views and could be seen from far away. Prominence and visibility were therefore clearly key attributes of at least the developed phase, and it is likely that power, display and impregnability were being projected by the occupants, however long or brief their sojourn at the site was.

Midsummer Hill fort occupies the summits of two parallel ridges (Midsummer Hill and Hollybush Hill) that form the central spine of the Malvern Hills and a close outlier. Its defences also include the upper part of a deep fold between these ridges. This involves a height differential of around two hundred feet (61 metres) between the western summit on Midsummer Hill and the main fort entrance nestling within and facing southwards down the fold. A further entrance provided access to the site from the ridge to the north. Again, a large number of platforms exist here, but many of these were linked by long narrow terraces.

Excavations at Midsummer Hill revealed the four-post foundations of several originally raised store-houses, and also the form and sequence of construction of the main gateway. Some of these buildings had been used as granaries. Grain was found associated with seven of the 31 four-post structures excavated, while nine produced potsherds, perhaps from storage vessels placed inside the structures.

Figure 12 Survey plan of
Midsummer Hill Camp,
with Hollybush Hill to
the right.

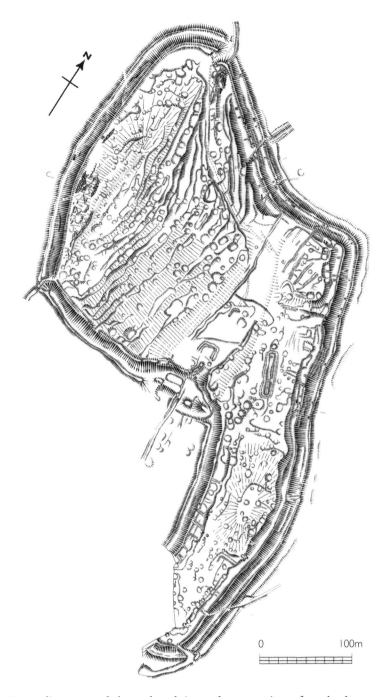

Long-distance trade brought salt in earthen containers from both
Droitwich in Worcestershire and Nantwich in Cheshire to the site.[17]

   In contrast to these now well surveyed sites, we know next to
nothing about Wall Hills Camp just to the west of Ledbury across
the river Leadon (panel 2). This is particularly unfortunate given

Figure 13 A fragment of the decorated rim of an Iron-Age pot from Midsummer Hill Camp. There were several sources for the pottery used in Herefordshire hillforts. While some were local to the Malverns, others came from further afield in Herefordshire, Gloucestershire, and even Shropshire, as indicated by the ground-up stone used to temper the vessels.

Figure 14 Wall Hills Camp from the air looking south. This view clearly shows the upper enclosure in the centre and the way in which the lower enclosure wraps around its north-eastern flank.

its geographical centrality within the upper Leadon area. Without detailed earthwork survey, geophysical survey or excavation, it is difficult to determine exactly how the fort developed, let alone to gain an idea of how the different areas within it might have been used.[18]

What is most interesting about Wall Hills Camp, however, is its location, which differs from the Malvern Hills ridge-top enclosures. The role of all three sites was quite probably broadly similar (panel 1), but in one respect there is a big contrast. Both British Camp and Midsummer Hill fort were built high above the Severn and Leadon river valleys. Wall Hills Camp also stands in an elevated position, but at much lower altitude and much closer to the everyday world of the farmed landscape. As such it would have served more effectively as a focal point for settlement.

Forts in the Ledbury Area

Two further forts are known in the district. Haffield Camp is an oval-shaped enclosure defined by a single bank and ditch. It occupies the northern end of an outlier ridge of the Malvern Hills on the eastern margins of Donnington parish two miles to the south of Ledbury. The site has the appearance of an Iron-Age enclosure, but is as yet undated. It now exists as a heavily landscaped earthwork within the grounds of Haffield House. Away to the east, Oldbury Camp, occupying the southern end of the

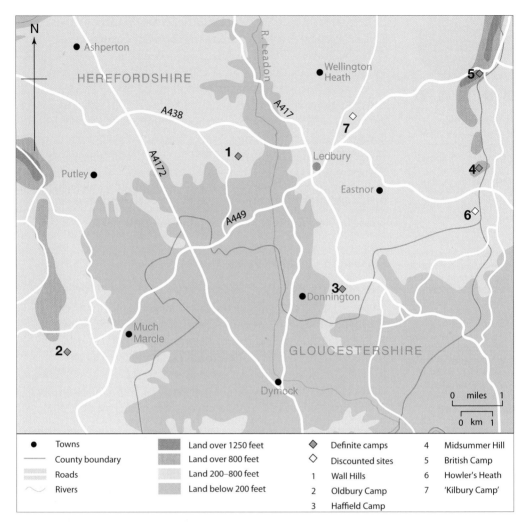

●	Towns	◆ Definite camps	4	Midsummer Hill
—	County boundary	◇ Discounted sites	5	British Camp
░	Roads	1 Wall Hills	6	Howler's Heath
∿	Rivers	2 Oldbury Camp	7	'Kilbury Camp'
		3 Haffield Camp		

Land over 1250 feet · *Land over 800 feet* · *Land 200–800 feet* · *Land below 200 feet*

Figure 15 The distribution of hillforts in the upper Leadon area. Among the known hillforts, Oldbury on the southern end of the Marcle Ridge frames the western margins, and British Camp and Midsummer Hill the eastern. In contrast, Wall Hills fort occupies a central location, immediately overlooking the Leadon itself.

Marcle Ridge, has all but disappeared due to ploughing. Its form is suggestive of an Iron-Age date but, again, there have been no investigations here that might provide a definitive answer.

Meanwhile, other sites have been proposed as Iron-Age enclosures, but do not bear close scrutiny. Kilbury Camp, for example, is a triangular topped hill lying to the south-east of Bradlow Knoll and at a lower elevation. Traces have been observed only of farming terraces on the slopes of the hill, and these may well have been mistaken for hillfort banks. Another alleged Iron-Age fort is said to have occupied the crest of the ridge at Howlers' Heath, Eastnor, but the feature concerned is of geological origin. An erroneous record for a second hillfort published for Donnington parish has resulted from a transposition of a record for a site in a parish with a similar name.[19]

INTO THE REALMS OF HISTORY

The Ledbury Area in the First Century AD

The proximity of the upper Leadon area to the Severn valley suggests that it lay within the sphere of influence of the late Iron-Age kingdom of the Dobunni. This was centred in Gloucestershire, but extended into Wiltshire, north Somerset, Worcestershire, and western Oxfordshire. The outline of the kingdom is perhaps traceable as the area within which early, locally-produced, coins were distributed as a means of asserting political authority. Dobunnic coins were struck and distributed from the 30s BC through to the Roman conquest in AD43. It may be that the upper Leadon area came only relatively late into the Dobunnic sphere of influence, since gold coins stamped with the letters EISV (an abbreviated form, denoting the last of the Dobunnic rulers) have recently been found not only near Ross-on-Wye, but also at both Dymock and at Ledbury itself where they were previously unknown.[20]

It has been suggested that at least a significant part of the Dobunnic territory was in treaty relations with Rome from an early point during the invasion period (AD43-55). This might explain why there was a major military base at Kingsholm near Gloucester, but no other forts until those known at Canon Frome, some six miles north-west of Ledbury. This is near where the Roman road from Dymock to Stretton Grandison and beyond crossed the Frome valley north of Ashperton. Standing above this route, Wall Hills was an obvious target for the Roman army as it advanced westwards from the Severn valley, and the reference to the discovery of human bones noted by members of the Woolhope Naturalists' Field Club on a visit in 1883 (Fig. A in panel 2) could have been a 'war cemetery', like that excavated at Sutton Walls just north of Hereford. Nonetheless, so far there have been no discoveries of Roman forts or marching camps from the invasion period in the immediate area.[21]

The recovery of Romano-British pottery from within Wall Hills fort suggests, as at Sutton Walls, that, despite any possible Roman military action at the site, domestic occupation resumed at some point. The re-occupation of at least some hillforts in the Roman period in Herefordshire is well-established, but some continued to be visited only for religious purposes as attested by the shrine excavated at Croft Ambrey north of Leominster.[22]

The Ledbury Countryside, AD100 to AD400

Distinguishing Romano-British from earlier, Iron-Age, fields and farms can be difficult. In practice, their occupation was often unbroken through the period 200BC to AD400. To the west of Wall Hills in the Putley area, the remains of three substantial farmsteads are known on the eastern slopes of the Woolhope Dome hills. These sites featured building stone and roof tiles, and this reflects both the wealth and the settled nature of the countryside here. The kilometre spacing, shared elevation (around the 250 feet contour) and east-facing prospect of these sites on free-draining gentle slopes suggest an ordering of the landscape in reference to the Roman road just over a mile away to the east.

That there were other rural building complexes is certain. For example, a sequence of farmstead-scale enclosures is evident from a site at Donnington. Four enclosures here occupy a slope beside the Leadon. Discoveries of Roman pottery and building materials were made here in the early 20th century. The remaining rural farming sites within the Romano-British countryside of the Upper Leadon are indicated by finds of Romano-British pottery recorded

Figure 16 Donnington: a group of early farmstead enclosures from the air. The course of the River Leadon is marked by the meandering line of trees. Dividing fences are visible within two of the enclosures, and these were probably created to facilitate stock-folding. They are commonly occurring features of Roman period farming sites in Herefordshire. See Fig. 18 for a map of the location.

in ploughed fields at several locations either side of the hills among which Ledbury town now stands.[23]

As to rural industry, a pottery or tilery was once thought to have existed at Marley Hall, just to the north-west of Ledbury, although the finds could simply represent the location of another farm complex. Evidence of ironworking could be expected from anywhere in the Leadon valley, given its relative proximity to the Forest of Dean iron ore sources. Whether or not any market centre local to Ledbury existed before the Roman invasion, it seems likely that the creation of the Roman road to the west of the Leadon and Wall Hills would have drawn trade towards it. Settlements are attested at Dymock on the Leadon only four miles (seven kilometres) south of Ledbury and in the Frome valley floodplain between Ashperton and Stretton Grandison five miles (eight and a half kilometres) to the north-west. Numerous early finds and the recent discovery of an extensive Roman-period cemetery to the west of Stretton Grandison add substance to the idea that it was a significant place.[24]

The Beginnings of English Settlement

The circumstances of the end of Roman Britain have been much debated. It seems likely that the political formation of the late Roman province of *Britannia Prima* centred upon Cirencester outlived the collapse of the market economy at the beginning of the fifth century AD. At Kenchester near Hereford, excavation at the west gate of the Roman town showed that life there continued well into the fifth century. Meanwhile at Stretton Grandison burials were still being made in the cemetery to the west of the settlement into the sixth century. South of the Wye, a bishopric, once under the care of Bishop Dubricius, is thought to have existed over the same period.[25]

Determining the date or the circumstances of Anglo-Saxon (English) incursions into the upper Leadon area is highly problematical, as in many parts of southern Britain. We have no written evidence to suggest particular patterns of land-seizure locally and as yet archaeology has thrown no light on the matter. There are, for example, no finds of Anglo-Saxon metalwork from the Ledbury district. Some clues concerning the direction of settlement into central Herefordshire may be gleaned from place-names that involved the recognition, naming and sometimes re-use of existing barrows by incoming Anglo-Saxons and occasionally the building of new ones. Three names ending in 'low' probably derive from the Old English word for 'barrow' or 'mound' (hlæw); Bradlow, Staplow and (less certainly) Huntley's Farm at

Much Marcle. They are but the most easterly examples within Herefordshire of a reasonably dense distribution of such names across the Frome valley landscape towards the lower Lugg area north of Hereford. The only trace of a possible pagan Anglo-Saxon barrow or mound so far uncovered through excavation in the county was a circular ditch formerly surrounding a mound at Sutton St Michael on the Lugg in the Marden area north of Hereford. A piece of early to mid-Saxon pottery was retrieved from the ditch, which was sealed beneath the remains of a deserted medieval village to the west of the church, in a location known to have been within a later royal manor belonging to the rulers of the Midland kingdom of Mercia.[26]

At the time of the migration of the first Anglo-Saxon communities into the upper Leadon district, probably not long after AD600, they doubtless existed side by side with the indigenous British people (whom the English soon denoted 'Welsh', meaning 'foreigner'). There was enough continuing British presence thereafter to ensure that a sprinkling of British (or sometimes Welsh) place-name elements survived. Local examples include Bronsil (Eastnor: incorporating the British personal name 'Branoc') and Walsopthorne (Ashperton: the Herefordshire Domesday Book version reading 'Welshman's apple-tree'). Meanwhile, Dymock has recently been read as 'Din Mocros' ('Fort of the Pigs'), its promontory location overlooking the Leadon from the west appearing to reinforce such identification. Moreover, among the customs noted in a 13th-century Ledbury rental was the allowance for some tenants to commute payments to provision

Figure 17   Aerial view of the possible early medieval linear dyke running north to south across the landscape south-east of Ledbury. Its course is marked by field boundaries in the present-day landscape to the north of Haffield park. Haffield Camp, a small oval enclosure defined by a single bank and ditch (left-centre), stands within woodland to the west of the course of the dyke. The dyke then crossed the parkland in the foreground, before continuing southwards towards the Leadon.

Figure 18   First Edition (1886) Ordnance Survey map of the Haffield House/Dingwood Park area. This shows the line of the possible territorial dyke as marked by field boundaries in the landscape in the late 19th century.

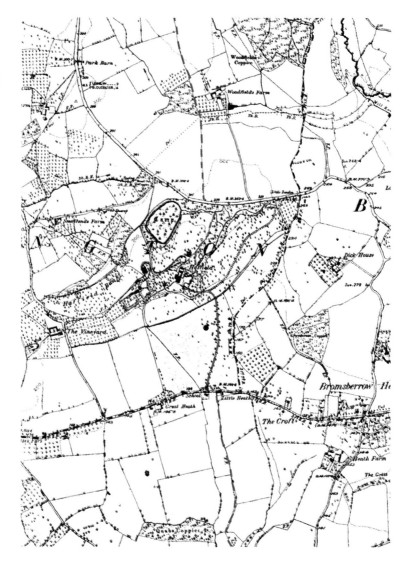

of honey. This was so characteristically a Welsh custom that it seems highly likely that it marks a continuing Welsh presence in the area.[27]

Boundary dykes are a feature of this 'migration period' in Herefordshire. There is a hint of the existence of one such feature in the Ledbury area, on a line occupied today by field boundaries extending southwards from Dingwood Park Farm just to the south of Ledbury, to the northern limit of the park at Haffield, close to the enclosure mentioned earlier in the chapter. A possible continuation of this line is evident in a boundary that until recently extended southwards from the southern boundary of the park. This continues to the south to meet a tributary brook that joins the Leadon at Callow Farm just to the east of Dymock. A record of a 'substantial boundary bank' running parallel to the stream for 360 yards (330 metres) through Dingwood Park Farm may represent an element of an early field system that the linear boundary dyke linked into, and a massive west-facing terrace on the line of the present field boundary was levelled only 20 years ago.

This putative territorial boundary, some four miles (six and a half kilometres) long, would have served to link the southern end of the Malvern Hills to the south bank of the Leadon as it curves eastwards towards the Severn. The relation of Haffield Camp to this possible dyke is interesting, since it stands on the most prominent hill along its course, and just 328 feet (100 metres) to the west of it, dominating the former heathland flanking the northern side of the Leadon valley east of Dymock. At present it can be regarded as no more than a possibility, but perhaps one worth exploring further, that this group of features was designed, or modified, to control movement in the post-Roman period east and west through the area between the southern end of the Malvern Hills and the 'fort of the pigs' above the Leadon at Dymock.[28]

Wall Hills and the Origins of Ledbury

If they could secure their tenure under a powerful lord, we know that coherent British (Welsh) communities could survive even in parts of Herefordshire north and east of the Wye at least to the 13th century, while being surrounded by English settlements. An example of a locality where they did just this was at 'Walshebroke' in Canon Pyon parish north of Hereford. Here a group retained their identity under the patronage of the descendants of Gruffyyd ap Maredudd, who held the place in 1086. While there is at the moment no evidence to support the view, we can perhaps identify at least a possibility that our 'Ledbury Welsh' supplying their honey as rent did not move far away from their former homelands.[29]

We can of course only speculate upon relations between the local surviving British population of the upper Leadon valley and the incoming English settlers in the period from AD600. Nonetheless, a significant question remains as to the fate of the fort at Wall Hills and of the descendants of the people who once inhabited it. It is difficult to avoid the impression that in the Iron Age the site was the centre for at least a sub-tribal grouping, such is the prominence of its defences, the size of the enclosed area, and above all its central location within the landscape. Nevertheless, before 1066, when Ledbury is first recorded as a settlement (in Domesday Book), Wall Hills lay abandoned and scarcely remembered. How did this come about?

Figure 19 Wall Hills from near Wellington Heath. This view from the north-east misses Ledbury (just out of view to the left) but shows the prominent wooded hill in the middle distance upon which the Iron-Age fort stands. This is just beyond the Hereford to Ledbury railway line viaduct visible at centre-left crossing the Leadon valley at its narrowest point.

It is highly likely that the spring-fed stream descending the small valley by the parish church in the centre of Ledbury would have attracted early settlement, although as yet there is no evidence for this. Nevertheless, there are some suggestive recent finds from excavations to the west of the High Street. Although none was associated with remains of structures, a later Iron-Age pottery fragment, and two definite (and two likely) pieces of Romano-British pot recovered here do hint at an early settlement focus. The only other early object found in Ledbury town itself is a spindle-whorl (a stone or piece of re-used pottery with a hole through it, used for spinning wool). Since it was not a find from an excavation, we cannot know whether it is of Iron-Age, or Romano-British, or indeed of early Anglo-Saxon date.

In conclusion we might simply observe the likelihood that Ledbury emerged where it did because it was not Wall Hills, but was a new site located in that same part of the valley where the upper course of the Leadon funnels through closely adjacent hills. The way in which Ledbury stands by an abundant source of fresh water with a fine south-westerly prospect in effect appropriates the entire locality. Its proximity to the meadows alongside the Leadon would have been an additional attraction to incoming Anglo-Saxon groups for their flocks of sheep and herds of cows.

Whereas Wall Hills could be perceived as standing aloof from the river itself, metaphorically looking backwards to the past, the site of the new settlement was closer to the river but

The Landscape of Wall Hills Camp, Ledbury

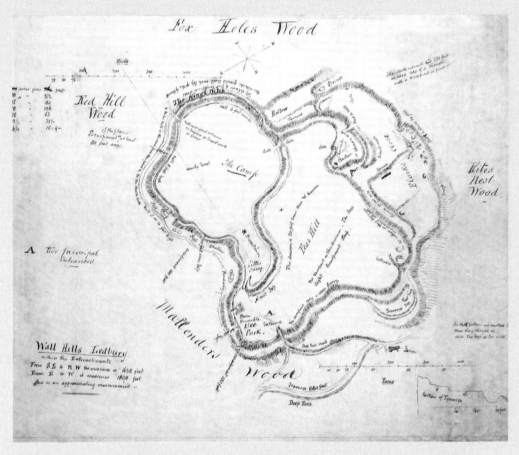

Figure A   A survey plan of Wall Hills Camp, produced in the 1870s by H.H. Lines. Note the military language of entrenchments, bastion, traverse and breastwork. Note also the possible incorporation of local tradition concerning burials, in the area near the main entrance labelled 'Church Yard'.

Wall Hills Camp is a complex of impressive earthworks covering the whole southern summit area of an almost level hilltop only a half a mile to the west of Ledbury across the Leadon. This part of the hill rises to just over 400 feet (122 metres) above sea level, over 250 feet (76 metres) higher than the surrounding land, overlooking the Leadon both to the east and the south. An upper enclosure is surrounded by a massive bank and a deeply cut ditch, while another enclosure is attached at a slightly lower elevation to the east and north. This may have been an addition, which rendered the approach to the north-eastern flank of the upper enclosure more difficult. It also doubled the enclosed space, and, since all

of this contained area is level or gently sloping, the fort was especially suitable for constructing dwellings.

There are three entrances into the upper enclosure, although it is difficult to determine which may be original based on the surface evidence alone. The eastern end of this enclosure is narrower than the rest, and the bank and ditch to both north and south pinch inwards at precisely the point where traces exist of what is either a natural linear hollow or perhaps an in-filled ditch. The outer enclosure defences dip down from a point just to the west of the north-facing entrance, to include the upper part of a side-valley that drops away northwards towards the Stores Brook and the Leadon valley. These

Figure B *The principal approach to the lower enclosure at Wall Hills was from the north. The approach picks up the line of a natural hollow, the top of which has been landscaped to channel movement in towards the gateway. Note the massive scale of the outer defences.*

outer defences are, for much of their circuit, no less impressive that those of the upper enclosure – despite the bank that once crowned the slope having being almost entirely levelled. Indeed, either side of the main north-facing entrance, the 'walls' tower over the long hollowed and curving track that leads up into the fort. This entranceway isolates an elevated triangular area to its north that offers a commanding view over the lower hill-slopes, and over the entrance itself.

It is worth reflecting briefly on how these massive defensive banks were built. It seems that in Herefordshire, a form of construction that only became common late in the Iron Age in central southern Britain was used from the outset. This is the glacis type of construction, which involved dumping the clayey rock and earth dug from the ditch directly onto the rampart, to present a smooth and continuously steep profile from bank top to ditch bottom.

on a well-drained and elevated site near it. As such it could
be regarded as looking in contrast forwards to a bright (and
of course a fundamentally English) future, achieved here as
elsewhere in the Malvern Hills region through the extinguishing
of indigenous British language and culture over the course of the
following centuries.

Chapter 3

Church and Parish to 1300

ANGLO-SAXON ORIGINS

Several distinguished historians have commented on the obscurity of the history of Anglo-Saxon Herefordshire, and the history of the Ledbury area is particularly poorly documented. We have seen in the previous chapter that prehistoric and Romano-British Ledbury seems to have centred on the hillfort at Wall Hills. At some point in the post Roman period, settlement shifted to the site of the present town which stands in a commanding position on a southern spur of the Malvern Hills, with a good water supply from springs and streams. A north-south road from Gloucester towards Bromyard runs through the later town just west of the church, and a minor east-west route from Hereford crosses it over the hills towards Malvern. The first clear evidence of settlement on the new site is the position of the parish church, in existence by the late 11th century; as we have seen, the archaeological evidence for activity before this date is inconclusive. The place-name Ledbury, discussed below, is Anglo-Saxon rather than British or Welsh and could have been formed at almost any date between about 600 and its first recorded use in Domesday Book (1086). It is likely, however, that the settlement shift at Ledbury, as elsewhere in the country, occurred early in the Anglo-Saxon period.[30]

The Malvern Hills form a natural boundary, one followed from Anglo-Saxon times by the boundaries of the dioceses of Hereford and Worcester and of the counties of Herefordshire and Worcestershire. Ledbury has probably always lain on the periphery of an area dominated by towns in the central plain of what is now Herefordshire. In the Romano-British and probably in the early Anglo-Saxon period the major settlement in the southern part of that plain was Ariconium (Weston-under-Penyard), which later gave its name to the British or Welsh kingdom of Ergyng or Archenfield. That kingdom may have extended as far east as Ledbury. If it did, that would strengthen the possibility that Ledbury and its church originated as a British ecclesiastical site, like some of the places and churches further west in Archenfield which were later associated with the bishopric of Llandaff. The power base of the earliest recorded ruler of at least part of the

Figure 20   This volume of the Gospels (Hereford Cathedral Library, MS P.I.2) is evidence of the interconnections of the British and Anglo-Saxon churches and cultures. It was made in England but close to the Welsh border in the eighth century and was probably given to Hereford cathedral by Athelstan, bishop of Hereford 1012-56. This is the opening page of the Gospel of Matthew.

later Herefordshire, the king or sub-king Merewalh (fl.625-85), lay further north, around Leominster and Maund and extended as far as Much Wenlock where he founded a monastery, but he also owned land on the River Monnow. Whether Merewalh was an incoming Anglo-Saxon or a Briton like the contemporary rulers of Ergyng is unclear, but he appears to have been subject to the rulers of the powerful Midland kingdom of Mercia. The exact extent of his kingdom is also unclear; it may not have included land as far south as Ledbury. Whatever their seventh-century position, in the course of the eighth century Ledbury and its surrounding area were absorbed into the territory of the people later known as the Magonsæte. They were important enough to have their own bishop from c.680.[31]

The only scrap of evidence for Ledbury itself in this period is the much later belief that it had once been the bishop's see or principal church. In 1173 Gilbert Foliot, bishop of London and formerly bishop of Hereford, wrote to the bishop-elect of Hereford, Robert Foliot, asking him to confirm the rights of the church of 'Lideburi' because of 'the episcopal seat [sedem] which it held long since and out of reverence for the holy bishops whose bodies lie there.' The medieval name 'Lideburi' could apply either to Ledbury or Lydbury North in Shropshire, but Gilbert Foliot was probably referring to Ledbury, since the suggestion that Ledbury had once been a 'cathedral' was made again in 1311, in the course of a dispute as to the status of the two priests who then held the estates of Upper and Lower Hall. There is no indication in this tradition as to when Ledbury had been the seat of a bishop. If, as suggested above, the later parish had remained under British rule in the seventh century, the bishopric might have been of the British church, like that at Welsh Bicknor. If, on the other hand, Ledbury was under the rule of Merewalh and his successors, the bishops might have been predecessors of the bishops of Hereford. Although 12th-century chroniclers assumed that the see of the Magonsæte had been at Hereford from its foundation c.680, the earliest bishops may have been based elsewhere. A case has been made for Leominster as the mother church of Herefordshire, but it is also possible that the see moved around during the seventh century, or that, in the absence of a fixed see, some early bishops chose to be buried at Ledbury. If so, Ledbury was of more importance in the seventh and eighth centuries than at any later time in its history. Indeed, it would have been in decline by the later Anglo-Saxon period; when the Shropshire landowner Wulfgeat made his will c.1000, he made bequests to four Herefordshire churches: Hereford cathedral, St Guthlac's in Hereford, Leominster and Bromyard minsters, but made no mention of Ledbury.[32]

Ledbury at Domesday

The estate at Ledbury was presumably given to one of the
Anglo-Saxon bishops of the Magonsæte or of Hereford by one of
the kings of Mercia. It certainly belonged to the church of Hereford
in 1066 when, with the church's other large manors along the west
flank of the Malvern Hills, it lay in the administrative subdivision
of the county called Winstree hundred. The meeting place for the
men of that subdivision or hundred, where courts were held, was
in Ledbury parish, at 'Wigmund's tree', the later Winsters Elms
Copse, a short distance north-west of the later borough. The only
non-episcopal manor in Winstree hundred was the large and
valuable Much Marcle, which in the 1040s had belonged to the
nunnery at Leominster. The nunnery was dissolved in or shortly
after 1046, and Much Marcle was held by Earl (later King) Harold in
1066 and by William I in 1086. Winstree hundred, excluding Much
Marcle, may represent the main part of the area dependent on an
early Anglo-Saxon royal or episcopal centre at Ledbury or perhaps
at the neighbouring Bosbury, where Bishop Athelstan of Hereford
died in 1056 (see below, chapter 6). Such an early administrative
area is likely to have extended further west, for in the 11th and
12th centuries the *parochia*, or area dependent on Ledbury church,
included Pixley, Aylton, Little Marcle, and probably Munsley,
all of which were in Radlow hundred in 1066. It may not have
included the northern parishes of Radlow hundred, however, as by
the 11th century several of those, including Tarrington where the
hundred met, were in the *parochia* of another minster church, at
Stoke Edith. Further north again, the Frome parishes seem to have
formed another *parochia* based on Bishop's Frome.[33]

In 1066 Ledbury was a substantial but not exceptionally large
manor, with no evidence of the beginnings of a small town. With
a recorded population of something over 26 it was less populous
than the neighbouring manors of Bagburrow (probably in Mathon),
Bosbury and Cradley (see below, chapter 6). In comparison with the
later small town of Bromyard, where there was a minster church before
c.840, Ledbury was at best a medium-sized place; it was assessed for
the geld, a land tax, at five hides to Bromyard's 30, and valued at £10
in 1066 and only £8 in 1086, to Bromyard's £45 10s. at both dates.
Bromyard had a recorded population of 65, including two priests and
a chaplain, and a total of 75 ploughs were employed there, compared
with 37 at Ledbury. One way in which Ledbury did stand out in 1066
was in the size of the endowment of its church in comparison with
the rest of the manor: its priest held land assessed at 2½ hides; at
Bromyard the two priests held only one hide and the chaplain 1¾ hide.
Ledbury's church was clearly an important one.[34]

THE CHURCH IN ITS PARISH

That church, and the bishops of Hereford who were lords of the manor as well as patrons of the parish church, played a major role in the development of early medieval Ledbury. People coming from the church's extensive *parochia* to attend its services probably boosted the town's market which in 1138 was held on Sundays. The importance of the parish church declined slightly with the size of its parish in the 12th century, but Ledbury soon acquired another ecclesiastical institution, the Hospital of St Katherine, founded by Bishop Hugh Foliot (d.1231), which attracted support from landholders over a wide area, mainly to the west of Ledbury. They included the influential baron Walter de Lacy who gave the new hospital the church and manor of Yarkhill and the church of Weston Beggard, and Geoffrey de Longchamp and his wife Isabel who gave the church and land in Kempley (Gloucestershire).[35]

Ledbury church stands on the east side of the medieval town. It now occupies a shelf of nearly flat ground which contrasts with the slope of the hill to the east and north, but this shelf may be the result of generations of digging in the churchyard. A stream, which has been dammed to form a pond in the garden of Upper Hall, flows down the hill and enters the churchyard immediately east of the church; from there it now enters a culvert and flows along the southern side of the churchyard to the Lower Cross and Bye Street. The existence of the stream may well have been significant for the church's founders, although when it was first recorded, as a boundary mark in the mid-13th century, there was no suggestion that it was considered holy.[36]

Figure 21 A detail from the enclosure map of 1816, showing the church, the vicarage and Upper and Lower Halls to the west and north of the churchyard. The plot marked 'Lady Gresley' to the south may have been the site of the bishop's manor house.

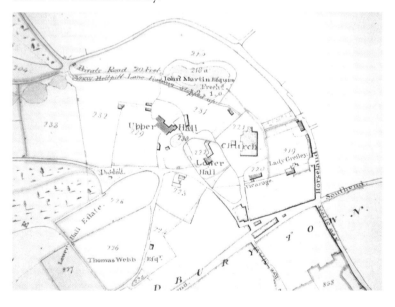

The origins of Ledbury church, as of most parish churches, are unrecorded, but certainly lie in the Anglo-Saxon period. The place-name 'Ledbury' may provide a clue to the status of the early church. The second element, 'bury' or 'burh' meaning an enclosure, was sometimes used in the eighth or ninth centuries to describe a monastery or similar religious foundation. There is a problem, in that in most such place-names 'bury' is compounded with a personal name (usually a woman's), whereas in Ledbury the first element is from the river Leadon. The same combination, with a river name as the first element, does, however, occur in the putative monastic site at Kintbury (Berkshire). The other hallmark of these religious sites of the middle Anglo-Saxon period is a church set in a large, roughly circular, enclosure. If the sites of the later ecclesiastical Upper and Lower Halls (the houses of the medieval priests called portionaries who shared the income of the church) are included, the early enclosure at Ledbury would be large, but irregular rather than circular. As mentioned above, there was certainly a ninth-century monastery or minster at Bromyard, and a smaller, 'family minster' at Acton Beauchamp (in Worcestershire until 1897) was founded in 727 and survived into the ninth century. The evidence is not conclusive, but it is certainly possible that Ledbury originated as a minster church.[37]

Whatever its origins, the size of its endowment, the number of its clergy, and the scale of the medieval church building confirm that the Anglo-Saxon church at Ledbury was an important one, a mother church which served a large, early *parochia* (see below). In 1086 a priest continued to hold 2½ hides of the bishop's Ledbury manor, an estate the size of a small manor and much larger than those held by most later medieval parish priests. By the mid-13th century the priests' houses were already known as the Upper and Lower Halls, suggesting that they were high-status buildings. Later medieval evidence (see below, chapter 7), confirms the large size of the portionaries' income from both land and tithes.[38]

Minsters were normally served by two or more priests. The first record of a priest at Ledbury is the inclusion of one among the tenants of the manor in 1086. He may in fact have been the head of a small college or community of priests, as 12th- and 13th-century evidence suggests that there were at least two priests at Ledbury. About 1160, two men who seem to have been vicars of Ledbury, Alfred and Robert, witnessed a grant of land. The appearance of two vicars is slightly surprising, as later there was only one vicar in Ledbury church; possibly the word 'vicar' in the document was only meant to apply to Robert. By the 1230s there were two rectors of Ledbury, that is, two priests who shared the endowment of the church, known as the rectory. Those two rectors look very much like the successors of Anglo-Saxon minster priests. From 1293 they appointed a single vicar, that is, a priest to serve the church. By 1311 the rectory (the land known as glebe and the right to tithe of grain which formed the church's endowment) was formally divided into two portions, of slightly unequal value. These portions gave their name to the two priests who shared the rectory and who were generally known as portionaries.[39]

Further evidence of the church's early status is provided by the size of its early medieval parish. From the 12th century until it was divided up in the later 19th century, Ledbury parish covered an area of 8,194 acres, including the detached area of Court-y-Park or Parkhold between Pixley and Munsley. Earlier, however, the area, which in the 12th century became the parishes of Aylton (812 acres), Coddington (1,064 acres), Donnington (808 acres), Eastnor (3,186 acres), Little Marcle (1,218 acres), and Pixley (655 acres), all seems to have been part of Ledbury's parish or *parochia*. When Coddington church was consecrated

Figure 22 The extent of Ledbury's early medieval parish (*parochia*) highlighted on a map of east Herefordshire. The parishes labelled in red are those parishes of the Winstree Hundred which were manors of the bishop.

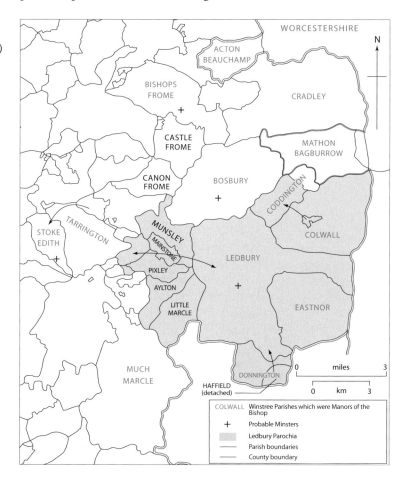

Figure 23 Pixley church dates to about 1260, although the bell turret dates to the restoration of 1865. The church is dedicated to St Andrew and stands adjacent to Pixley Court Farm.

in the mid-12th century, a pension of 2s. a year was reserved to the portionaries of Ledbury, presumably in recognition of their rectorial rights. At some time, probably in the 13th century, part of the tithe of Aylton, Pixley and Donnington was assigned to the vicar of Ledbury to increase his income, an arrangement which indicates that the tithe of those parishes had belonged to Ledbury church. Donnington church was called a chapel in the mid-13th century, and from the mid-14th century the portionaries of Ledbury presented priests to Donnington and Aylton chapels. As late as the later 16th century Aylton, Donnington, Little Marcle and Pixley were all described as chapels of Ledbury. The evidence for Eastnor is slighter, but persuasive. In 1460 the bishop, in allowing an exchange of benefices between the incumbents of Eastnor and Hanwell, reserved the pensions or portions due from Eastnor to the portionaries of Ledbury. Although there is no documentary evidence to connect them with Ledbury church, the later parishes of Colwall (3,771 acres) and Munsley (1,228 acres) also seem on topographical grounds to have been taken out of Ledbury's early *parochia*. The late Anglo-Saxon and early Norman church of Ledbury thus served an area of 20,936 acres, the southern half of the later Radlow Hundred.[40]

The House of God

The church fabric is an important source of information. By examining it closely, we can see that what is visible today is the

Figure 24 Plan of the
church, redrawn from a
measured survey by the
Royal Commission on
Historical Monuments in
1932. It shows the major
phases of development.
Note the change in
alignment of the nave
between the 11th and
12th centuries.

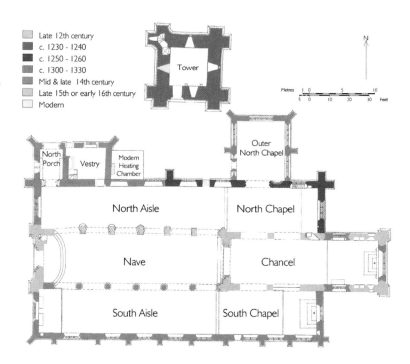

result of six or more medieval building programmes, carried out
over more than 500 years. Each century made its own contribution,
altering previous features in a way which makes it complicated to
understand what the early church builders achieved. We also have
to take into account alterations, both recorded and undocumented,
made after the Reformation and the efforts made by the Victorians
to restore or recreate medieval features.

About the time of Domesday Book a very large church, with a
long nave probably flanked by two narrow aisles, was begun on the
same site as the present church. The clue to the size and plan of that
building is the survival of bases of four large circular piers which
supported an arcade separating the nave from a north aisle; those
bases can be clearly seen at the foot of new piers constructed when
the aisle and its arcade were rebuilt later in the Middle Ages. Any
trace of a contemporary south aisle has disappeared and so has the
original east end of the north arcade so we have little evidence of what
the rest of the 11th-century church was like and whether it was ever
completed. The church was clearly very important within its county
and may have had minster status, so it is likely it followed the pattern
of such churches and had a cruciform plan, with arms (transepts)
projecting north and south and a chancel as the eastern limb. Where
such transepts intersected with the nave they usually formed what is
called a crossing, which was strongly marked with larger piers at each
angle and often crowned by a tower. We do not know whether this

arrangement existed at Ledbury and was demolished or whether it was planned but not finished. It seems likely that the church was intended to be cruciform and that its crossing filled an area which stood partly over the west end of the present chancel.

The 11th-century church was probably completely rebuilt late in the following century. The chancel and much of the west end survive from the late 12th-century building, the high quality of their masonry and decoration indicating the huge investment made in the grand new church. It was laid out on a new alignment. No doubt it was intended to rebuild the 11th-century aisle arcades to conform with east and west ends but, because the arcades were replaced in the 14th and 15th centuries, the only clue left is the clustered shafts (responds) where arcades met the chancel. The style of the southern one suggests that work was not finished until after 1200. Whether the choir was aisled is less certain. The evidence that it was can be seen high up on the walls that face the north and south chapels. Each wall has a row of carved heads (corbel table) which ran under the eaves of the original roof. Below that is a moulded course of stones, which it has been claimed, marked the height of the 12th-century aisle roofs. But the arcades and the walling below these features have been so altered that it is difficult to draw firm conclusions. The round arcade piers stand on high pedestals of classical form, which might have been created to abut new pews perhaps when the chancel was beautified in 1810,

Figure 25 The west front of Ledbury church, showing the three main phases of the medieval building and post-medieval restoration work in medieval style. In the centre, the narrow 12th-century front of the nave flanked by turrets and with a highly decorated west doorway; the window above is 19th-century. The aisles to either side of the nave are both early 14th-century, as can be seen most clearly from the traceried windows, which were modified in the late 19th century. The fourth gable belongs to the north porch, added about a century later than the aisles.

Figure 26 A 12th-century carving of St Peter, identified by the key over his right shoulder, on the north jamb of the chancel arch at Kilpeck, Herefordshire.

Figure 27 A bishop, followed by clergy and laity, consecrates a church in this 13th-century manuscript of the Decretals of Gratian from Hereford Cathedral Library.

and there are indications that the north and south walls were solid and were pierced only by windows. If so the arcades must have been inserted later and made to look Romanesque since then. Unfortunately documents about changes made to the church after 1550 are few and no drawings showing the church interior before the late 19th century have been discovered.[41]

The west front was designed to impress those approaching from the town. The carving on the west doorway, which includes chevron as well as foliage and faces on the capitals, is less exuberant than that found at many contemporary Herefordshire churches but of great sophistication. The chancel stood considerably higher than the west entrance and must have been an imposing sight from there, with its pointed chancel arch decorated with alternating red and white stones and clustered columns, and rows of tall narrow windows at the east end, and perhaps all along the sides as well if traces of a window on the north side have been accurately identified.

The figures behind these ambitious building programmes were presumably the bishops of Hereford, as lords of the manor and patrons of the living. It is tempting to associate the late 12th-century work with Bishop William de Vere (1186-98), who had been a canon and clerk of the works at Henry II's new Augustinian priory (later abbey) at Waltham in Essex. One of the most unusual features of the church is the extremely long chancel, much longer than is usually found in a parish church of its date, and at 74 feet (22.5 metres) only 16 feet (4.8 metres) shorter than the nave. The unusual length suggests that several clergy officiated at services there, perhaps reflecting the unusual organisation of the clergy at Ledbury, with two (often absentee) portionaries, as well as a vicar, deacon and the chaplains assisting them at services.[42]

The church building also provides evidence for Ledbury's continuing importance in the 13th century by which time, if not before, it was dedicated to St Peter or to Sts Peter and Paul although more recently it has been known as St Michael and All Angels. In about the 1230s a massive, detached, bell tower was built in the churchyard to the north of the north aisle. Marshy ground to the west and south prevented a tower being attached to the west end of the nave in a conventional fashion, or to the south aisle. Indeed a detached tower might have been easier to build than one incorporated into existing fabric. The tower has a solid sculptural form, its thick walls pierced only by small lancet windows. It was crowned until the 18th century by a short, shingled spire, so its original form was squatter and less elegant. It may have been the first among several detached church towers in the county. Certainly Ledbury was a prominent enough church

Figure 28   The south elevation of the detached bell tower. There are 15 such towers in England, eight of them in Herefordshire. The roughly-coursed yellow sandstone masonry in the lower section is similar to that in the chancel, suggesting that work on both was undertaken at a similar period in the early 13th century.

to set a fashion, and Herefordshire has more such towers than any other county except Cornwall. The work may be associated with Bishop Hugh Foliot (1219-34) or possibly with his successor Bishop Ralph of Maidstone (1234-9). Hugh Foliot seems the most likely candidate, as his interest in Ledbury is shown in his foundation of St Katherine's Hospital. Alternatively, the tower may have been built by the portionaries, anxious to proclaim their right

Recording the Church

Figures A and B *The west end of the parish church of St Michael and All Angels Ledbury, photographed and drawn in 2008. Both photography and measured drawing are important elements of historic building recording and can highlight different aspects of the building's history. The stone-by-stone elevation drawing above highlights fabric changes such as the missing string course on the south (right-hand) aisle and the curves of two early windows, replaced by the inserted window above the west door. The drawing also highlights changes in alignment such as the west door and inserted window above and emphasises the changes in the size of the stone coursing. The photograph highlights the condition and quality of the stonework and can point to historic fabric which may have been restored during the 19th century.*

Historic building recording is considered a specialist subsection of archaeology or architectural history, designed to apply archaeological and architectural recording techniques to historic standing buildings. This process is intended to aid the understanding of the history of a building by identifying features which date the building's construction and phases of alteration.

Building recording provides a lasting record of the building as it is today and where possible can also be combined with analysis of documentary sources, historic maps and plans and landscape survey to provide a full history of a structure. This can be a rewarding process in itself, but it can also aid in the

understanding of a building to inform processes of restoration or alteration – to prevent modern work impacting upon the most significant historic elements of a building.

The detail in which a historic building is recorded can take many different forms or levels depending on the age, size and complexity of the building and the purpose of the survey; but the Survey Report usually includes a photographic record, a drawn record in either outline or detail and phased plans and elevations, combined with a written description and interpretation. English Heritage's *Understanding Historic Buildings: A Guide to Good Recording Practice* details the different levels of historic building recording in order to ensure

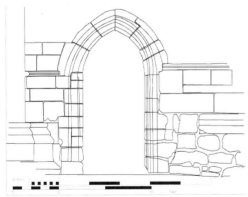

Figure C   *The south doorway of Ledbury parish church. This measured drawing highlights the irregular nature of both the arch and moulded door jambs, possibly indicating that this doorway was reconstructed reusing earlier fabric.*

that there is consistency in the completed reports and records. Once completed the record can be held by the owners of a building, submitted to the Historic Environment Record or published in local or national journals, to disseminate the information to as wide an audience as possible.

At Ledbury church a volunteer team worked with professional archaeologists, recording the exterior of the building and also looking for clues which may reveal more about the history of this important building, which was much altered during five major phases of building. Accurate, measured outlines of the church's elevations were produced, noting and recording architectural features of different dates and their relationship to each other in addition to anomalous features which highlighted phases of alteration.

These techniques can be applied to any historic building to reveal more about its history, providing an important tool for people involved in the conservation of the historic environment.

to hold the main services in the parish and to ring bells to summon parishioners to them. At the foundation of St Katherine's, *c.*1230, the portionaries had given permission for mass and other services to be held in its chapel, saving the rights of the parish church. When in 1303 Pope Boniface, at the request of the master of the hospital, confirmed the portionaries' grant, he included permission to ring a bell. Although the bell was not mentioned in the original grant, that charter was later endorsed with a note that it granted permission for mass and divine service, and for a bell. Was the hospital's bell a bone of contention from an early stage, to be countered by the provision of a prominent *parochial* bell tower?

Twenty or thirty years after the building of the bell tower more work was done on the north side of the church: the north aisle was rebuilt and the north chancel chapel added in a style closely connected to that of the north transept of Hereford cathedral, probably commissioned by Bishop Peter de Aigueblanche (1240-68). It was followed in the 14th century by major remodelling of the rest of the church, to be described in chapter 7.[43]

Men of God

The wealthiest and most important priests associated with Ledbury were the two portionaries, sometimes incorrectly called prebendaries. Their income was such that the bishop seems to have coveted it, and in 1276 Bishop Cantilupe obtained papal permission to appropriate, or take the income from, the livings of Ledbury and Bosbury to supply food for his table. The bishop may have taken the revenues of Ledbury for a short period, since in 1281 he owed Master Adam de Filaby, canon of Hereford, 40 marks (£26 6s. 8d.) for the profits of Upper Hall. The previous year the bishop had collated Adam to the office of dean of Hereford, although the former dean, John de Aigueblanche, was still alive and in possession of it. By 1307 John was a portionary of Ledbury. It seems likely that he had held that living since the late 1260s and that Bishop Cantilupe had intruded Adam de Filaby into Upper Hall as well as into the deanery, though this probably had nothing to do with the proposed appropriation. Ultimately the permission to appropriate the rectory was not acted upon, and the portionaries of Ledbury continued to enjoy the endowments of the living without actually serving it. Those portionaries, like John de Aigueblanche, were usually senior clerics, often related to the bishops of Hereford. They included Philip de Braose and Thomas Foliot who held the rectory at the time of the foundation of St Katherine's Hospital, about 1230. Thomas was presumably a relation of Bishop Hugh Foliot; he had been appointed precentor of Hereford cathedral in 1223 and became treasurer sometime between 1230 and 1234. Philip, who seems to have been related to Bishop Giles de Braose (d.1215), was a canon of the cathedral. In 1280 Bishop Thomas Cantilupe deprived the portionary James de Aigueblanche, archdeacon of Shropshire and a great nephew of Bishop Peter de Aigueblanche, of his portion of Ledbury for not residing in Ledbury. James's fellow portionary was Nicholas de Anne, a member of Oxford University who held a succession of livings in Oxfordshire but had no other known connection with Hereford diocese. He seems to have continued his studies while he held the Ledbury portion; when he witnessed a Ledbury charter during his tenure of the living he was described as 'dominus', but by the time of his death in 1277 he was a Master of Arts.[44]

Although only James de Aigueblanche was actually accused of non-residence, the 13th-century portionaries seem to have been non-resident most of the time, leaving the church to be served by a vicar. In 1288 Roger the vicar held half a town property or burgage in Middle Town or the High Street, next door to Richard the deacon. From 1293 or earlier the portionaries appointed vicars regularly. The exact status of the portionaries and whether or not they ought to serve the cure was disputed in the late 13th and early 14th centuries, but in 1311 it was agreed that they had no cure of souls, that is they were not required to take service and minister to parishioners themselves.[45]

In addition to the portionaries and the vicars, a number of chaplains were recorded in Ledbury in the 13th century. Some served side altars or cult statues. John, 'chaplain of the blessed Mary of Ledbury', who witnessed a grant of land in the parish around the year 1280, served an endowed chantry or service. He and his successors were paid at least partly out of rents from land in and around Ledbury which had been given to support them. The chaplains held land in Eastnor field by 1316. A candle of the Virgin, also supported by rents, presumably burned before her statue; in the later 13th century arable land outside the town paid 2d. a year to 'the wax of the blessed Mary' in the parish church. Although not specifically recorded until the later Middle Ages, the light of St Peter, the church's patron saint, presumably dated to the 12th or 13th century. It may well have been the 'light of the church of the blessed Peter of Ledbury', to which John Gersant paid 14d. a year from another piece of arable land. St Peter's statue would have stood by the high altar, presumably with the light before it. A light of St Radegund had been endowed with rents from another piece of arable before 1250. At St Katherine's Hospital in the mid-13th century there were lights of St Katherine and of St Mary Magdalene.[46]

Figure 29 St Radegund from the frontispiece of the *Lyfe of Saynte Radegunde* by Henry Bradshaw.

The Virgin Mary was the most popular and highly regarded saint in the medieval church. The two saints honoured at the hospital were also universally popular. St Mary Magdalene, from whom Christ cast out seven devils, was identified with the sinful woman who anointed Christ's feet, and was thus the type of the penitent sinner. St Katherine of Alexandria was a probably mythical saint whose alleged virginity, skill in debating with philosophers, and torture on a wheel made her the patron of young girls, students and clergy, nurses, and craftsmen such as wheelwrights and millers. St Radegund, on the other hand, was a sixth-century Frankish queen, known for her piety and charitable works, whose cult does not seem to have been widespread in England. Religious houses in Cambridge, Thelsford (Warwickshire), Bradsole (Kent), and Usk (Monmouthshire) were dedicated to her in the 12th century, and she had chapels in St Paul's, Lichfield and Exeter cathedrals and, perhaps significantly for Ledbury, in Gloucester abbey (now Gloucester cathedral). Did Radegund's cult reach Ledbury from Gloucester, or possibly Usk, or was it introduced by the Savoyard Bishop Peter de Aigueblanche (1240-68) directly from the Continent? Could the existence of a chapel of St Radegund at Ledbury have influenced John Grandison, bishop of Exeter? He had been born at Ashperton near Ledbury in 1292 and 20 years before he died in 1368 he had built a chapel dedicated to St Radegund at Exeter cathedral to hold his body when the time came.[47]

Other priests or chaplains assisted the vicar and the portionaries if they were in the parish, with the services in the chancel. Walerand the chaplain, who was involved in a lawsuit over land in the town in 1255, was sacrist of the church. As such he would have been responsible for the vestments and vessels used at mass and for the relics which the parish church, like St Katherine's Hospital, would have held. The title 'dominus' given him in one document may mean that he was a university graduate, although it was a common term of respect for those clergy made 'gentle by occupation'. Gilbert, chaplain of Ledbury, who witnessed a deed about 1240, may also have assisted in the chancel, as may Roger, then chaplain of Ledbury, who was present at the payment of a rent to St Katherine's Hospital in 1234. Some of the chaplains were probably freelance, owning land in the borough and earning money by saying prayers and masses for their fellow townsmen. Aluric the chaplain, son of Aluric reeve of Ledbury, was probably one such; his father was an important man in the town and Aluric himself sold a total of 11 acres of arable and three quarters of a burgage plot in the mid-13th century. One Ledbury man seems to have used his property in the town to endow a position for himself in the church. In 1279 John de Preston was ordained subdeacon at Newent 'to the title of a burgage and land which he appropriated to the church of Ledbury'. Shortly afterwards Margery daughter of Osbert Joce of Ledbury sold to John de Preston, chaplain, a house and land in New Street adjoining his own house; was John replacing the estate he had given the church? Some clerics led less than perfect lives: in 1288 Simon the clerk, who owned a house in Ledbury, abjured the realm for felony.[48]

Surviving registers show that the bishops of Hereford visited Ledbury regularly from the 1270s, staying in their manor house, later, anachronistically, called a palace. Earlier bishops probably did likewise, although the only evidence of such a visit is Bishop Richard de Capella's death at Ledbury in 1127. Bishop Hugh Foliot was presumably in the town for the foundation of St Katherine's Hospital about 1230. Bishop Thomas Cantilupe

Figure 30 Bishop Thomas Cantilupe and Archbishop Thomas Becket, depicted on early 14th-century glass in the church at Credenhill, Herefordshire.

dated letters at Ledbury on 22 December 1275, 15 January 1276, and 10 October 1288. On the Monday in Holy Week 1278, he heard a legal case at Ledbury manor house, and in March 1280 he held an ordination in Ledbury church. His successor Bishop Swinfield held an ordination at Ledbury in March 1283.[49]

ST KATHERINE'S HOSPITAL

The foundation of St Katherine's Hospital by Bishop Hugh Foliot provided the people of Ledbury with another focus for their religious devotion and with a purchaser for their land in the town and elsewhere in the parish when they needed to raise money. Bishop Hugh bought 1½ burgage plots in the town from John Gersant as part of the original endowment of the hospital; later John, who seems to have been a prominent inhabitant of Ledbury, sold to the hospital other land, including a pasture in the neighbouring parish of Eastnor. William of Ockeridge, whose holding of four yardlands by knight service was the largest in 'Ledbury Foreign' (the area of the parish outside the town) in the mid-13th century, was a more substantial donor, giving a house and three acres of land in Ockeridge as well as an assart (land cleared from woodland) for the souls of himself and his wife. Philip Ruddoc in 1242 sold to the hospital a long lease of land in Hole meadow; later he granted the land outright. About 1240 Roger of Northinton (Netherton), for the 'health of his soul', gave the hospital a rent of ½lb of pepper which his sister paid him and another

Figure 31　The exterior of the 13th-century building of St Katherine's Hospital from the west. The bell tower is a later addition.

Figure 32   Bishop Foliot, founder of St Katherine's Hospital, from a 16th-century panel which once hung in the Master's House and is now in the chapel of the hospital.

rent of 4d. a year, both from land in Netherton. Later the hospital had to pay his widow Alice to give up her claim to several parcels of arable land. Another early donor or seller of land to the hospital was Aluric son of Aluric the chaplain whose grant of three quarters of a burgage plot with the buildings on it may well have been worth more than the 2½ marks (£1 13s. 4d.) which the hospital paid him. In 1261 Peter of Donnington in his 'great necessity' sold the hospital a lease of his mill. The hospital benefited indirectly from the poverty of Juliana daughter of Alan of Wellington. Adam Beyvin, a canon of Hereford, bought a rent of 8s. from her in her 'great necessity' and gave it to the hospital. Ledbury people would have attended services in the hospital chapel: Adam de Street's grant of rents to maintain a wax candle burning in the church of St Katherine in Ledbury reads like a grant to a local parish church.[50]

Bishop Hugh's foundation charter for St Katherine's had provided for a warden or master and for two chaplains, one of whom was to pray for the bishop's soul, the other for the souls of the hospital's other benefactors. The chaplains' prayers, and those of the poor inmates, must have been a strong incentive to give to the hospital, and presumably only a small gift was needed to secure the prayers. All did not always go smoothly, however, even in the relatively early days of the house. A visitation by the dean and the archdeacon in 1297 found that Brother Henry, the master, was not acting on the advice or with the consent of the brothers in matters relating to the government of the hospital. From the hospital's revenues he was supporting his sister and her children and was also maintaining the son of William Eseger, a prominent Ledbury layman. He had so neglected the hospital's manors that the land lay uncultivated and the livestock had gone; he had also misappropriated goods and money to the value of 120 marks (£80). Even the hospital buildings were in poor repair. All in all, the visitors were told, matters were going from bad to worse and would continue to do so until the master was removed. What happened next is not recorded.[51]

The story of St Katherine's Hospital and the spiritual life of the people of Ledbury will be taken up again in chapter 7.

Chapter 4

Growth of the Borough

LEDBURY BEFORE THE BOROUGH

The entry for the bishop of Hereford's manor of *Liedeberge* in Domesday Book described the manor in the standard fashion, listing the numbers of tenants and types of land and mentioning two mills. The church was not mentioned, although there is a clue both to its existence and its importance in the fact that a priest held a considerable portion of the land in the parish. But there is nothing at all to suggest any sign of urban development; it is not even clear from the Domesday account whether there was a village or whether the 100 or more inhabitants were scattered in individual farms across the manor. Another feature of the later life of the town, the bishop's hall or palace, is also absent from the Domesday account, though in all likelihood it was there too, as the administrative centre of the manor, where rents were paid and courts held, and as an occasional residence and (probably) a hunting lodge. Whether the presence of such a centre had a year-round, permanent impact on the population of the manor, we cannot tell. The ground on which the town of Ledbury was to be founded, about forty years after the Domesday survey, is not at first sight an obvious one for a new planned town and emphasises the fundamental importance of the church in the location of the settlement, although it is on a spring-line and minor streams flow at intervals off the high ground down to the Leadon. One such rises in the gap between Dog Hill and Coneygree Wood, supplying a chain of fish-ponds before flowing around the south side of the churchyard and across the built-up area. The town's axis is formed by a north-south road that forms part of a long distance route between Gloucester and Bromyard. This section of the road clings to the eastern side of the Leadon valley, about a kilometre from the Leadon brook itself, following the base of the steep gradients up to (from north to south) Frith Wood, Bradlow Knoll, Dog Hill, and Coneygree Wood. This chain of hills runs roughly parallel to the main range of the Malvern Hills about five kilometres further east, and the gap between Dog Hill and Coneygree Wood was used by the west-east road linking Hereford and Worcestershire, on its way to cross the Malverns at Little Malvern. Ledbury's church stands in this gap, 656 feet (200 metres) away from the main road.

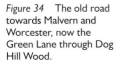

Figure 34 The old road towards Malvern and Worcester, now the Green Lane through Dog Hill Wood.

PLANNING THE BISHOP'S BOROUGH

The act of founding a borough at Ledbury went unrecorded, at least in the surviving sources, though in 1138 Bishop Robert de Bethune was granted permission by the king to hold a weekly Sunday market there. This probably confirmed a situation that had already existed for around a decade. The 1130s were troubled years, a most unlikely time in which to found a new town, whereas the more peaceful 1120s were distinguished locally by the episcopacy of Bishop Richard de Capella, a well-connected and experienced administrator responsible for securing a number of royal grants for the development of markets and fairs around his diocese. He may well have acted as agent for Henry I in the foundation of a borough at Leominster about 1123, and is the most likely individual to have developed the borough at Ledbury around the same time or shortly after.[52]

Along with many other manorial medieval new towns established by the local lords, in this case the bishop, the development of a formal borough at Ledbury was successful enough to have been followed, probably quite quickly, by a series of planned extensions to accommodate the demand for plots within easy reach of the market place. This process, in Ledbury and elsewhere, is not documented, though historical records can occasionally provide dates by which certain streets had appeared and were being built up. The sequence of extensions may, however, still be worked out from clues in the present or recently recorded layout of the streets and their house-plots; these were often known as burgages – town plots that, unlike much rural property, could be freely passed on to the next generation and carried certain legal rights within the borough. The terms used to distinguish the urban and rural areas of Ledbury were 'Borough' and 'Foreign', and persisted in use and significance until the late 19th century.[53]

It is possible to use the present-day townscape to reconstruct arrangements made 800 years ago because a large body of experience shows that, once established and built up, urban property boundaries are extremely persistent. Even though original plots may be subdivided, or amalgamated, a proportion of the original boundaries along a street will remain unchanged. As a result it is often possible to work out the original systems of measurement used by the medieval surveyors. These men were professionals, sometimes referred to as *locatores*, who would not only stake out the new plots and organise any necessary building work (bridges, drainage, quays, defences and so on) but would promote the new venture throughout the district to potential settlers. The units they used to plan new towns and town extensions were often multiples of the statute perch of 16½ feet (5.03 metres). The bishop of Worcester, for example, had his new borough of Stratford-upon-Avon laid out in the 1190s with plots with 3.5-perch frontages, and these can still be traced in the modern town. Burford in Oxfordshire was originally planned with plots measuring 1.5 perches wide by 22 to 28 perches deep; later extensions had plots measuring 3 perches wide by 14-19 perches deep. Examination of existing plot boundaries suggests that Ledbury, too, was at least partly planned with regular measurements, and there is a reference in an early 15th-century copy of a late 14th-century rental to the use of measurement 'by the king's perch'.[54]

Surviving townscape is not the only source from which the growth of a medieval town can be reconstructed: archaeological excavation, too, has a part to play. Individual excavations can occasionally transform our understanding of the way a place has developed; more often such a transformation comes about by the slow accumulation of results from a series of excavations spread over many years, and several locations. Between 1995 and the beginning of the community archaeology campaign of 2008, some 23 archaeological investigations took place in the historic core of Ledbury, mostly responses to new developments in the town and improvements at the church. Most have been of limited scope, constrained by the needs of particular developments, and scattered unevenly across the town centre, wherever building work happens to be taking place. In consequence, while there have been five

Figure 35 A map of
the principal features
of medieval Ledbury,
showing property
boundaries surveyed in
the late 19th century,
many of which are likely
to be of medieval origin.
The map also shows the
measurements of those
property boundaries as
surveyed in 2009.

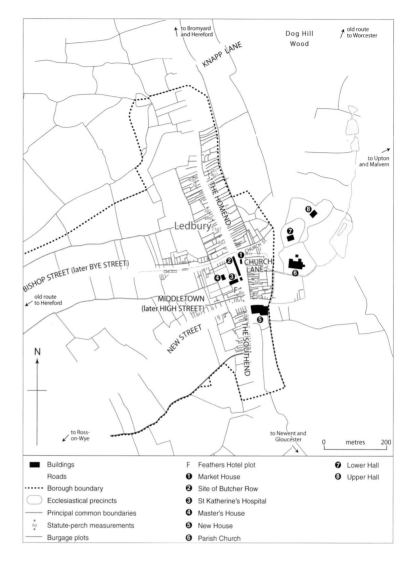

individual excavations along or just off Bye Street, other streets are
barely represented at all. Medieval pottery has been found on 13
out of the 23 sites. Medieval pottery dating from the first century
of the borough has now been found widely across the inner town
centre: at the church, south of the churchyard at the Priory, at
the former cattle market, west of the cattle market on the Market
Theatre site, in Ledbury Park, behind the *Feathers Hotel* on High
Street and at St Katherine's. The community excavations in 2008
also found 12th-century pottery in the grounds of Abbot's Lodge
on the west side of the churchyard (panel 3).[55]

However, before exploring the creation of the new borough, it is
first necessary to review the pre-existing features of the site that the
town was planned around.

The Ecclesiastical Quarter

The origins, characteristics and many of the problems of
Ledbury's ecclesiastical institutions have been discussed in the
preceding chapter. Nevertheless, it is difficult to discuss the
shaping of the town without some further reference to what
geographers would term the 'pre-urban nucleus', the institutions
that were present before the town was founded, and around
which the town grew – in other words the church of St Peter,
the portionaries' halls, and the so-called bishop's palace or
manor house.

To some extent the present topography reflects an ancient
pattern. Clearly the church has been on its present site since at
least the late 11th or early 12th century (the date of the earliest
extant dateable architectural features) and it would be surprising
if it were not also on the site of its Anglo-Saxon predecessor,
though no trace of this has ever been recorded. The surrounding
churchyard is now a polygonal area of about 2.2 acres, bounded
on the south by the stream that runs down the valley between
Dog Hill and Coneygree Wood, eventually crossing Ledbury
High Street at the Lower Cross. This feature of the churchyard,
at least, is of some age as it was commented upon in 1781:
'The church is strong, and well built, and detached from the
steeple and spire. The church-yard is flanked on one side by a
wet fosse, and on the others by well-built houses, which give it
the look of a cathedral close'. It is now certain that the present
churchyard was once more extensive than it is now. This became

Figure 36 The church
and its immediate area
looking west. The rough
ground rises steeply to
the east from the present
churchyard boundary,
marked by trees. The
trees to the left of the
church mark the line
of the stream. The plot
surrounding the brick
house top left may have
been the site of the
bishop's manor house.
The former vicarage is
immediately west of the
church, pierced by the
spire in the photograph.
To the north, on the right
of the photograph, is
Lower Hall. The drive at
the bottom right leads to
Upper Hall.

clear during the excavation of three test-pits in the garden of
Abbot's Lodge, immediately west of the churchyard, during the
community excavations programme of 2008. Once the topmost
garden soil had been removed a typical churchyard soil, full of
many small pieces of disarticulated human bone, was exposed
and tested to some depth. Abbot's Lodge, the former vicarage
house, is, in origin, a timber-framed 15th-century hall and must
have been built on part of the cemetery. Where, then, did the
western boundary of the medieval churchyard lie before the
Abbot's Lodge was built? The western boundary of the Abbot's
Lodge plot shared the boundary between Ledbury Borough and
Ledbury Foreign, so it seems likely that this was also the original
churchyard boundary.[56]

In Ledbury, as in Bromyard and in Ross-on-Wye, the houses
of the clergy that served the minster churches stood close by, on
sites adjoining the churchyard. This seems to reflect a common
pre-Conquest settlement pattern of linked enclosures, though
in not one of these instances are the actual boundaries clear. At
Ledbury, only Lower Hall has, on 19th-century maps, anything
resembling a discrete enclosure around it, with an oval plot
located immediately north of the churchyard. The Upper Hall in
contrast sat within a more amorphous property on the northern
slope of the small valley overlooking the largest and lowest
fish-pond. Below it was Hellpitt Lane, leaving the Worcester Road
at a junction near the upper ponds and following the stream
down to the churchyard boundary where it apparently stopped.
The 1816 enclosure map shows a total of four ponds in the chain;
nowhere else in the immediate vicinity of Ledbury was there
scope for a series of ponds, and it seems probable that these
were part of the bishop's estate, the bishop being able to offer to
guests pike and tench from his stews (fish ponds) in 1289-90 (see
Fig. 21). This raises what may be the single most vexed question,
the biggest mystery, of Ledbury's medieval past – where was the
bishop's hall?[57]

The 17th-century historian Thomas Blount was in no
doubt. The bishop's hall 'was on the south side of the church
but now utterly demolished'. It seems most probable that the
hall, like the portionaries' houses, stood in close proximity to
the church, probably actually adjoining it. This has recently
(2008-9) been found to be the case at Ross-on-Wye, where a very
substantial medieval building, identified as part of the medieval
bishop's palace, has been found by excavation immediately
west of St Mary's church, standing within a former Roman
stone-walled enclosure. At Ledbury there is no such evidence
of a Roman background but the large plot known as the Priory,

immediately south of the churchyard, has, at least superficially, all the requisite characteristics for the site of the bishop's hall or 'palace'. Historical evidence seems to point in exactly this direction. A 17th-century book of leases includes an indenture of 1616 concerning property in the tenure of Edward Hill on Horse Lane (Worcester Road) that included 'the garden called the Lord's orchard' and 'two parts of a barn called the lord's barn'. This seems to be identifiable with 'one garden in lord's manor with the parcel of barn at the entrance of the said manor' for which a two-shilling rent was paid in 1495, and the 'garden of the lord of the manor with a parcel of barn next the gate and entry of the said manor for which two shillings was paid for herbage (grazing)' in 1537. The only problem is that a 75-foot (23-metre-long) trench dug in the centre of the plot in 2005 and monitored by archaeologists, produced results that were, at best, ambiguous. Subsoil containing crushed sandstone and small stones was found, together with some animal bone and charcoal, but only a single piece of cooking pot, dated to the 10th to 12th centuries. No features (pits or ditches for example) were found and the results were consistent with medieval cultivation activity. So, while it can be argued that the substantial buildings to be expected of a bishop's residence – a great hall, chamber block, kitchen, lodgings and stables – could well lie elsewhere within this large plot, the negative archaeological results give pause for thought.[58]

Other sites have been considered as possible candidates for the location of the bishop's hall. Attention has in particular been drawn to the unusual siting of St Katherine's Hospital, occupying valuable land on the west side of the market place rather than the extramural and peripheral sites most commonly associated with medieval hospital foundations. It has been suggested that the hospital took over the original site of the bishop's hall, which was then relocated to Ledbury Park, specifically the site of New House, built in about 1590 on the corner of the Southend and Horse Lane (Worcester Road). While the location of St Katherine's is indeed very unusual, there is no other evidence to support the idea that it superseded the bishop's hall, and its separation from the church and the park by the main road is problematic. Nor is there evidence that the hall was ever moved. The New House site on the corner of the Southend appears unlikely to have ever accommodated the hall as it is now known to have been divided into burgage properties in the Middle Ages. In short, a degree of uncertainty still surrounds the location of the bishop's hall and, until it is resolved, one of the most significant factors in the history and planning of the town will not be fully understood.[59]

Church Street-Church Lane

This tiny triangle of land bounded by High Street, Church Street (to the north) and Church Lane (to the south) may be a much more significant element in the town plan than its size at first sight suggests. Church Lane is the principal access to the church from High Street, while Church Street was the beginning of the main road to the east before it was supplanted by Horse Lane (now Worcester Road) further south.

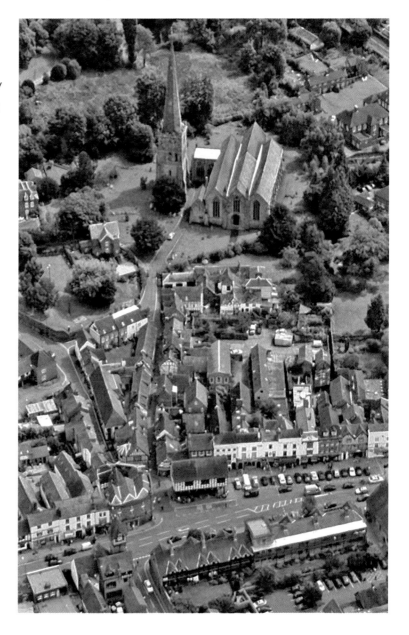

Figure 37   Church Lane runs eastwards from the market place to the church. Church Street (formerly Back Lane or Hall End), to the left, now performs a dog-leg turn around 18th-century infill buildings immediately to the north of the Market House.

Figure 38 This view
from the church tower
shows Dog Hill rising
to the north-east of the
town. The large building
in the foreground is
Lower Hall, immediately
to the north of
the churchyard.

It has been suggested that the Church Lane-Church Street
triangle represents an infilled pre-Conquest market place
developed at the gates of the minster precinct. While this is
perfectly possible, it must be said that there is no historical or
archaeological evidence to support it. In fact, the town-plan
evidence, such as it is, points in a different direction. 'Market infill',
the building of permanent commercial structures in medieval
market places, is usually distinguished by the presence of buildings
without plots, yards or gardens. This does not seem to be the
case here, where at least a proportion of the buildings sit within
distinguishable plots with boundary walls and yard areas. If,
therefore, the triangular block was not a market place, it may have
been a cluster of small plots developed either to face south onto the
access lane to the church, or north onto the road over the end of
Dog Hill towards Worcester.[60]

A complicating factor is the presence of a culvert running along
the north side of Church Lane found under the Old Grammar
School when it was restored in 1977-8. Though now dry, the
culvert appears to have formed one branch of the watercourse
running down the valley and around the churchyard before

crossing the main road at Lower Cross. It is not known whether the channel was open until the time the Grammar School and the earlier phase of the nearby council offices (1 Church Lane) were both built in about 1500; nor is the precise route by which water was fed from the churchyard into this branch of the watercourse. Both buildings belonged to the parish and were part of a concentration of parish property in this area: whether this is because they were both built by the parish, or whether there is another explanation for the concentration of parish property here – for example, former guild property – is also uncertain. The development of this crucial area will only now be understood by archaeological excavation. The presence of the culvert and the suspected former stream should mean (if the stream is close to or still in its natural course) that there has been much infilling of ground here and that deep archaeological deposits, potentially well-preserved and waterlogged, could one day be found here.[61]

THE STREETS OF THE NEW BOROUGH

High Street

High Street has, since its foundation, been the heart of the town of Ledbury, its commercial and ceremonial core, a distinctive wedge-shaped market place whose limits were marked by a cross at each end. The street slopes down from the site of the High or Top Cross, at the junction with New Street and Worcester Road (formerly Horse Lane), to the Lower Cross at the junction of Bye Street (the medieval Bishop Street) and Church Street (formerly Back Lane). Close by the Lower Cross it was crossed by the shallow stream that flowed past the churchyard and continued westwards down Bye Street towards the Leadon.

Although its outlines have hardly changed at all, the market place itself has changed quite substantially in the centuries since it was first laid out. Not only have the crosses gone, so too have the shops and stalls that were erected in it, only the early 17th-century Market Hall surviving clearance in the early 19th century. Such shops and stalls, a distinctive feature of so many English medieval towns, are generally termed 'market-place encroachments', though the term is misleading, in the sense that it suggests a surreptitious, even illicit, process rather than a very deliberate speculative venture by the lord of a manor to increase his rent rolls – which is more likely in most cases to be their origin. There appears to have been one such development in Ledbury market place, the Shop Row (*Schopprewe*), first referred to by name in a lease of 1370. Its position can first be identified from the conveyance of

Figure 39 An aerial view of the market area looking north along High Street and Homend. Bye Street can be seen coming in from the west at the clock tower. Church Street is marked by the row of brick houses centre right. The long burgage plots on the east of High Street are clearly seen.

two shops within the row in 1451-2 which were said to extend 'from the common place where meat is sold in the front as far as the common street leading to the hospital at the back'. These structures, or predecessors on the same site, were probably in place by the 1280s, and account for some of the selds (stalls) and butchers' shambles listed at the end of the bishop's rental.[62]

The exact nature of the seld or market stall is difficult to determine. In truth, the word probably covered a variety of things, ranging from the temporary booths erected for fairs to substantial buildings akin to market halls. For example, during the 13th century the king regularly allowed the men of Hereford to gather twigs and alder wood in the Hay at Hereford to make their booths and hurdles (*seldas et cleyas*) for the fair. Sometimes they were referred to as shops (*schoppas*) rather than stalls or booths (*seldas*). Many weekly market stalls would also have been temporary affairs, trestles and boards brought out for the day, and the word seld might refer both to the stall and the pitch on which it stood. This may be the case in Ledbury in the report of Thomas Lorymer to the bishop in 1537 where he accounts for 'the farm [lease] of a burgage called le Bothall with the farm of selds'. This carried on into the modern period, with the trestles and boards being stored in the 'Booth Hall' (the seat of government – see below chapter 5) until the early 19th century. However, it is clear that many selds were permanent structures, whether individual small shops or buildings containing a number of stalls, akin to a market hall. It would seem that the development of the Rows in Chester arose from selds of the latter sort.[63]

In Ledbury in the late 13th century the *Red Book* shows a variety in value, and therefore presumably size, and location of the selds. In Middle Town (now High Street) John de Homme had a seld, while Nicholas of Worcester had two, but only Philip de Erdesley's was specifically described as being 'in front of his burgage'. Philip also held two other selds in the unassigned part of the rental – presumably in what came to be called Shop or Middle Row. He paid 4d. a year for the one in front of his house, but only 2d. a year each for the other two. There is an intriguing possibility of a two-storeyed seld in High Street in 1314, when a rental of the property de of the hospital listed 'from the upper seld which is next the seld once William Wynyard's in High Street, 15d., at each of four terms; from the lower seld next the aforesaid seld 18d. at each of four terms', although it could mean the ones up and down the slope of the street, on either side of William Winyard's, which is more likely. This also suggests the increasing value of commercial property on High Street. In the 1280s, however, the majority of the 42 selds paid far less; seven paid 6d. a year, the remainder, including the shambles and butcher's selds, paid 4d. a year. There were no selds in Southend, New Street, Homend or Bishop Street. In the *Red Book* the majority of the selds were listed after various unassigned burgages, and can assume to have been the Middle (or Shop or Butchers') Row and the Shop Row, the latter demolished in the early 17th century to make way for the new market house.[64]

The burgages lining the market place were listed under Middletown, the medieval name for High Street, where there were 26 tenants, a small number that becomes explicable if it is assumed that much of the western side was unavailable for settlement – or had even been cleared of plots – because it was occupied by the hospital. The west-side plots, south of the hospital, probably ran back to the current rear boundary of the *Feathers Hotel* plot, which at that point is 243 feet (70 metres) from the frontage. The property boundaries continue south to New Street, though the plots south of the *Feathers* may have lost ground at the rear by having a plot facing south to New Street cut out of them. The significance of this rear boundary is that it appears to be a southward continuation of the common boundary at the rear of the west-side Homend plots, and indeed to have continued further south, across New Street, bounding the rear of the Southend plots. In short, it looks as if it may have been a primary component of the planned town, an outer boundary perhaps framing all its new plots. The High Street plots also have signs of regular measurements in their layout, the distance between the New Street corner and the boundary between 23 and 24 High Street being almost exactly eight statute perches (*c*.132 feet/40.24 metres). Within this, the combined frontage width of nos 22 and 23 (occupied by a 16th- and a 17th-century building respectively) works out as close to two statute perches (c.33 feet/10.06 metres). While this does not tell us what the width of the original plots was, it is at least an indication that their measurements are likely to have been deliberately planned.

The east side of High Street is occupied by plots sharing a number of short common boundaries, as seen in Fig. 35. It is difficult to know whether they originally shared a continuous rear boundary, although the longest of these back boundaries, shared by nos 9-15, occurs 195-200 feet back from the frontage and, as on the west side of the street, appears as if it may have been planned as part of a single boundary uniting all the plots from the Homend to the Southend. Again, there are tantalising signs of plots planned in regular multiples of the statute perch: for example the width of numbers 19 and 20 combined, at 49 feet 2 inches (14.98 metres), is within 4 inches (0.1 metre) of 3 statute perches, while that of nos 12 to 15 at (82 feet 8 inches/25.19 metres) is within 2 inches (.05 metres) of five statute perches. The problem is the same as on the west side: regular measurements seem to be embedded in the current townscape, though to what dimensions the first plots were laid out remains obscure.

The Homend

This was, from the historical evidence alone, the longest built-up street of medieval Ledbury, stretching north from the market place in the direction of Bromyard. The west-side plots form a homogenous series for about 842 feet (300 metres) north from Bye Street, sharing a common rear boundary parallel to the main road. This regular series of plots comes to an end at the point where the road bends slightly to the east; beyond this, the maps made in the early 19th century show the road frontage only intermittently occupied, and it may be that this marks the outer limit of occupation in the medieval period. Beyond this, the historic maps reveal a pattern of small closes along the road extending back to another common boundary. This is much more irregular than the common back-fence line to the regular plots to the south, though it is interesting to note that it prolongs the same NNW-SSE alignment.[65]

The west-side plots also appear to have had an element of regular planning in their layouts, beyond the provision of an accurately rectilinear form. A number of the plots, or combinations of adjacent plots, have frontage width measurements that are

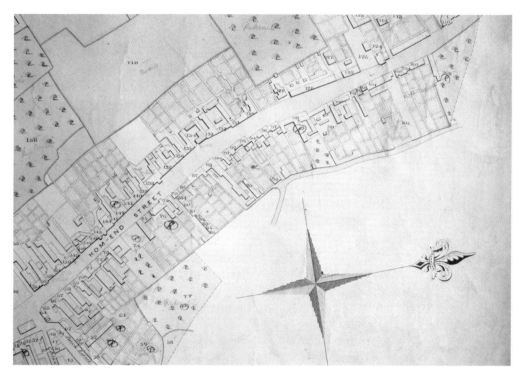

Figure 40 This section of the 1840 tithe map clearly shows the slight change of alignment part way along Homend. To the north (the right of the illustration) the plots are not as regularly laid out.

accurate multiples of the statute perch of 16½ feet (5.03 metres). So, towards the north end of the regular plot series, nos 78 to 82 have a combined width close to 49 feet (15 metres) (three statute perches are 49 feet 6 inches/15.09 metres), 74-6 are together 48½ feet (14.78 metres) wide, and 38 and 38a in combination measure 15.13 metres, while nos 32 to 36 combined measure 99 feet 2 inches (30.22 metres), almost precisely six statute perches (99 feet/30.18 metres). This quite convincingly suggests that the original surveyors were using a three-perch module in this part of the town. However, further south this is less clear, nos 14 to 30 having a combined measurement of 180 feet 1 inch (54.88 metres) (possibly representing 11 perches at 181 feet 6 inches/55.33 metres) and nos 6 to 12 a combined width of 130 feet 9 inches (39.85 metres), possibly representing an original width of eight perches (132 feet/40.24 metres). These plots, towards the south end of the street and the market place, have suffered a greater degree of amalgamation and may less reliably reflect their original planning than those further north.

The east-side plots were occupied for a slightly greater distance (about 1,010 feet/360 metres) out from the centre in 1816. As on the west side, the plots for the first 842 feet (300 metres), as far as the bend in the road, share a common parallel rear boundary and are uniformly rectilinear in form. Further out, beyond the bend, the plot outlines are less regular, with a greater number of curving individual boundaries. The anomaly here is that the line of the common back boundary is continued much further north (to Knapp Lane, 1,685 feet/600 metres from Lower Cross) by a common rear access lane connecting south-east to Green Lane. This may once have been common to the whole plot series but been lost by encroachment at the rear of the continuously occupied plots at the south end. The presence of the lane probably implies a single planned origin for the series as a whole, and Homend may be an example of a medieval planned street where plots were provided on both sides but a rear-access lane on only one (as in Corve Street, Ludlow). It may also imply that settlement was originally envisaged to extend as far north as Knapp Lane, and either never fulfilled its designer's expectations, or contracted in the later medieval period. Curiously, there is much slighter evidence on this side of the street of regular statute-perch multiples having been used by the bishop's surveyors. The combined frontage width of nos 133-5 is 32 feet 6 inches (9.9 metres) – which may relate to an original measurement of two perches (33 feet/10.06 metres), but this is by no means certain. Likewise, immediately to the south, numbers 127-31 sit within a plot 64 feet 2 inches (19.55 metres) wide at the frontage, perhaps representing an original measurement of four perches (66 feet/20.12 metres), although the discrepancy is greater and may be deceptive.

By 1288, the date of the surviving rental, there were 78 tenants holding plots along the Homend, though it is not at all clear what this implies in terms of lengths of occupied frontage. The evidence of the surviving townscape – there having been far too little archaeological investigation along the Homend for this source to contribute to the discussion – is in many ways ambiguous. The form of the present plots suggests that the medieval built-up area stretched north as far as the bend in the road, and this was (roughly) as far as the Borough extended into the Foreign, though there are other indications that the built-up area once extended, or was intended to extend, for twice that distance. Further, the provision of continuous back-lane access to the east-side plots is a sure sign of an organised origin, though measurement of the plot frontage widths has not yielded further evidence of this. But on the west side, without the provision of a rear lane, the evidence that the width of the plots was carefully specified is much stronger.

The Southend

As the name suggests, this is the road south, taking traffic from the Upper Cross towards Gloucester. Its most striking characteristic

Figure 41　This shows the Southend curving gently north-eastwards towards the town. The buildings on the left occupy medieval burgage plots, while the trees on the right grow on the site of houses demolished to make way for the grounds of Ledbury Park. See the map (Fig. C) in panel 5.

today is that it is only built up on one side – its western, down-slope side, the other being occupied by Ledbury Park.

The formation of the plots on the west side is complex, with strips running off the frontage angled slightly to the south to bring them perpendicular to one of a number of common rear boundaries and parallel to New Street. In the late 19th century the majority of the Southend plots ended at a common boundary that appears to have been a southward extension of the principal rear boundary of the Homend plots as well as those on High Street south of St Katherine's. There are signs of statute-perch based multiples in the lateral measurements of the Southend plots (the *Royal Oak Hotel*, for example occupying a plot 81 feet 8 inches (24.89 metres) wide, almost exactly five perches), though no overall scheme of measurement can now be discerned.

Although the Southend is now only built up on the west side, this was not always the case and it was part of the Borough. Deeds from between 1582 and 1621 show conclusively that there was then a row of at least five and a half burgages from the corner of Horse Lane (Worcester Road) southwards down the Southend; these were gradually cleared to create Ledbury Park. There were 20 tenants in the Southend at the time of the Bishop's rental of about 1288; some, at least, would have lived on the east side of the street. Because these plots were cleared at such an early date we know almost nothing of them. However, the Borough boundary recorded on the Tithe Map of 1841 includes a block of parkland extending roughly 786 feet (280 metres) south from the Upper Cross and some 225 feet (80 metres) wide into the park from the main road. This, in all probability, was all land that was once occupied by burgages, and its depth (roughly that of the east-side High Street plots) suggests that the High Street plots and the Southend plots were all conceived as a single scheme.[66]

THE LATER MEDIEVAL STREETS

In its first phase, the bishop's new borough appears to have been a linear settlement disposed along the main north-south road. But by the time of the surviving rental of 1288, two further streets, Bye Street (Bishop Street) and New Street, had come into existence and been built up to the west of the main axis (Fig. 35). For a number of reasons, these can be recognised as additions to the original town plan. First, they are both constricted as they cut through the properties on the north-south alignment of the Southend – High Street – the Homend, but widen out beyond the back boundary of the pre-existing plots. The plots developed at the eastern end of both streets are very short, biting into the rear of the corner plots of the properties on the main frontage. Westward of the common rear boundaries of those properties, the side streets had full-length plots. This pattern of development is also entirely consistent with that of the other Herefordshire market towns of Leominster and Ross, so much so that the term 'the Ledbury model' was coined many years ago to characterise this pattern of development. Finally, the street name New Street is a giveaway: medieval New Streets can be found on the growing edges of small towns from Beccles, Suffolk, to Birmingham, whose own New Street (perhaps one of the most widely known) was added to that new borough by the end of the 13th century at the latest.[67]

Bye Street

Bye Street, or Bishop Street as it was known in the Middle Ages, was, with New Street, one of two routes approaching Ledbury from the west; it led to Church Street on the other side of High Street and hence to the chain of hills to the east of the town. Bye Street's origins as a road therefore lie in the pre-urban past, though there is evidence that it was adapted for the needs of townspeople at an early stage in Ledbury's growth. This can be discerned from the abrupt widening of the street about 308 feet (110 metres) from its junction with High Street, its width increasing from less than 22 feet (8 metres) to more than 58 feet (20 metres). The enclosure

map of 1816 (made before the canal had been cut through)
shows that this enlarged section continued for nearly 842 feet
(300 metres) before the road narrowed again, and that then, as
now, there were rows of buildings standing in the middle of the
enlarged street. There is little doubt that this was a market place,
and, given its position on the edge of town, that it was a secondary
market developed to relieve pressure on the main (High Street/
Middletown) market place. It can also be suggested that this was
a cattle market: on the grounds that the stream that ran down the
street would have been ideally suited to watering livestock; because
of the close proximity of the Victorian cattle-market, and because
in the history of English towns, large and small, it was invariably
the cattle trade that was the first to be banished from the centre to
the periphery, for obvious reasons of space, mud, pollution and
traffic management.

The 19th-century maps all show the street relatively lightly built
up with plots of quite disparate character facing the road. Thus,
on the north side, close to the junction with the Homend and
High Street, there are a limited number of very short plots that
were clearly contrived by the sub-division of the last of the long
plots facing east onto the Homend. Opposite, on the south side
of Bye Street, is another series of short plots ending at a common
boundary running parallel to the street, separating them from the
St Katherine's Hospital precinct behind. These plots, at least in the
early 19th century, did not belong to the hospital; archaeological
investigation of one towards High Street end confirmed that it had,
as expected, been built up within the medieval period.[68]

Figure 42   The widening
secondary market place in
Bye Street, looking west.
Note the later row of
infill shops in the centre.

In contrast to the fairly regular appearance of the plots at the eastern end of the street, the plots on the north side of the market place were notably irregular, though nothing is known of their origin. On the opposite side of the market place, excavations on the street frontage of the Victorian cattle-market suggested that medieval development in this area got off to a slow start. Natural hollows had first been filled in the 12th or 13th century, after which a number of pits had been dug before the site (or at least the rear of the plot) was put down to cultivation. More intensive occupation began later in the Middle Ages although the excavated remains – a wall near the frontage, gullies, post-holes and ditches – had been badly damaged when the cattle market was built. One medieval building, of 15th-century date, survived on Bye Street long enough to be recorded in the 1930s: this was the so-called 'Bishop's Palace', a wealthy hall house with decorative cusped timbers. Whether it had any connection with either the bishop or the hospital to its rear is however doubtful.[69]

How much further out the street was plotted and built up in the Middle Ages is uncertain. By the time of the surviving rental of about 1288 there were 56 tenants living along the street though, as in the Homend, this cannot easily be translated into precise lengths of occupied frontage, even assuming that the built-up area was continuous, and not intermittent nearer the edge of town. The fields either side of the street, mapped in the 19th century, provided boundaries equidistant from and parallel to the street for a distance of around 1,965 feet 6 inches (700 metres), right out to the edge of the Leadon brook floodplain. It seems highly unlikely that the built-up area ever actually extended anywhere near that far; whether the field boundaries were planned with the possibility of one day accommodating that many plots is, however, another, intriguing question – the whole of the area was included within the bounds of the Borough.

Bye Street was distinguished by the watercourse that ran down it, from Church Lane via the Lower Cross towards the Leadon. Although unusual today, except in small villages, the sight of an open channel running down a town street would have been common in the Middle Ages, as streets often provided natural drainage routes and a flow of water could be useful for many trades (tanning or dyeing, for example) or for carrying away waste. Such was the case on the north side of Bye Street in the late 19th century, where a tannery functioned on the corner with the Homend until demolished and replaced by the Barrett Browning Institute in 1895. It had, however, been a local health hazard; the minutes of the Ledbury Board of Health in 1844 recorded that the drain or 'mouth of the town ditch' at the bottom of Bye Street should be covered, that the water raised by pump in an adjacent cottage was putrid, and that a row of houses had been built in the middle of the street over the ditch with cellars which 'were very obnoxious'. The bishop's rental of about 1288 included payment by a weaver of a penny for using the *fossatus* (ditch), probably a reference to this stream. Archaeological monitoring of a trench dug across Bye Street found that much of the street had been cut away in the early 19th century when the stream was first culverted. The stream can still be heard to this day, particularly in wet weather, by standing on one of the inspection covers in the middle of the street.[70]

New Street

New Street, like Bye Street, is part of the pre-urban landscape of Ledbury, a road bringing traffic from the west (ultimately from the Ross-on-Wye direction) to the Upper Cross and thence, via Horse Lane, towards the Malverns. The street maintains a fairly constant width until a point 230-40 feet (70·3 metres) from High Street where it narrows, in part because it passes through the rear boundary of the High Street and Southend plots into the more congested townscape of the axial street, in part presumably because of successive encroachments, the final phase of which is wonderfully represented by 1 and 2 The Southend oversailing the pavement (Fig. 43).

The street was never completely built up in the medieval period. Building had begun by 1174-86 when a burgage, later to form part of the endowment of St Katherine's, was granted by Bishop

Figure 43 New Street looking westwards from the Top Cross.

Robert Foliot. There were 35 tenants in the street at the time of the bishop's rental of about 1288, but four selions (agricultural strips) were recorded there in about 1300; in 1359 it was still incompletely built up.[71]

Archaeological sources have little to contribute to this at the moment: a building contractor's trenches monitored by archaeologists at the rear of no. 26, about a hundred metres from High Street, produced pits containing domestic pottery of the 13th to 14th centuries and fleeting glimpses of masonry rubble structures; trenches excavated further to the west, behind Linden House, revealed medieval ploughsoil, cut by an east-west gully, also of medieval date. The plots associated with this street are generally short, irregular in their layout and were probably contrived at the expense of much larger, more formally planned plots facing east onto High Street and Southend.[72]

THE NEW BOROUGH: DEVELOPMENT AND DECLINE

As first conceived, it appears that the new borough of Ledbury was a linear settlement, extending north and south from the wedge-shaped market place with an almost continuous boundary delineating the town plots. There are signs of measurement in regular multiples of the statute perch in the planning of the burgages throughout the town, but only on the west side of the Homend is the evidence complete enough to suggest the actual multiples concerned – in this area, three statute perches. As has long been suggested, the streets extending westwards from the main road were built up as a secondary phase in the early growth of the borough, though this had been accomplished – at least partly – before the end of the 13th century. Archaeological discoveries do not, at the moment, significantly alter or expand our knowledge of the extent of the medieval town though they certainly support the evidence of the 1288 rental in showing that the town centre was no less extensively built up by 1300 than it was in 1800. It is, however, not yet possible to confirm or refute the linear extent of building along the Homend or the Southend. Nor – and this is undoubtedly the greatest failing of archaeological, historical and topographical research to date – can we yet be absolutely certain about the location of the hall of the medieval bishops.

While the initial planning of the borough in the 12th century and its growth up to the end of the 13th can be illuminated from topographical and historical sources, the later development of the town and, in particular, how it fared in the 15th and 16th centuries when many towns experienced economic

The Community Archaeology Project

Figure A   *Volunteers learn how to set out a test-pit.*

England's Past for Everyone volunteers carried out some small-scale test excavations within the town, in the gardens of a number of willing residents. The aim was to determine, through the pottery assemblages uncovered, how the built-up area of Ledbury has expanded and contracted through the centuries. Staff of Herefordshire Archaeology provided them with training and equipment so they could confidently continue the investigation without the presence of an archaeologist.

A two-day training event was organised within the grounds of Abbot's Lodge, where four trenches were excavated. The volunteers were taught by a member of Herefordshire Archaeology how to decide on a trench location and then measure it out. Each trench measured one metre square and could not be excavated beyond a depth of one metre because of health and safety requirements. With the trench marked out, volunteers began to remove the turf, stacking it neatly on a ground sheet so as not to disturb the surrounding garden. The underlying soil could then be excavated, removing a 3.9 inch (10cm) spit at a time and recording each spit's colour, compaction, inclusions

(for example, stones) and finds. The artefacts excavated from each spit were then stored in labelled bags ready for cleaning and professional interpretation.

The overall results showed that across Ledbury during the post-medieval period a substantial amount of landscaping and construction had taken place. This was represented by a mixed clay layer with inclusions of brick, tile and mortar found in all of the trenches up to a depth of at least one metre. Due to the depth of this deposit no in-situ medieval or earlier archaeology was encountered. The artefacts recovered from the post-medieval soil were typical of the period, consisting of fragments of clay pipe, glass and a mix of pottery sherds from various vessel types.

Although the excavations failed to uncover any earlier deposits, a number of medieval pottery fragments mixed within the post-medieval soil were uncovered. These would have been disturbed during later post-medieval activity. It is perhaps not surprising that almost all of the medieval pottery came from the centre of Ledbury in gardens close to St Michael and All Angel's Church. The largest concentration came from the grounds of Abbot's Lodge: a mix of coarse black cooking-pot (probably 12th- to 13th-century), two fragments of finer green-glazed tableware and a fragment of glazed roof tile, all of which date to around the 14th century.

Though the findings of the investigation were not spectacular they have contributed to our understanding of the layout of Ledbury over the centuries. The overall depth and spread of the post-medieval deposit throughout Ledbury, consisting largely of 17th- to 18th-century material, was quite astonishing. Works linked to construction and landscaping were widespread throughout this period and would have contributed

Figure B   *Medieval pottery from the Abbot's Lodge trenches, 12th- to 14th-century. Cooking-pot fragments (left), part of a roof tile (right).*

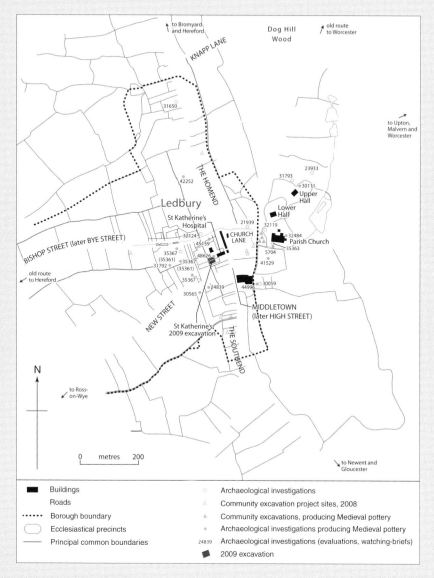

Figure C *Map showing the areas in Ledbury where archaeological evaluations, watching briefs, excavations and community projects have been carried out. The majority of 12th- to 14th-century medieval pottery excavated during the test pit investigation came from the grounds immediately to the west of St Michael and All Saints Parish Church.*

greatly to Ledbury's current appearance. Despite the medieval material not being in its original context, it is likely that it had not moved a great distance from where it was first buried. The finer tableware pottery fragments and the glazed roof tile indicate relatively wealthy settlement around the church in the 14th century.

The greatest legacy of the investigation may be the involvement of the community of Ledbury; it was through their hard work and dedication that the results were produced, and they will support and inform any future archaeological investigation within the town.

Christopher Atkinson, Community Archaeologist, Herefordshire Archaeology.

stagnation or contraction, remains largely obscure. There are, however, hints that Ledbury, too, was in decline in this period. The abandonment and clearance of burgages on the east side of the Southend points in this direction. Although we only have definite evidence of the loss of five and a half burgages between 1582 and 1621 (see above), the extent of the Borough boundary here suggests that these were merely the last survivors of a much greater number. The historic buildings of Ledbury also hint that the late medieval town was not a prosperous place. Although Ledbury is justly renowned for its many black and white, timber-framed buildings, it is notable that these were, with very few exceptions, products of the years from 1580 onwards. The 15th century, which is well represented in the domestic architecture of, for example, Leominster and Ludlow, is virtually absent from Ledbury. In part this may be a tribute to the dynamism of the late Tudor town, but it seems likely that it is also a reflection of its relative poverty in the period following the Black Death. This difficult subject remains another significant challenge for future archaeological research.

Chapter 5

Town Life, 1200-1500

RUNNING THE TOWN

Villages, market towns, cities and ports were all meshed in a web of connections, economic, legal and cultural. There were many overlapping layers of government. The counties of England were divided for judicial and administrative purposes into hundreds, a term which primarily expressed an administrative unit rather than a coherent geographical area in the later Middle Ages. Ledbury was in the Radlow hundred. The men of the settlements or 'vills' within the hundred were responsible for responding to royal demands for taxes and soldiers (or the money to support them), and were also responsible for the maintenance of bridges and for keeping the peace within their bounds. The men of the vill would meet to discuss matters and to elect officers. The town of Ledbury, often called Ledbury Denizen or Ledbury Borough, was described as a vill for the purposes of royal taxes and the raising of troops. So, too, were Massington, Ledon, Wallhills and Wellington in the Foreign. Interwoven with, sometimes indeed replacing, the royal, public, administration mediated through county and hundredal institutions were manors, private estates which had varying degrees of control over the lives of their tenants. Ledbury, as we have seen, was part of – indeed gave its name to – a large estate belonging to the bishop of Hereford who was in fact the most powerful figure in the area. The episcopal manor included a number of sub-manors. The manor of Hazle predated the Norman Conquest, whereas the first reference to the estates held by knight service at Wellington and Massington as actual manors was not until 1401. The bishop exercised wide powers for his manor of Ledbury, claiming in 1292 to have a gallows in Ledbury as well as assize of bread and ale. He also had a prison there.[73]

The bishops of Hereford appointed officers to oversee the running of their estates, as did the portionaries of the Upper and Lower Hall and the master of St Katherine's Hospital. In the 13th century there were references to the bishops' reeve (*prepositus*) but thereafter the term bailiff (*ballivus*) was used. The *Red Book* (see panel 5) mentions both Geoffrey *prepositus* and Thomas *ballivus*. Other entries in the document refer to Robert Furches as bailiff. These officials undertook the legal aspects of holding the bishop's courts, recording land transactions and dealing with infringements of the customs of the manor, as well as drawing up the annual financial accounts. They were also held responsible for keeping prisoners, like the unfortunate William Collyer, who was indicted for having let the felon Robert Ryan escape in 1390. In 1408 Bishop Mascall appointed James Blount as bailiff of Ledbury and ordered his tenants 'to be obedient to and counsel the said James'. Not all bailiffs were equally respected. Thomas Lorymer was bailiff of Ledbury in the 1530s and may have obtained the bailiwick of Hampton Shelwyk and Tupsley, near the city of Hereford, by underhand means. He was described in unflattering terms by Richard Sparcheford, writing to Edward Fox, bishop-elect of Hereford:

> Here is one Thos. Lorimere, dwelling in Ledbury, a tall man, but a coward of his hands, of an excessive prating and dissimulate fashion, not fit for your service. As soon as the late bishop died he went to Court, and by means of Mr Knottsford, your acquaintance, obtained the King's grant for the said bailiwick and discharged this bearer; but when your temporalities are restored, you may make what officers you please. Lorimere dwells 10 miles away, and wishes to serve by deputy. He will poll and bribe the tenants.[74]

The Booth Hall   The Booth Hall was the building in which the manorial and hundredal courts were held and perhaps the meetings of the men of the vill as well. In 1375 it was referred to as the hundred house of the town, near the 'hospital house'. Twenty-five years later the bishop granted to Richard Glover, about whom nothing else is known,

> A messuage called le Bothall in Ledbury Denzein for 40 years from Michaelmas next; rent 6s. 8d. Reserved to the bishop, a certain place to hold the hundred and court for service to the lordship of ancient custom, and a small place there to keep and guard prisoners. At Michaelmas next Richard is to build at his own expense, a house of three bays and four roof trusses [*unam domum de tribus spacis de quatuor copulis*], except that the bishop shall give Richard an oak. And he will also build a solar above the said place within the said messuage where the court shall be held. In the event of default Richard will forfeit 40s. of silver.[75]

This building would have been on the west side of High Street, overlooking the market place, to the south of the hospital chapel, as the land to the north was occupied by the hospital. In 1537 the Booth Hall was let to one John King; in 1619 James Bonde, who also held the *Plume of Feathers* (now the *Feathers Hotel*), had the

lease of it. In 1698, Thomas Pantall, landlord of the *Feathers*, also
leased the Booth Hall 'always reserved the Court Chamber, the
Prison House, the Park House with the said Boothhall House upon
all occasions for the keeping of all Courts to be kept in the said
Manor and Burrough'. Twenty years later, when Pantall assigned
the lease of the *Feathers* to Humphrey Owen, it included 'the
boards and trestles that are in and about the said messuage and
outhouses thereunto belonging for standings to be used in the fairs
and markets'. In the early 19th century ownership of the *Feathers*
passed to John Biddulph, and the land tax records make it clear
that property to the north belonged to the lords of the manor, and
was occasionally described as 'the lords' house'. From 1786 to 1802
it was occupied by Richard Grinall, but was vacant in 1814. In 1815
a terrier of the estate of John Biddulph showed that Giles Taylor
occupied the *Feathers* and also 'The Boothall or Manor house
adjoining to the *Feathers Inn* with Garden thereunto belonging'.
He paid £92 a year for the Booth Hall, an indication that it was a
substantial property. It would seem that the Booth Hall was the
timber-framed building which now forms the northern wing
of the *Feathers*. Whether it was completely rebuilt in the early
17th century (perhaps the work of James Bonde), or whether it still
contains the kernel of Richard Glover's three-bay property, remains
to be investigated.[76]

Figure 44   The north
range of the *Feathers
Hotel*, on the site of
the Booth Hall. This
17th-century building
may contain elements of
the medieval building at
its core.

Crime and Punishment

Medieval towns, like their modern successors, had their share of
social problems, some endemic and others the product of local
events. In Ledbury, as elsewhere, there were thefts and murders,
disputes and violence between individuals and between factions.
It was said that Herefordshire was a particularly lawless area, made
worse by the periodic incursions of the Welsh into the county.
The brunt of those attacks was felt by the western districts, with
occasional forays to Hereford, but the major outbursts such as the
rebellion of Owain Glyndwr in 1401 must have had a destabilising
effect throughout the county, though only intermittently. Internal
strife also had its impact on Herefordshire. In 1321 Roger
Mortimer, nephew of Roger Mortimer of Wigmore, and Adam de
Orleton, bishop of Hereford, were involved in the rebellion against
the king and terrorised the countryside. Amongst other crimes,
Roger and his men stood accused of taking beef and pork, bread
and ale and brass pots from Roger Fortrich of Ledbury. Even before
the long-drawn-out struggles between the houses of York and
Lancaster flared into open warfare, the king complained in 1438 of
the intractable nature of Herefordshire people. In 1446 the clergy
and people of all the dioceses of Wales and those of Coventry
and Lichfield and of Hereford made one of their regular, perhaps
formulaic, appeals to the pope, complaining of the increasing
number of 'murderers and ravishers of virgins … thieves and
robbers' making life unsafe.[77]

Felonies were dealt with by the royal justices as they made
their slow rounds of the country. When the justices came to
Herefordshire in 1292 there were a dozen serious cases to be dealt
with involving Ledbury people. The circumstances ranged from
accidental killing, through domestic violence to violent affray and
the punishments meted out varied accordingly. Some culprits were
hanged, some outlawed and some banished. Outlaws' goods were
confiscated and they themselves were placed outside the protection
of the law. They could then be legally killed by anyone who met
them. Hanging was not that frequent, though William le Little
Harlot was hanged for having killed John of Oxford in Ledbury.
Hugh the Cobbler of Ledbury and Vincent son of Thomas Smith
of Wellington who killed Adam le Taskere were outlawed. Walter
Melksop of Shropshire killed Richard de Colemer in the Foreign of
Ledbury. He fled and was outlawed in his absence.

Some of those who fled the scene of crime sought sanctuary
in the parish church. Hugh Basset of Ledbury killed William
the chaplain of Eastnor in Ledbury. He then fled to the church
of Ledbury and his punishment was to 'abjure the land',

Figure 45 A king
condemning a man to
execution, 14th-century,
from a manuscript of the
Institutes of Justinian at
Hereford cathedral.

meaning that he had to leave England and never return. As it
had happened by day, the town of Ledbury had to pay a fine for
not having captured him. When John Syrecock and William his
brother killed John de la Street in Ledbury, John fled and was
outlawed, but William sought refuge in the church. He then
admitted the crime to the coroner, the elected legal officer who
kept the record of all these crimes to be presented to the justices.
When a felon confessed to him, it was his duty to make the
arrangements for the felon to abjure the land. Other perpetrators
fled and were never found, like William le Mareschal who had
killed Walter le Staniale in the town of Ledbury and then fled.
Some affrays seem to have involved a number of people. A
particularly violent dispute took place when Gilbert le Forester of
Malvern and his wife Agnes, her sister Juliana and their mother
Isabel met Richard le Fauconer and his son Richard and Henry
son of Hugh de Fetberton in Ledbury one day. A dispute broke

out amongst them. Gilbert le Forester killed Richard le Fauconer and fled at once. He was outlawed but the others were acquitted. Gilbert had no chattels of value but he did own property in Ledbury, which was seized by the court. No doubt other crimes occurred through the centuries, though few have left traces in the records. One other bloody affair has. About the year 1550 Richard Walwyn, then sheriff of Herefordshire no less, and his uncle Giles were violently attacked by a mob while visiting the home of John Knight, the bailiff of Ledbury. There is no indication of the cause, perhaps some personal feud or sense of grievance felt by the ring leader, John Lyngyn, esquire, but Richard and his uncle were badly beaten and robbed, and a warrant was issued for the arrest of Lyngyn.[78]

THE TOWN AT WORK

Craftsmen in wood and metal made items for household and farmstead. Weavers, dyers and fullers worked the wool of the district into cloth. Flax, too, was grown and woven by linen weavers and sold by mercers. Skinners, tanners and leatherworkers turned the pelts of animals into useful items of clothing or harness. Other people were concerned with the preparation of food and drink or with administrative tasks relating to the estates of the bishop or the hospital. Many were in holy orders (see chapters 3 and 7). This range of occupations is one of the factors that distinguished a town from a village, even if the overall number of inhabitants was quite small. Ledbury may have had a population of about 1,000 in the late 13th century, declining in the following century as a result of poor harvests, famine and plague, and not reaching similar figures again until about 1600. A certain amount of evidence for the occupations of townsmen (and, to a lesser degree, townswomen) can be gleaned from surnames. The detailed list of tenants of Ledbury, recorded in the *Red Book* in the late 13th century, included many names which indicate trades, occupations or office holding (see panel 5). Property deeds and wills sometimes recorded the occupations or status of the parties involved. Lists, such as of those assessed for tax, regularly used such appellations to distinguish between two people of the same name. None of these sources for Ledbury is comprehensive enough to enable an analysis of the number of people engaged in different occupations at any time, but together they provide an insight into some of the trades of Ledbury. This scarcity of documentation also makes it difficult to trace in detail the fluctuations in the fortunes of the town, but it certainly seems to have been markedly less prosperous in the 15th century than in the early years of the 14th.[79]

Figure 46 A carpenter working at his bench, from a manuscript of *c*.1225 which may have been written and illustrated at the Cistercian Abbey of Dore, Herefordshire.

Trades and Crafts

Trades and crafts can be arranged into broad groups of those working with cloth, leather, metal and wood, and the preparation and supply of food and drink.

Wool and Clothing   Herefordshire wool was traded widely and there was trade between London and the regions in finished cloth, both home-made woollens and imported fine linens and silks, usually the trade of mercers. Richard Unet of Ledbury was described as a mercer in 1417 and in 1446 Edmund Ekeney 'citizen and draper or merchant of London' was at Ledbury. There are later records of a number of Ledbury men becoming merchants in London. The way into this was by apprenticeship. For example, Thomas Bracy, son of John Bracy of Ledbury, was described as a mercer of London lately discharged of his apprenticeship in 1535 when he began a law-suit regarding some property in Ledbury. The *Red Book* shows that Oldred le Mercer had a burgage next to the two occupied by William le Folur (fuller). Their names do not occur under named streets and they may have been in the Church Lane-Church Street area, as neither of these streets was named in the rental. Three weavers were listed in the *Red Book*. John le Webbe (weaver) paid for the use of a ditch, which may have been the 'town ditch' or stream running down Church Lane, across the market place and down Bye Street. Henry le Webbe had a half burgage in the Homend, and Adam Webb held two separate half burgages nearby. He also had a seld, or stall, in the market place. Once the woollen cloth had been woven, dyed and fulled, the nap would need to be sheared and perhaps that was the task of Nicolas Napper in the Homend. Then the cloth would be made up into clothes.[80]

The production of clothing was of vital importance, not just to individuals, but to the economy as a whole. The Latin *Cissor*

Figure 47   Women carding and spinning wool from the 14th-century Luttrell Psalter.

The *Red Book*: A 13th-Century Rental

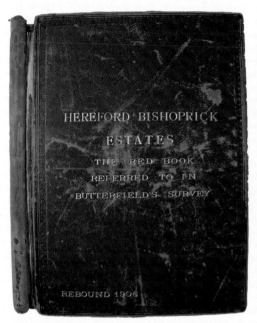

Figure A and B   *This small volume (only 11in x 9in, 28cm x 23cm) binds together six medieval documents relating to the bishop of Hereford's estates; the pages were numbered in arabic numerals much later. Swithun Butterfield, who made a more detailed survey of those estates in 1577-8, called it the* Red Book. *Pages 47-206 contain rentals for the bishop's manors. Each entry is in a different hand and they seem to have been written at different times, but further research, for example into known people's names, help to date it. Also, there is a note about certain rents due for the first six years of Swinfield's episcopate, 1283-8, which suggests that the rental was made shortly after 1288, although probably incorporating older lists.*

Rentals are valuable sources of information about the tenants and the layout of property. They include personal names and sometimes give titles or occupations, which shed light on the social structure of a place. The wealth of individuals and of the whole community can be gleaned from the size of properties held and the amounts of rent paid. Other forms of rent other than cash are also listed, whether payments in kind or services rendered to the lord of the manor. Where complete rentals survive from two different periods they are useful for assessing changes over time in the size or social composition of a place.

The Ledbury rental in the *Red Book* begins with the town or the Borough and the entries are laid out by street: the Southend, New Street, Middle Town (High Street), Homend and Bishop Street (Bye Street). After that there is a group of names not headed by a street, presumably those living in the Church Lane and Church Street area, and then the list of those holding selds or stalls. Each tenant is named, with a brief description of what they held – everything from an eighth of a burgage to three burgages together – and how much rent they owed at each of the four quarter days. The values of the rent were totalled for each street and then the final entry for the Borough stated, 'Total sum of the value of the borough by estimation £27 10s. 7½d.' After that, there is a list of those holding land by knight service, the free tenants and the copyhold tenants in the Foreign, the rural part of the parish. What the *Red Book* has to say about that is discussed in chapter 6.

Matilda of Wolputtor [?Woolpit] holds half a burgage, rendering thence at the feast of St Andrew 1½d., at the feast of the Annunciation 1½d., at the feast of the nativity of St John 1½d., at the feast of blessed Michael 2½d.

Hugh of Alderton holds half a burgage, rendering thence at St Andrew 1½d., at the Annunciation of Mary 1½d., at the nativity of St John 1½d., at the feast of the blessed Michael 1½d.

Obayn [Owain?] de Walinter [?Wellington] holds half a burgage and owes at the feast of

Andrew 1½d., at the feast of the annunciation of blessed Mary 1½d., at the feast of St John 1½d., at the feast of blessed Michael 1½d.

John Cobet holds half a burgage and owes at the feast of blessed Andrew 1½d., at the feast of the annunciation of blessed Mary 1½d., at the feast of the nativity of St John 1½d., at the feast of blessed Michael 1½d.

Reynold of the Wood [de Bosco] holds a burgage and a half, rendering at the feast of blessed Andrew 4½d., at the feast of the annunciation of blessed Mary 4½d., at the feast of St John 4½d., at the feast of blessed Michael 4½d.

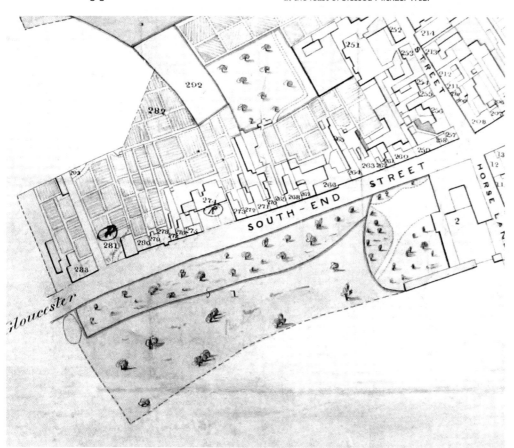

Figure C   *Southend in 1841. The burgage plots are still to be seen on the west (top). The boundary of Ledbury Park (bottom) reflects the back boundary of the eastern burgages.*

Sources: HRO A59/AA/1, *Red Book*; A.T. Bannister, 'A Transcript of "The Red Book", A detailed account of the Hereford bishopric estates in the thirteenth century', *Camden Miscellany*, vol. XV (1929).

was used to describe John Tailor in New Street, but whether
he was a tailor or that was a surname is not clear. There is no
doubt, though, 40 years later, about William Berde '*le tailur*', also
in New Street. There were specialists in making different types
of garments, from hoods to gloves and those who specialised in
making decorative trimmings. Surnames in the *Red Book* suggest
such occupations – William and Alice Capron (hood maker),
Geoffrey le Parminter (fancy tailor or maker of trimmings),
Alditha Glover. Household linen, sheets, towels and napery, were
the province of the linen weavers, but were often made up by the
women of the household. The making of blankets was a specialist
trade, probably followed by Warin le Chaloner. Whoever was
making them, Bishop Swinfield paid 14d. for stockings and shoes
bought in Ledbury in 1290.[81]

Leather   Leather was used for shoes, of course, but also for
belts, straps, bags and vessels of all shapes and sizes. The skinner
(*pelliparius*) and the tanner (*tannator* or *whitawer*) prepared the
leather for use by the shoemaker, cobbler and harness maker.
Most of the leather would have come from beasts killed for
meat or from horses too old to work. However, in 1290 Bishop
Swinfield paid 6d. for 13 fox skins to be dressed in Ledbury. The
widespread use of the surnames Skinner and Tanner is evidence
of how ubiquitous the trade was. When Bishop Swinfield paid
2d. for mending the harness for his cart and 20d. for the cook's
saddlebag in 1290 it may have been to Richard Tharcenor
(harness maker) who occupied a burgage in New Street about
this time. In many towns the stinking trade of the tanner was
relegated to the outskirts, but in Ledbury it appears to have been
based along the banks of the stream running down Church Lane
and Bye Street until well into the 19th century.[82]

Figure 48   The sole
of a late 13th- to early
14th-century shoe,
excavated from Drybridge
House in Hereford in
1977. It is the sole for the
right foot of a pointed
shoe, with narrow
heel-seat and edge flesh
stitching around the
sole. A hole bored close
to the heel from within
the shoe suggests the
attachment of a repair
piece at the heel seat,
which is worn. Fashions
for pointed shoes were
common in the medieval
period and became
particularly pronounced
with 'poulaines' which
extended the point of
the shoe several inches
beyond the toe.

Metal- and Wood-Work   Both Bishop Swinfield and the duke of
York paid for shoeing horses in Ledbury. A new body (*caretillus*)
was required for one of the bishop's carts, too, and tallow was
bought to grease the axles. There would also have been work for
the two wheelwrights Walter Wheolare and Robert Rotarius. The
bishop paid 3d. for a 'hammer and other things for the marshalcy'
– in the 1280s there were a number of men who bore the surname
Marescall or Marshall (farrier). Other related trades were those
of lorimer and spurrier, makers of stirrups and bits, and spurs
respectively. Apart from the heavy work of the general smith
(*faber*) and the farrier, more delicate metal work was done by
cutlers. Geoffrey Goldsmith (*aurifaber*), with his burgage in the
Southend and a seld in the market place may indeed have been a

Figure 49 A medieval spur found at Tretire, Herefordshire.

goldsmith. There was a goldsmith called Adam who had a seld at Ross, too. Many people probably combined a craft with a certain amount of farming (see chapter 6).[83]

Food and Drink Trades These trades were an important part of the economy of any town. Farmers brought the raw materials to market but then they had to be processed in a variety of ways and finally cooked. The trading of cattle and the processing of skins has already been touched upon. The beasts were slaughtered in the shambles in the market area. These shambles, and the neighbouring butchers' stalls, which would originally only have been erected on market days and then taken down, were built as permanent structures and became a row of little shops, known as Middle Row or Butcher's Row until it was finally demolished in the 1830s. In the 1280s there were five shambles (*shomeles*) and 14 butchers' selds (*selde*), which equates well with the 15 shops in Butcher Row taken down in the 19th century. Poultry was also supplied, by people like Geoffrey le Polter in the 1280s, and eggs were bought by the score for large households. Although fish was regularly traded in Ledbury, no one seems to have been called a fishmonger until Edward Barret, who made his will in 1591.[84]

Grain was a staple, both for bread and pottage, and lords jealously guarded the obligation of their tenants to grind corn at their mills. In the *Red Book* the water mill in the Borough was valued at 53s. 4d. and the windmill at 26s. 8d.; another mill at 'Wymondestr' in the Foreign was valued at 4 marks (£2 13s. 4d.). The latter may have been near the site of the old hundredal meeting place of Wygmund's tree. In many manors the lord also controlled the public oven or bakehouse, but in Ledbury in the 1280s Robert Moreb paid the bishop 8d. a year for an oven and a seld. The bishop himself then had to pay to have his bread and pies baked when in Ledbury, unlike when he was at his other manors, when only the flour for the bread making was accounted for. By the 1380s there was at least one cook shop in Ledbury, for the widow Alice Gruys sold hers in New Street to William King, a neighbouring butcher. Cookshops prepared cooked food for travellers and those in a hurry – like a 'take-away' today. In many other towns there is often evidence for women being heavily involved in the food and drink trades, as baxters and brewsters, or as hucksters, retailers in a small way. The Ledbury material is disappointingly meagre, except in this reference to Alice's cook shop.[85]

Wine and ale figured largely in the household accounts of the Middle Ages. Ale was brewed both in great households and by lesser folk in towns and villages. Wine was regularly imported

Figure 50 Depiction of a miller, from a manuscript of *c.*1225 which may have been written and illustrated at the Cistercian Abbey of Dore, Herefordshire.

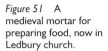

Figure 51 A medieval mortar for preparing food, now in Ledbury church.

from France, but some was produced locally. In 1290 Bishop Swinfield's household drank many sesters of wine from the store at Bosbury (presumably imported wine) but also seven doles (a large measure of liquid) of 'white wine of Ledbury and almost an eighth of verjuice [liquor from sour grapes] from the vineyard of Ledbury'. In the autumn of 1276 Bishop Thomas Cantilupe wrote to his steward in Ledbury giving instructions about the making of a vineyard there, or more likely about enlarging an existing one. Over a hundred years before, Gilbert Foliot (bishop of Hereford 1148-63) had mentioned Robert his 'vine dresser' at Ledbury. The vineyard was certainly productive when the rental of the manor was drawn up in the late 13th century, for the vineyard on new ground (*in vine de terra recenti*) covered 12 acres and was valued at 100s. a year. The rental also recorded that the customary tenants of Bishops Frome and Cotyntone [Coddington] owed work at the vineyard in Ledbury. The Bishops Frome entry noted that this was 'an ancient and proven custom'. By 1404 it seems that the production of wine had ceased, as the vineyard was only valued at 3s. 4d. a year and again, in 1495, it was described as pasture called Vineyard, valued at 6s. 8d. By 1537 no rent was recorded for the vineyard itself, but there was reference to a parcel of 'forlet land next Wynyard' let for 10½d. a year. The medieval documents do not make it clear where the vineyard was, only referring to it as 'at Ledbury'. It has been assumed that this was on the south-west flanks of Haffield, now in the parish of Donnington, where there was a vineyard in the early 18th century, still in 1838 called Vineyard Bank. The tithe map also shows a plot which suggests another possible vineyard in

Figure 52 A skillet for boiling or stewing food from Hereford, dating to the 14th or 15th century.

the parish, though of uncertain date. This plot (no.582) called 'Vineyard and Oldbury' was in the north of the parish, just to the north-east of Prior's Court.[86]

Brewing and the sale of ale and wine were regulated by assize and lords of many manors had jurisdiction in their courts to punish those who offended against the assize. It seems that amercements (fines) for brewing contrary to the assize became, in effect, a payment for a licence to do so. In Ledbury in 1292 Walter Caperun of Ledbury was charged with having sold three tuns of wine contrary to the assize. Control of the standards of goods for sale and of the weights and measures used to dispense them was very important and the bishop of Hereford appointed a commission in 1442 to enforce the assize and regulation of bread, ale, wine and all other victuals, and of weights and measures, in his manors of Prestbury, Bromyard, Ledbury, Ross and Bishops' Castle 'and all others', though there are no records of the procedure.[87]

Figure 53 A modern vineyard at Coddington, four miles from Ledbury. In the 13th century tenants of Coddington were obliged to do a day's work at the bishop's vineyard in Ledbury.

MARKETS AND FAIRS

Ledbury was only one of 35 places in Herefordshire for which evidence of a market between 1086 and 1516 has been found. Some were very short-lived, probably founded by enterprising lords

in the hope of yielding profitable toll revenue, but which never throve. Others were active over some decades or even centuries. However, only nine can with certainty be said to have survived as markets into the second half of the 16th century: Bromyard, Kington, Ledbury, Leominster, Pembridge, Ross-on-Wye, Weobley, Wigmore and Hereford itself. In addition, within a radius of 15 miles or so of Ledbury, there were thriving markets at the cities of Gloucester and Worcester and the towns of Upton-on-Severn (Worcestershire), Tewkesbury and Newent (Gloucestershire) and, slightly further to the west, Monmouth (Fig. 55). The markets that were established earlier tended to survive the longest. It would seem that well established markets were better able to withstand the economic difficulties of the mid-14th century than were newer foundations. However, early establishment was not the only factor. A more significant factor would seem to be that the markets which did best were distributed relatively evenly around the countryside. They also benefited from the patronage of a powerful lord, in whose interest it was to foster the market and to ensure its good management. The markets of Ledbury, Ross and Bromyard were promoted by the bishop, while that at Leominster belonged to the abbot of Reading. The market at Hereford belonged to the king himself.[88]

Each market had a natural hinterland, dictated by topography, ease of travel and population density. Local trade was conducted within a radius of six or seven miles, a relatively easy journey even when driving cattle or carrying goods. Indeed, medieval law regarded six miles as a reasonable distance between markets. Larger market centres, or places which served other important functions of a legal or religious nature, might typically be 15 to 20 miles apart.

Travel   Although it was not easy before the days of properly maintained roads and accurate maps, people did travel sometimes considerable distances on foot, on horseback and in carts. Travellers between south and mid-Wales and the midlands and south-east England passed through Herefordshire and some came through Ledbury. For example, in 1409, when Edward, duke of York (d.1415) moved his household from Cardiff to Hanley Castle, Worcestershire, about ten miles over the Malverns, they came through Ledbury, where they had supper and stayed the night; they paid 1s. for the hire of beds, though it is not clear where they lodged. Men of substance arranged their journeys so that they could stay on their own estates wherever possible. So it was when Richard Swinfield, bishop of Hereford, passed through Ledbury in the winter of 1289/90 on his way to London. His next stop was at his manor of Prestbury, 29 miles to the east. The abbot of Reading also passed

Figure 54   A green glazed jug made by the Worcester potters in the late 12th to 13th centuries was found in the Kings Ditch in Hereford in 1931. The jug has a spout, handle and a thumbed-frilled base, and has been decorated with rilled lines and a roller-stamp design, and the whole then coated in a dark green glaze. It is a fine example of the type of large jug or pitcher commonly used during the 13th century.

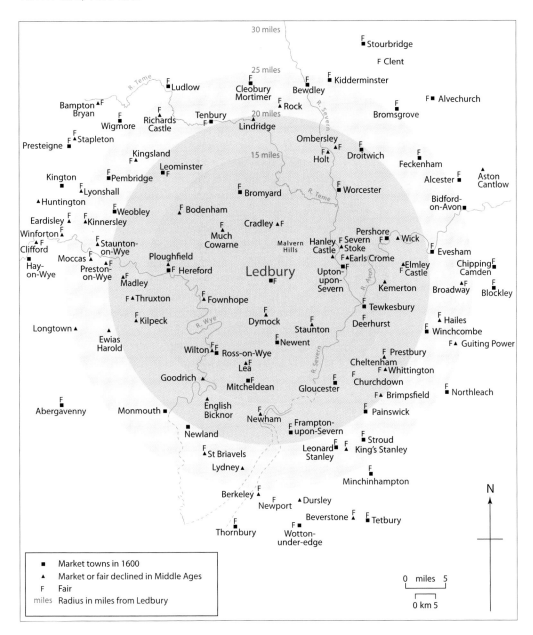

Figure 55 A map of Herefordshire, western Worcestershire and Gloucestershire, showing markets and fairs within a 30-mile radius of Ledbury.

through Ledbury in April 1290, presumably on his way to visit the dependent priory at Leominster, and was accommodated by the bishop. It is more than likely that Henry III and Edward II also stayed at the bishop's manor house, wherever it was, as they passed through the town. (See discussion in chapter 4.) The dating of royal letters enables us to determine the routes taken by kings. In 1232 Henry III travelled from south Wales, through the Forest of Dean, stopping at St Briavels, then Ledbury, en route to Worcester.

The following year, during his struggles with the earl of Pembroke in his castle at Usk, the king stopped at Ledbury on a number of occasions, passing repeatedly between Gloucester, Hereford and Worcester.[89]

Water transport was a cheaper and easier way of transporting many goods, especially grain and timber, and many rivers were navigable far inland. Ledbury is not on a navigable river, but sits between the Severn and the Wye. Although a common right of Wye navigation was recorded in the time of Edward I (1271-1307), when it was stated that no weirs or other obstructions were to be erected and any already in existence were to be removed, the river was never as important a route as the Severn. Both rivers formed barriers to easy east-west travel by road, necessitating many ferry crossings in their lower reaches, but they provided a means of transport north-south. The Severn, in particular, brought goods, including imported wine, upstream from the docks at Bristol and Gloucester to Tewkesbury or Upton-on-Severn, whence they could be taken by road into Herefordshire as well as into Gloucestershire and Worcestershire. Even Hanley Castle had a small quay, although unfortunately the 360 hens eggs destined to be delivered there in 1410 were lost overboard and sank into the Severn, at a loss of 2s. 8½d.[90]

Market Charters   Often the first reference that survives to a market or fair is a charter granting it privileges, but this may only be a later regulation of an existing market that had grown gradually from the regular coming together of people at religious centres or at crossing places of rivers and roads. This is likely to be the case in Ledbury, with its important church. The first formal mention of the market at Ledbury occurred about 1138, with a grant by King Stephen to Robert de Bethune, the bishop of Hereford. This established a market on Sundays, with assurance that all frequenting it should have royal protection. At the same time the bishop's market at Ross was confirmed on Thursdays on similar terms. Some fifteen years later, Roger, earl of Hereford, granted to the see of Hereford an eight-day fair at Ledbury, running from the feast of Sts Peter and Paul (29 June). The September fair, held on the feast of St Matthew (21 September), may have existed already, as it was later described as a prescriptive fair. Certainly the town must have prospered, for in 1234 the tolls of the St Matthew fair were said to be worth £7 to the bishop, a not inconsiderable sum. For comparison, fifty years later the major fair of St Ethelbert at Hereford brought the bishop £20. A third Ledbury fair was granted to the bishop in 1249, on the vigil, feast and morrow of the beheading of St John the Baptist

(29 August). The grant also conferred a market on Fridays. This was probably instead of the Sunday market, as Sunday trading was increasingly frowned upon by the church. It was important that markets in nearby places should not be on the same day, causing undue competition. In 1237 Henry III had upheld the complaints of his citizens at Hereford, who were suffering because of the Saturday market held by the abbot of Reading at Leominster. The king ordered the abbot to hold his market on Fridays instead.[91]

Trading was followed by regulation. The 'peace of the market', freedom to trade and regulation of sharp practice, was offered by the lord of the manor in return for tolls. This was often symbolised by the erection of a market cross, as a reminder that all human

Figure 56   The market house was built in the early 17th century to provide a more convenient place for the sale of grain and other goods. It stands on the north-east corner of the market place, where some earlier buildings were removed to make room for it.

affairs were under the oversight of God and at which oaths could be made regarding deals struck. The first known reference to a market cross in Ledbury is in a deed of 1584, when Edward Bennys sold to Edward Skinner a messuage in the Middle Row 'near unto the Condycte [conduit] or Market Cross there', near the gate of the hospital. Many earlier appellations of people as 'of the Cross' or 'at Cross' may refer to the two cross roads at either end of High Street, rather than a standing cross.[92]

No doubt most of the goods sold at these markets and fairs were the produce of the surrounding countryside – wheat and oats, pigs and poultry. Sheep and cattle were traded over much longer distances. A series of markets and fairs throughout Wales and the Marches facilitated the movement of beasts from the pastureland of Wales into the more arable and urban areas of England. In the spring of 1290, the bishop of Hereford's household accounts recorded the expenses (22½d.) of Harpin and 'certain shepherds' in bringing ewes and lambs from Montgomery (where there was an annual three-day fair at the beginning of May) to Ledbury. The real value of sheep, beyond their meat and milk, was in the renewable resource of their wool. The fine, long-stapled wool of Herefordshire was dubbed 'Leominster ore' and trading in it did indeed make the fortune of many a merchant, including that of William Eseger of Ledbury. He seems to have had connections with Northleach, Gloucestershire, as in 1312 he exchanged land there for a yardland in Ledbury with John de la Hasele (Hazle in Ledbury). In 1337 the king authorised merchants (including Eseger) to purchase wool

Figure 57 This Ryeland breed of sheep originated from Herefordshire in the mid-14th century and was best known for its production of fine wool.

throughout the land, and the price to be paid in each county was recorded. The highest price of all went for Herefordshire wool, at 12 marks the sack. This compared favourably with 10½ marks for Gloucestershire and 9½ marks for Worcestershire wool, but even the famed fleeces of Lincoln could only command 10 marks a sack, while those of Durham made a mere five marks. The following year the merchants of the Peruzzi, Italian financiers who lent large sums of money to Edward III, were permitted to buy 200 sacks of wool, including 15 at Ledbury and 16 at Upton, and fully 35 at Wigmore in north-west Herefordshire, near the borders with both Shropshire and Wales.[93]

Fish was a staple of the medieval diet, especially eaten on the weekly non-meat fast days stipulated by the church, and was regularly traded over long distances. Freshwater fish was not abundant in Ledbury, other than a few small varieties from the Leadon or larger ones from specially stocked fish ponds or stews. Salmon would, no doubt, have come from the Wye or the Severn. Sea fish for sale in the market would also be brought overland from either Tewkesbury or Upton. In February 1290 the bishop paid 17s. for 17 cod, compared with 1½d. for minnows (perhaps a catch-all term for all small fish), at the same time as having six small pike and nine tench from the stew. Other more exotic items of food, such as sugar, dried fruit and spices would have been traded through the greater markets and fairs of Worcester, Gloucester and Hereford. Shopping was no easy matter. The accounts of the household of the duke of York regularly show payments for the cost of a man to travel from Hanley Castle for one or two days through the district procuring food. This meant regular trips to Worcester, Gloucester and Tewkesbury, as well as to smaller markets like Upton and Ledbury. In November 1409 one man spent five days travelling the district looking for victuals for Christmas and the purchases included rice, currants, dates and sugar. Nearer to Christmas there were frequent trips to Ledbury for more mundane items. Oats were regularly bought at Ledbury, wheat, less often; 72 per cent of the household's oats were bought at Ledbury but only 55 per cent of the wheat. Other purchases included barley and green peas, salt and mustard, poultry and milk. Finer items would be bought at major international fairs, such as Stourbridge fair in Cambridgeshire, or from retailers in London. Richard Swinfield's agent bought clothes, furs and spices for the bishop in London and arranged for them to be transported to Bosbury on 'long carts'. The household accounts of both the bishop of Hereford and the duke of York also contain references to payments for goods and services in Ledbury.[94]

CONCLUSION

The bishop's rental of about 1288 and two sets of accounts for 1495 and 1537 have been used in this book to unpick the social and economic make-up of Ledbury. They are separated not only by 250 years but also by the chasm of the catastrophes which struck Europe in the first half of the 14th century. Poor harvests and waves of sickness, animal and human, swept the country from the 1310s to the 1350s. Although there is no direct evidence for the impact of the plague, generally referred to as the Black Death, on Ledbury, its progress can be surmised in the number of ordinations and appointments of new priests that are recorded in the bishops' registers. Neighbouring Bosbury, for example, had four new priests appointed in only five months in 1348/9. The loss of population led to stagnation of trade and struggling communities.[95]

In late 13th-century Ledbury there was a good diversity of trades, a flourishing market and well-established fairs. It was a reasonably prosperous town. Despite the difficulties of the 14th century, the town did not wither completely. Some men, like William Eseger, became wealthy merchants. Members of his family and others had sufficient money to endow chantries and to pay for work at the church. However, the town was no longer expanding. The streets laid out in the 12th century were not substantially added to for nearly 700 years. In the late 15th century there were signs of a decay that had probably set in long before. Richard Berde's accounts drawn up for the Upper Hall portion in 1495 list cottages destroyed, although there was also a new tenement and garden in New Street. When the under bailiff, Thomas Lorymer, returned his accounts to the bishop in 1537, he noted a number of vacant burgages in the town; no rent was received for 'divers shops in the middle of the borough because their buildings have fallen to the ground'. The tolls of the St Matthew fair were only worth 10s. The Palm Sunday fair (not otherwise recorded) had made no profit at all. The town needed a change of fortune.[96]

Chapter 6

Woods and Fields

The land of Ledbury and its environs has been exploited and farmed for millennia, long before Ledbury itself even existed. This chapter will look at how the people of the district fitted into the landscape, exploiting its favoured position between areas suitable for agriculture and those rich in the natural resources of woodland and water.

THE DOMESDAY LANDSCAPE

In 1086, when the Domesday clerks wrote their lists of manors and tenants, mills and ploughs and woods and meadows, their intention was not to describe the countryside but to record for the king, as the Anglo-Saxon Chronicle put it, 'what or how much, in land or livestock, everybody had who was holding land in England, and how much money it was worth'. In Herefordshire they recorded this information in a variety of interlocking ways: by hidage, a form of assessment for tax purposes based on the notional unit of land sufficient to support a single free household (five hides being enough to support thegnly, i.e. noble status); by ploughs or ploughteams, which cultivated the arable land; and by valuation, which perhaps represents an annual rent. A careful reading of this record can give some indication of types of landscape and farming as well as of social organisation, population and wealth. It also gives information about changes following the Norman Conquest. The landholders at the time of King Edward as well as in 1086 were noted and any difference in the value of the holdings between those two dates. The entries for Herefordshire were grouped according to the tenant-in-chief, beginning with property in the king's own hands, ecclesiastical bodies, including the bishop and canons of Hereford, the greater lords like Ralph de Tosny, who had land in many counties, down to a certain Stephen who held just one virgate (notionally a quarter of a hide) in Marden directly from the king.[97]

In pre-Conquest Hereford, a distinction had been made between the lands held by the bishop and those held by the canons who served his cathedral. In the Domesday record most of these lands were listed under the canons, but this seems to have been an error; in fact many were held by the bishop, his knights (*milites*, fighting men), and his clergy. The nine estates of the bishop in Winstree (*Wimundestreu*) hundred in south-east Herefordshire formed a compact block of land stretching along the western flanks of

Figure 59 The
Domesday record of
Bishop of Hereford's
manors in Winstree
hundred (South-East
Herefordshire).

	Bagburrow*	Bosbury	Coddington	Colwall
Taxable Hides	5	6	3 (½ waste)	3
Demesne ploughs ≠	2	2	2	2
Tenants' ploughs	30	23	7	11
Recorded tenants ‡	2 knights 2 radmen 16 villani 13 bordars	1 priest 17 villani 1 bordar	1 radman 6 villani 1 bordar	1 radman 8 villani 8 bordars 6 slaves
Mills	1 – 32d. 1 – 16d.	1 – 30d.	0	1 – 16d.
Meadow	8a.	8a.	3a.	8a.
Wood	Pays nothing	Pays nothing	Pays nothing	0
Value 1066	£7 15s.	£6	£2 5s.	£3
Value 1086	£7 15s.	£6	£2 5s.	£3

* Bagburrow may be identified with the area of Bagburrow Wood (SO 74 45) in the parish of Mathon, which straddles the Herefordshire/Worcestershire border.
≠ Demesne ploughs of sub-tenants are counted with tenant ploughs.

the Malverns and reaching to the river Leadon (Fig. 59). Almost certainly ancient possessions of the see, they comprised Ledbury itself, Bagburrow, Bosbury, Coddington, Cradley, Donnington, and Eastnor, together with Hazle (part of Ledbury), and Colwall (part of Cradley). The last two estates, together with Coddington, had been annexed by Harold Godwinson, presumably after he became earl of Hereford in 1055, but had been returned to the bishop after the Conquest. Because of this, Hazle and Colwall were recorded separately from the manors to which they belonged and have separate valuations. If, therefore, we count their hidages as additional to those for Ledbury and Cradley, the total assessment of the bishop's Winstree holdings amounts to the round sum of 40 hides, a further indication that, as suggested in chapter 3, they may once have formed a single early territory.[98]

Cradley	Donnington	Eastnor	Ledbury	
			Ledbury	Hazle
12 (1 waste)	1	4	5	1
3	1	3	2	3
39	7	15	29	3
1 priest, 1 reeve 2 knights, 1 radman 23 villani 3 bordars 6 boors 5 slaves	6 villani 6 bordars 6 boors 5 slaves	1 knight 1 mason 8 villani 9 bordars	1 priest 2 knights, 1 radman 10 villani 7 bordars 1 boor	4 villani
1 – 32d.	0	0	1 – 32d.	1 – 2s.
7a.	8a.	6a.	7a.	7a.
I league x ½ league Pays nothing	0	4 furlong x 2 furlongs	½ league x ½ league Pays nothing	0
£10	£1 5s.	£4	£10	£1 5s.
£10	£1 5s.	£4	£8	£1 5s.

‡ These figures represent simply the head of tenant households and in any case are not complete; there are several references to 'others' sharing ploughs; subtenants of knights etc are generally not recorded. Population may be calculated using a factor of 4.5 for all recorded tenants (excluding slaves who were counted individually), but such an estimate is very conservative.

Ledbury was almost certainly the focal point of this complex of estates (see above, chapter 3). Although assessed at only six hides, the combined estate (i.e. including Hazle) was clearly a significant holding. As we have seen, it had easily the richest church in the area and was perhaps held, like Donnington, by one of the bishop's clerks. Ledbury was also one of the few Herefordshire estates to have a relationship with the salt-town of Droitwich (where, like Eastnor and Bagburrow, it had part of a salt-pan). Again, this was a sign of importance because salt, a highly valued commodity in the early Middle Ages, had traditionally been subjected to strict royal control. The combined estate's tenants numbered at least 26 and included four of relatively high status, the priest, two knights, and a radman, a free man who probably owed a mixture of money rents and unservile services, such as riding as messenger or escort for

his lord. Most importantly, it was well endowed with ploughteams: five held 'in demesne' by the lord, and 32 by his tenants. Its total value, which included two mills worth 4s. 8d., was put at £9 5s. in 1086, although £11 9s. in 1066. All this compares interestingly with Bosbury, assessed at six hides. Bosbury had a priest with a holding of a hide, 34 tenants, none of higher status than villein (peasant farmer), and two slaves; two ploughteams were in demesne and 22 held by tenants. It had a mill worth 2s. 6d. and its total annual value was put at £6. This record of the two estates' respective assets suggests that Ledbury, with its important church and relatively grand tenants, was assessed preferentially. That is clearest if we calculate the ratio of ploughlands to the taxable hide – in Ledbury with Hazle 7.4 (assuming an assessment of five hides) but in Bosbury only 4.2.

It is also worth comparing Ledbury with Cradley, the other major manor among the bishop's holdings in Winstree. Cradley had clearly once been of considerable importance; besides the main estate, assessed at 12 hides, a high rating for the area, it had two dependencies, Colwall and Hanley's End (now lost). By 1086, however, the bishop held only Cradley and Colwall, which together were assessed at the round figure of 15 hides, i.e. three times the minimum for noble status. Like Hazle, Colwall had been annexed by Earl Harold but later returned to the bishop. One indication of Cradley's continuing importance in 1086 is that the bishop's reeve, his official agent there, unlike many of his colleagues on other manors, had a substantial holding assessed at half a hide. Yet, unlike Ledbury, Cradley with Colwall did not have a privileged fiscal status; even allowing for one hide being treated as untaxable waste, the ratio of ploughteams to the hide was just under four. Significantly, although Cradley had a priest, his estate was assessed at only 1½ virgates, far less than his counterpart at Ledbury. It may be that it was the presence of a favoured episcopal clerk at the latter that helps to explain its preferential assessment. Interestingly, the most favourable ratio of ploughs to the hide (8:1) was at Donnington, which Domesday expressly says was held of the bishop by one of his clerks.

Here, as elsewhere in Herefordshire, the bishop's estates had a distinctive tenurial structure. An unusually large number of priests, clerks and chaplains were recorded as holding property, either in their own right or as glebe (property for the support of the church). As we have seen, one of the bishop's clerks held the small manor of Donnington, but the richest was undoubtedly the priest, who perhaps represented a religious community and was a tenant at Ledbury with a holding assessed at 2½ hides and valued at 50s. None of these clerks was named and nothing more is known about them. There was, however, a great difference in status between the simple village priest from one of the local villein families and a career clerk in the service of the bishop, like the one at Donnington and, presumably, those at Ledbury and (perhaps) Bosbury.

In contrast to these clerics, there were comparatively few knightly tenants on the bishop's estates – only 15 throughout the county, compared with over 50 on the bishop of Worcester's similar-sized estates. The bishop's estates in Winstree hundred contained two knights at Ledbury, Bagburrow and Cradley and one at Eastnor, all probably of foreign extraction, followers of the Conqueror, and generally holding property assessed at between a half and a whole hide. There were also six native freemen or radmen, based at Ledbury, Bagburrow, Coddington, Colwall and Cradley, with very similar holdings. Eastnor had one unusual subtenant, a mason (*cementarius*), who was probably of similar status, with a holding of just over half a hide.

The bishop farmed directly a certain amount of land in demesne in all his Winstree manors, except Donnington, much of the work being done by the unfree tenants, who included the peasant farmers known as villeins, lesser tenants such as cottagers (*bordarii*) and freedmen (*buri*), and – at the bottom of this hierarchy – the serfs or slaves (*servi*). The grander tenants, the bishop's clerks, knights, radmen and reeves, had their own demesne and, often, subtenants, but the latter were not fully recorded since they did not directly contribute to the wealth of the manor. At Ledbury, for example, the priest, knights and radman were said to have 10 ploughs in demesne and seven cottagers 'with others' a further eight; at Cradley, the reeve and grander tenants had five ploughs in demesne and their unspecified number of cottagers another six. On all the manors except Hazle, a majority of the ploughteams were held by the unfree. Most of the manors had mills where the corn produced on both the demesne and the tenanted land would have been ground.

The amount of meadow was reasonably consistent across the eight manors, though, as one would expect, Donnington, in the lush Leadon valley, had a higher proportion than in the hillier areas, where rougher pasture would have been available. Such grazing was an important element of the pastoral farming of the time. Native types of livestock fed on a wider range of material than their more refined kin today, happily browsing on holly, bracken, bark and the young growth of trees. The woodland, too, would have supported

Figure 61 Cattle resting in the daffodil-strewn woodland to the south of Ledbury. This landscape is typical of wood pasture, with its ancient trees giving shelter to the deer, cattle or horses that grazed beneath it.

many beasts in the clearings, for we are not to imagine a dense covering of wood, but rather an area of a few large trees, bosky thickets and grassy clearings. It is difficult to tell how extensive this wood pasture would have been. The Domesday entries only gave measurements for three woodlands, at Ledbury, Eastnor and Cradley. It is perhaps understandable that there was no mention of woodland in Donnington, in the vale, but it is surprising that none was recorded at Colwall, on the higher ground towards the Malverns.

The value of the woodland lay not only in the grazing of cattle and feeding of swine, but also in the timber itself, for building and for fuel. The furnaces of the saltpans of Droitwich, Worcestershire, consumed vast quantities of wood. In return for sending cart-loads of fuel to Droitwich a number of manors in the surrounding area received salt, which was vital for flavouring and preserving food. Some of the bishop's land had connections with the Droitwich salt industry. On his Winstree manors, Ledbury, Eastnor and Bagburrow each had a share in a salt pan.

MANAGING THE LAND

The Domesday clerks said nothing about the field system or systems by which the land was cultivated, other than making the distinction between land in demesne (under the direct management of the lord) and that in the hands of tenants. In 1086 only a small proportion of the land in Ledbury was held in demesne. By the time a rental was drawn up of the bishop's estate in 1288 (panel 5), the bishop held in demesne 479½ acres of arable, 28 acres of meadow and 23½ acres of pasture, with 12 acres of vineyard and an unspecified amount of woodland (about 550 acres in total). Eight named tenants held land from him by knight service, their holdings varying in size from one yardland to 1½ hides (six yardlands). Translating yardlands into acres is difficult, as the standard varied around the country and over time. The yardland or virgate in Worcestershire and Warwickshire was often between 25 and 30 acres, whereas on the manors of St Katherine's Hospital, it appears to have been 60 acres. This is further complicated by the erratic size of the acre itself, to say nothing of the difficulty of accurate measurement. Speaking, then, in the crudest terms, in the late 13th century the manor of Ledbury was reckoned to contain some 5,500 acres (compared with a measurement of the parish at 8,184 acres in 1887), and the bishop of Hereford farmed about one tenth of the area in demesne.

In 1288 the Hazle was said to contain 'one knight's fee [probably 12 yardlands], whence are owed two suits of court at Hereford from month to month, and two suits at Ledbury when it happens, and two heriots …' (the obligation of the tenant to attend the manorial courts and to pay a form of death duty to the manorial lord). The fact that it owed two suits of court, two heriots and two reliefs suggests that it was already held in two halves. This was made explicit in a list of those who held from the bishop of Hereford by knight service in 1304: Sir Grimbald Pauncefoot held one half of Hazle and John Sollers the other. The amount of land, including the Hazle, held by knight service in 1288 was 31 yardlands. The free tenants held 24½ yardlands, in plots ranging from three acres to one ploughland (four yardlands) and a further 120 acres in plots of six or 12 acres; the customary tenants held 22 yardlands, in holdings from ¼ to one whole yardland, with another 159 acres being held in small plots of three to 18 acres.[99]

There are no detailed records of the other sub-manors within Ledbury, although the detached portion of the parish known as Court-y-Park, to the north-west, and two tenements in the north-eastern part of the parish called Wellington and Massington are mentioned, and there is a single reference to a manor at Pesebrugge in the west. By 1439 Wellington itself was subdivided. The estates of the portionaries of the Upper and Lower Halls probably grew out of the 2½ hides held by the priest at Domesday and there are a few surviving court rolls and accounts for both of these. The most prolific set of surviving records are those for the estates of St Katherine's Hospital. The land which the hospital held in Ledbury lay for the most part in the north-east corner of the parish, and in adjoining Eastnor. These lands were managed as a single unit and the records give an insight into how interconnected the land holdings and farming practice were between these two parishes.[100]

Surveys and rentals were periodically drawn up, recording who held what land, on what basis and what they paid for it, in cash, kind or service. This might happen when a new lord took possession or when a new official was appointed. For example, it was noted in 1400 that the bailiffs of Upper Hall and of each part of the Hazle made new rentals on first coming into their bailiwicks. The bailiffs also drew up annual accounts which recorded the rents received, perquisites of court and any other income of the manor as well as expenses and outgoings. These records are not generally common before the mid-13th century. The manor courts, usually held every three weeks, recorded transfers of ownership and regulated the customs of the manor. From documents such as these, where they survive, a great deal can be learnt about daily life and the running of agricultural estates. There are a handful of such records for Ledbury and its sub-manors, mostly from the 15th and early 16th centuries.[101]

The Bailiffs

The bailiff or steward, as well as having judicial responsibilities (as discussed in chapter 5 above), was responsible for the management of the estates, and on large estates had assistants, called reeves, to manage individual manors. These were the men who had regular contact with the tenants and saw to the day-to-day allocation of work. The bailiff collected the rents and made up the accounts. Rents were payable in cash and kind. Payments were usually made at the four quarter days, the feast of the Annunciation, otherwise known as Lady Day (25 March), the feast of the nativity of St John the Baptist or Midsummer's day (24 June), the feast of St Michael, known as Michaelmas (29 September) and Christmas day (25 December). Some customary payments, including the Ledbury rents, were payable on the feast of St Andrew (30 November) instead of Christmas day. From the late 13th-century rental it appears that the free tenants of Ledbury paid at a rate ranging from the 4s. a yardland paid by Richard le Falconer to the 27s. 7d. paid by Gilbert Eseger. The differences no doubt depended on the mixture of arable and meadow land and the quality of it. At this time the demesne land was valued as 4d. an acre for arable, 18d. an acre for meadow and 8d. an acre for pasture.

The Tenants and their Dues

The customary tenants, who held property by the custom of the manor, regulated and recorded by the manor court, paid money rents and owed certain other dues. Payments 'of gift and honey' (*de dono et melle*) and 'for fish' (*pro pisce*) were made in four of the

Figure 62 A section of the 13th-century rental showing payments for fish and honey due from the customary tenants.

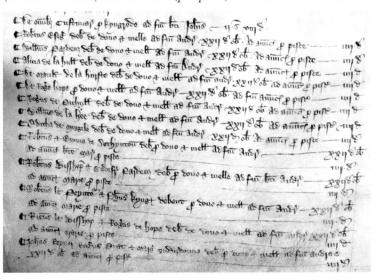

bishop's manors. At Bosbury 28 people made similar payments as gift and honey and for fish. At Colwall 24 tenants paid 2s. 1d. each as gift and honey at St Andrew and 1½d. each for fish at the Annunciation. At Eastnor 13 tenants paid 1s. 9d. as gift and honey at St Andrew's. In Ledbury 17 tenants paid between 1d. and 1s. 10½d. a year as gift and honey and 21 paid 4d. each for fish. These four manors form a compact geographical group in south-east Herefordshire. Such archaic payments, typical of many Welsh tenurial systems, perhaps indicate that these manors were originally all in one hand, and that Welsh occupation survived relatively late on this early estate. There are other examples of 'Welsh' communities and customs surviving well within 'England' and of English communities to the west of Offa's Dyke (see chapter 2). It is not clear from the manuscript whether the scribe meant for fish (*pro pisce*) or for fishing (*pro piscaria*), since the terms *pisce* and *piscar* seem to be used indiscriminately. Were the tenants expected to give a gift of fish worth 4d. or were they paying 4d., in effect, for a licence to fish? As *pisce* appears twice as often as *piscar*, it seems likely that the former was meant, especially as no mention was made of the river. At Hampton (Bishop) the fishing of the Lugg (*de piscaria de Lugge*) produced 22d. a year.[102]

Boon Works   These were work obligations owed by customary tenants to their lords. The majority were days spent working for the lord on the demesne land, supplementing the work of slaves and later of servants. As farming became more commercial in the 12th and 13th centuries more and more rent was paid in money rather than in kind or in service. By 1288 in Ledbury 44 customary tenants of the bishop paid solely a money rent for their holdings. Ten people who held only between three and 12 acres apiece also owed boon works. The three who had 12 acres each owed two days a week from Michaelmas (29 September) to the 'gules' or 'mouth' of August (1 August), less the three festival weeks, making a total of 82 days. The tasks to be performed were not specified, but would have been given under the direction of the reeve and would no doubt have included sowing and weeding, mowing and mucking, hedging and ditching.

On some of the bishop's Herefordshire estates (Bishops Frome, Ledbury and Whitbourne) the ploughing work was done under an arrangement called 'the Rede' (*rede* meant a small furrow in Old English). The Ledbury entry in the 1288 rental regarding this service is somewhat difficult to interpret, reading: 'And be it known that the ploughing service called the Rede is allowed to all the customary tenants in one [of two] times. And concerning the other time [*de cetero*], it is not necessary to mention the

Figure 63 Harvest work, still in the 1930s, as in the Middle Ages, a strenuous task for men and horses.

ploughing service, the said Rede, in the account [*compoto*], and of the will of the customary tenants the rent is divided equally at four terms'. This seems to suggest that by 1288 the tenants were 'let off' the ploughing at one season (it does not say whether spring or autumn) and that a cash rent was paid in lieu of the other. The entry for Whitbourne gives more detail, saying that the tenants of eight named virgates were liable to plough eight acres and sow them with their own corn and harrow 'which is called the Rede'.[103]

All the customary tenants, except Hugh de La More, Roger son of Alice of Walsued, Matilda de Walsued, and those doing minor works, also had to plough and sow 23 acres with their own wheat, and to plough 22½ acres for oats in Lent but not to sow them. The three who did not have to follow this prescriptive sowing paid an extra 6d. on St Andrew's day (30 November). In addition, the customary tenants owed 16 days' work at harvest. Those who held six acres and even the three who only had three acres each owed half this amount. The day works were valued at ½d. each and the harvest works (very hard work indeed) were valued at 1d. each. The valuation may be more than just a matter of accounting, but imply that it was at least possible for the tenant to pay in cash rather than do the work himself. The one woman in this group, Matilda de Leadon, especially, may have paid someone to do her service for her or paid cash in lieu.[104]

Other Duties Two of the customary tenants also had other duties to perform, reflecting a higher social status. Gilbert of Dunbridge, who held 12 acres, 'ought to summon the court of Ledbury at the steward's order'. Alured of the Frith, who also held only 12 acres, seems to have had particularly responsible charges. He had to guard the lord's corn in the fields at harvest, to carry the bishop's letters within the bishopric at the order of the bishop or his bailiff and to guard thieves within the court of Ledbury. If they escaped he had to answer for it in court. An Elured had been reeve at some point in the mid-13th century, when he witnessed a deed. Perhaps it was this same Alured, or his father, and the services were therefore part of his duties as reeve. How duties such as summoning the court became attached to particular holdings is now lost to us.[105]

Decline of Service   The erosion of boon works by economic trends was hastened by the after-effects of the Black Death in the late 1340s. As the population fell, tenants found themselves able to make more favourable arrangements when taking on leases of land. Boon works and other customary services dwindled in the second half of the 14th century, though with regional variations in the pace of change. In 1404, when a survey was taken of the value of the bishop of Hereford's estates during a vacancy in the see, although the sum of the rents of both freemen and customary tenants was not dissimilar to those in 1288, no mention was made of the value of boon works. On the other hand, an account made in 1495 which referred to the rents, for both freemen and customary tenants, as being based on a rental made one hundred years before, did refer to 30s 2½d. being paid for works before autumn and 117 works in autumn. By 1537 Thomas Lorymer was only able to account for 24 harvest works sold at various prices amounting to 30s. 10½d. Similar trends were to be seen on the manors of St Katherine's Hospital, too. When Swithun Butterfield drew up a survey of the bishop's estates in the 1570s he studied the old records and recorded that:

> In the old court rolls appeareth that many Custome Tenants have forsaken the Custome lands they occupied And would not hold it for the Rent they then paide whereby the Lord was forced to abate his Rent for lacke of tenants.[106]

Exploiting the Land

Where was the arable land and how was it arranged? Field boundary patterns reveal the legacy of the furlongs into which the landscape of medieval open fields was divided. Within the upper Leadon valley the influence of these former furlongs is pervasive in today's field boundaries. There is a strong indication in some places, and especially in the Mathon basin, of the relatively late enclosure of the formerly extensive medieval open-field landscapes here.[107]

Aerial photography helps to identify areas of open-field farming and deserted settlement sites. Place names also offer a clue to their location. Such places often include the suffix *tūn* (town). There are a number of examples in the parish of Ledbury: Wellington and Massington, already mentioned as manors, and also Netherton and Suthinton, the latter of which became the farm now known as Siddington. Other local place names or locative surnames which occur regularly in medieval documents include Mitchell, Ockeridge, Wall Hills, Fairtree and Playstow. Some of these settlements remain as clusters of cottages, or as individual farms, such as Ockeridge or Playstow. Others have become deserted, like the settlement on the borders of Ledbury and Eastnor, just south-east of Lower Mitchell Cottages. It seems likely that these small settlements outside Ledbury itself, dotted around the Foreign of the large parish, some associated with sub-manors, had their own field systems. Tenants then had separate strips of land scattered in the furlongs which made up the common fields. Evidence for these strips comes from deeds of gift, sale and exchange which describe land, usually 'acres' or sometimes 'rugges' (ridges) in such and such field, bounded by land of other people on either side or by natural features in the landscape. One example is the land described as 'three selions lying in a field of Eastnor between the land of Robert de la Geldepirye and the land of the chaplain of the blessed Mary of Ledbury, and it extends from land of the rector of the church of Eastnor to Brankeswallessiche'. Such plots were often marked out 'by metes and bounds'. The names of fields, traced from medieval documents to modern maps, can also give clues to the location of these open fields.[108]

Figure 64 The ridges and furrows of medieval ploughland running up to the western edge of Frith Wood just north of the present Frith Farm.

As climate, population and economics dictated, the edges between ploughland and woodland ebbed and flowed. Under pressure of expanding population, land was won back from

woodland and waste in the 11th and 12th centuries, a process known as assarting. In the mid-13th century William of Ockeridge (in the north-east of the parish) gave to St Katherine's Hospital 'all his assart with a certain moor and all the appurtenances within the ditch and inclosure of the said assart'. By the early 14th century the extent of arable land throughout England was probably at its maximum. High on the Malverns there are the remains of terraces, known as lynchets, made to wrest a few more acres of tillable land from the steeper surrounding countryside. The effort involved in creating these works, despite the poor returns from the thinner soils, was driven by a greater demand for food as the population had grown considerably by 1300. Even the wet soils in valley bottoms, suitable for meadows, were sometimes put under the plough. There are areas of ridge and furrow still visible on the flood plains of the Wye and the Lugg, although not the Leadon. The people of Ledbury constructed a series of massive lynchets at the southern end of the hill now covered by Frith Wood, closest to the town but closer still to what is now the Frith farm, from which they were probably worked. These lynchets form a series of five terraces cut into the hill, each up to eight feet (three metres) high and 14 feet (five metres) wide and over 421 feet (150 metres) long. Although not as remote as those higher up the Malverns, being only half a mile from the town, they cannot have been easy to work, let alone to construct. They were abandoned after the mid-14th-century collapse of population.[109]

Figure 65   This map of the parish of Ledbury, drawn in 1816 at the time of enclosure of the common waste, still clearly shows separate strips of land the fields at Ludstock, in the south-west of the parish. The gently curving flattened 'S' of the strips reflects the slow progress of the medieval ox team up and down the land, still followed by the 19th-century horse plough, and leaving its mark on the divisions of the land.

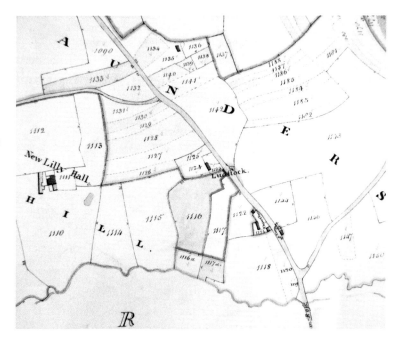

The arable land was arranged in large fields around the settlements, individual tenants holding a number of selions or strips in different fields; ploughing, sowing and harvesting would have been arranged communally. Meadow, too, was divided amongst the tenants and access to the open common land, often called the waste, was related to the amount of land held and was regulated by manorial customs. Although there were large fields lying in strips, it was not a completely open landscape. Some, at least, of the arable fields themselves seem to have had hedges around them. In the mid-13th century there were references to selions and acres in Wellecroft with 'foreland and hedges adjoining' and to five selions in Wetecroft running next to the hedge. In addition, there was any number of small closes, sometimes called *parrocs*, for specialist crops or for controlling livestock; for example, one of the parcels of land exchanged by the hospital in 1300 was called Calverparruc (Calves Close).[110]

There is evidence to suggest that people were exchanging land, consolidating their holdings and enclosing areas of arable land from an early date. In 1350 John de Calhulle let all his enclosed land at Wall Hills to John atte Nash and his wife Emma. This may have lain within the pre-existing earthworks (panel 2); note also that there are visible lynchets and ridge and furrow on the north-east face of Wall Hills. The process of enclosure was certainly under way by the early 16th century, for in 1537 the steward failed to collect the rent for 'ploughland lately enclosed by Hugh Carewe because it is not known where it lies'. It has been suggested that Herefordshire, like most western counties, was heavily enclosed by 1600, though (as Fig. 65 shows) this process was not complete even in the early 19th century, when an Act of Parliament in 1813 permitted the parcelling up of the last remaining open common land in Ledbury.[111]

Crops   Wheat, barley, oats and rye were the main field crops of the Middle Ages, the particular ratio of one crop to another depending in large measure on soil type and climate. The central Herefordshire plain was well suited to wheat, although oats were also grown in considerable quantities. Wheat was sown after the autumn ploughing, oats in the spring. Peas, beans and vetches, also spring-sown, began to be much more widely grown by the late 13th century. There is clear evidence for such crops in Ledbury itself at this time. In 1289 the bishop's household spent 4d. on a bushel of peas when staying in the town and when John de Aigueblanche (dean of Hereford and portionary of Ledbury) died in 1320, he left bequests of bushels of corn and peas to the poor of many parishes where he had connections, including

Ledbury. The detailed survey of the possessions of St Katherine's Hospital in 1316 shows that on their manors in and around Ledbury, they were growing 51 per cent wheat, 28 per cent oats and 21 per cent peas and beans. In contrast, 11 years later, the Leominster priory estates, in north Herefordshire, do not appear to have grown any pulses at all, growing 48 per cent wheat and 52 per cent oats. This, despite the proportion of arable land on their estates being remarkably similar, 88 per cent of St Katherine's and 87 per cent of Leominster priory, with similarly close proportions of meadow, pasture and moor. This pattern of cropping suggests a three-course rotation of two crops and a fallow, providing pasture on the fallow, which also had the benefit of allowing the animals to dung the fields.[112]

There are a number of references to gardens (or possibly orchards). The earliest dates to around 1242 when Richard le Wyte of Ledbury granted to William de Norton and Alice his wife a plot of land in Church Lane stretching 'between the house of Richard le Long and the stream flowing from Upper Hall, in width from the middle of the well (*fontis*) to the said stream, and in length from the garden of Lower Hall to the highway'. In the early 14th century the Berde family had three large gardens, including a 'new' garden, adjoining their tenements in New Street. Unfortunately none of these records gives any indication of what was being grown in the gardens. The two belonging to the bishop in 1288 were said to be worth 4s. 6d. yearly. This was quite likely to have been for the pasture, as certain later documents make clear: in 1404, in 1495 and again in 1537, the herbage and fruit of one garden were valued at 2s. Many medieval gardens contained areas of grass with a few fruit trees and the herbage was a valuable addition to the grazing for animals. No doubt many people kept hens and pigs in their gardens, too; good for the pot, if not for the growing plants! The late 16th-century tithe book makes it clear that people grew hemp, flax and even corn in their gardens, as well as vegetables like leeks and fruit trees. This was no doubt true in earlier centuries and evidence from elsewhere suggests that onions, garlic and 'coles' or cabbages would have been grown. In seigneurial gardens and perhaps even those of wealthy merchants some flowers and sweet herbs would have been grown, too. It has been said that 'small towns stimulated horticulture in their vicinity' and this may be true of Ledbury. In 1485 Martin Bracy rented a garden called 'ympey' for 6s. a year. The name 'ympey' suggests that it was being used as a nursery garden of some sort, as 'imp' means a slip, shoot or sapling. He still had the garden in 1499 and then it was described as being at Haffield.[113]

MEADOW AND PASTURE

Meadow land produces lush grasses suitable for cutting for hay. It needs to be well watered and is usually found in the valleys of streams and rivers. The Leadon itself has a wide, level valley through which it meanders and no doubt most of the meadow mentioned in Domesday Book (14 acres in Ledbury and eight in Donnington) would have been in this valley. In the hills to the east streams rise in the north and form narrow valleys with a certain amount of meadow on their verges. The Glynch brook, especially, was bordered by meadows, described in the mid-13th century as 'brademedwe (broad meadow) lying near the water of Glenche between the land of Osbert de Suthinton and the meadow of Robert and William de Goldhull'. In 1288 there were 28 acres of meadow recorded in Ledbury Foreign, although in the rental and many of the earlier deeds the meadows are not named or clearly described, so it is difficult to locate them. Some areas of meadow were close to the town, on the south-west: Upper Hall had meadow in Mabel's furlong and there was meadow to the south of New Street, near a place called 'Lonecotes', which was part of the manor of Hazle.[114]

The value of meadow and pasture was in the number of beasts that it could support. Horses were pastured but also fed hay and oats in winter; Bishop Swinfield's household, staying in Ledbury in December 1289, brought hay from the farm and bought three quarters of oats for 44 horses. Oxen were used for ploughing and were valuable beasts. The custom on the bishop's manors was for the best ox to be paid as heriot, the fine paid after someone's decease so that their heir could take over their land. When Thomas Bracy died in 1485 his son Edmund gave a red ox, valued at 10s. – perhaps an ancestor of the modern Herefordshire red cattle. There is little evidence for dairying in the medieval period, though the bishop's household did spend 20d. on cheese at Ledbury in 1289. There are occasional references to cows being stolen, which proves their value but tells nothing of their management. Sheep were probably kept for milk and cheese as well as for meat. (The importance of wool has already been discussed in chapter 5).[115]

WOODS

The woodland on the hills to the east of Ledbury, partly in Ledbury and partly in Eastnor, was a vital resource for grazing as well as for timber. Woods were used as rough pasture for cattle, sheep and horses and pannage for pigs, which enjoyed rootling for acorns and beech mast in the autumn. What is now Frith Wood, 5,615 feet

Figure 66   A hollow way through Frith Wood, half a mile to the north-east of Ledbury town. Woodland boundaries were marked by banks and ditches like this one on the west of Frith Wood. This was made sometime after the mid-14th century when the hollow way path from Le Frith was no longer being used to reach the arable lynchets which slowly became clothed in scrub and trees.

(two kilometres) long and 842 feet (300 metres) wide, may retain at its core something of the wood described in Domesday Book as being 'half a league by a half' (a league was usually three miles, 4.8 kilometres). The size and shape of the wood have changed over the years, as has the composition of its vegetative coverage, but it is likely that the ridge, surmounted by an ancient boundary bank, has remained permanently clothed in trees, being too steep and narrow for any other use. There were other patches of woodland scattered around Ledbury and the surrounding parishes, especially on the hilly ground around the parish boundaries, like Haffield to the south and the western flank of Wall Hills, known as Tyrrell's Frith. The 1404 inquiry into the estates of the bishop of Hereford referred to 'a several wood called le Parc', meaning an area owned by several people and kept separate. But none of it was 'wild wood'. It was a managed landscape, carefully guarded by both custom and by physical boundaries. The value of every blade of grass, acorn, twig and tree was accounted for.[116]

Figure 67   A coppiced stool of hazel in Frith wood. Trees were cut down short, on a regular cycle (often seven years), and then the young shoots sprouting from the 'stool' were harvested to make laths and poles.

Timber   Provision of timber for building is perhaps the first use of woods that comes to mind. Certainly most of Ledbury's buildings, as generally in the west midlands, were timber-framed at this time. In chapter 5 we saw how the bishop gave Richard Glover an oak towards building the new Boot Hall. The king regularly gave trees from the royal forests to favoured subjects or to pious purposes like building or repairing churches and monasteries. Ships, too, required large timbers and many great trees from the nearby Forest of Dean went for this purpose over the centuries. But to have large trees of straight growth in steady supply requires

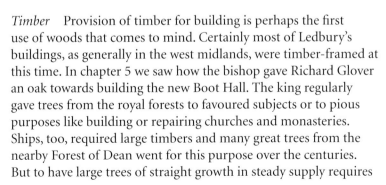

careful management. Standards were selected for their good shape, the surrounding lesser wood being coppiced, cut back regularly, to allow light and space for the main trunk to develop.[117]

Undergrowth and Coppiced Wood   This had many uses. Young pliant stems of hazel and alder were used for making hurdles and baskets, as were the withies or willows which grew near the river. On a number of occasions the bishop allowed the citizens of Hereford to gather alder boughs in the wood by Hereford to make hurdles and stalls or even booths (*schoppas*) for fair days. Bishop Richard Swinfield's accounts show a number of payments for collecting brushwood for mending hedges on his estates. Bark was gathered for tanning and nuts for eating. The bracken which grew in the open areas between the woodland stands was collected for litter for cattle or to be burnt and the ashes used to make a form of soap. Nothing was wasted.[118]

Charcoal   This was another by-product of the woodland. Charcoal has been in use since at least the time of the Romans. Their iron works in the Sussex weald and the Forest of Dean depended on a regular supply of this steadily-burning efficient fuel. As with all

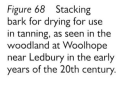

Figure 68   Stacking bark for drying for use in tanning, as seen in the woodland at Woolhope near Ledbury in the early years of the 20th century.

aspects of woodland work, patience is required in the production of charcoal. An area of level ground is first selected (or levelled as so many woods are on hillsides), covering an area of 14-28 feet (5-10 metres) in diameter. The coppiced wood is then carefully arranged in a pyre, covered with turf and lit, then left to slowly combust anaerobically. The clamp needs to be checked regularly. It is not possible to date the charcoal burning platforms in Frith Wood – they could be from any period from Domesday to the late 19th century when John Masefield the poet observed them at work, for the technique changed little over the centuries. In 1289 Bishop Swinfield paid 5d. for three loads of charcoal at Ledbury and 1d. more for carriage; a cryptic entry in the household expenses mentions a charcoal burner who went to London on the bishop's business. Surnames such as Coleman and Collier or the designation *carbonarius* refer to charcoal burners.[119]

Deer   Deer were important creatures in the medieval landscape of wood pasture. The Domesday entry for Eastnor mentioned two *haga*, which means, literally, a hedge, but was used to refer to hedged enclosures, perhaps to be identified with the later Deerfold near Bronsil Castle. There were many '*haga*' or 'hay' references in the Domesday entries for Herefordshire, Worcestershire and especially Shropshire; in these border counties the word often seems to have meant enclosures for the control of deer. Later on the term was used in these counties for larger enclosures in areas that had once been royal forest, such as the Hay of Hereford.

Figure 69   Deer in Eastnor Park in the early 20th century. Although a newly created 18th-century park, this landscape of open glades and stands of trees would have been similar to that of the medieval chace.

Figure 70 Men hunting a stag with bows in an early 14th-century manuscript now in Hereford cathedral. Note the rabbit peeping from its burrow.

Malvern Chace was part of what had once probably been a much more extensive royal forest, subject to special laws, and included parts of Eastnor and Ledbury. It was granted by Edward I to Gilbert de Clare, earl of Gloucester, on his marriage with Jean d'Acres, the king's daughter. From that date it ceased to be under true forest law. In 1278 the earl began a long legal dispute with Thomas Cantilupe, bishop of Hereford, over rights in the Chace. The bishop maintained his rights on the western side of the hills, and popular legend has it that the earl cut the Shire Ditch to mark the division between the two counties (chapter 2). In the 1390s a later bishop, John Trefnant, also had to take legal action to urge his claim 'to a free Chace there for wild beasts with all other usual privileges and prerogatives'. The difference between deer kept in enclosures and parks and those roaming wild is demonstrated in the household records of Richard Swinfield, where it was recorded that the bishop's household had fat does from the parks of Colwall and Dingwood and lean ones from the open chace.[120]

Rabbits   Rabbits were introduced by the Normans in the 12th century and became a lucrative stock in the late 13th and early 14th centuries. They were farmed, artificial burrows being made for them in 'pillow mounds'. There are the remains of such mounds on either side of the Malvern Hills, on Hollybush Hill in Eastnor and

near the British Camp on the Ledbury side. There is also a distinct
mound near the deserted village at Massington in the north-east of
the parish. The Coneygree wood to the south-east of Ledbury and
the slopes below it still teem with rabbits and further investigation
may locate pillow mounds here, too. In 1409 John Baynham was
appointed warden of Malvern Chace and surveyor of the warren
of Ledbury. This was no sinecure post, for medieval court records
show a number of cases of poaching and breaking into parks.
One of the most dramatic occurred 55 years before Baynham's
appointment, when the bishop prosecuted Walter Morton in the
king's court at Westminster, because he had entered 'with force and
arms' into the bishop's free warren at Ross, Upton, Ledbury and
Eastnor, and chased hares, rabbits, partridges and pheasants. On
the Monday after St James's day (30 July) 1352 he took 500 hares,
1,000 rabbits, 1,000 partridges and 200 pheasants. Walter was
himself 'taken' and the bishop was awarded damages.[121]

From the banks of the Leadon to the crest of the hills, the land
was intensively farmed and managed. When Piers Ploughman fell
to dreaming one May morning on the Malverns the 'fair field' he
saw was indeed 'full of folk working and wandering'. It was also full
of noise and activity.[122]

Chapter 7

Spiritual Life

Figure 71 One of two sundials, sometimes referred to as mass-dials, scratched onto the fifth buttress from the east on the south side of Ledbury parish church. The gnomon is long since gone, but, when there, its moving shadow would have allowed priest and parishioner alike to calculate the passing of time and the hours for the services.

As we have seen in chapters 3 and 4, the church played a very important part in forming and shaping Ledbury as a town. Physically the small town was dominated by two large ecclesiastical buildings: the parish church of Sts Peter and Paul and the hospital of St Katherine, with its stone-built chapel abutting the market place. As a manor belonging to the bishop of Hereford, Ledbury was subject to the temporal as well as the spiritual direction of the church. Religious life and observances permeated the life of the townsfolk and surrounding villagers. The rhythm of their year was shaped by the seasons and by the liturgy of the church. The stages of their lives were marked by the sacraments of baptism, marriage and last rites, their earthly remains consigned to the sacred ground of the churchyard. They earned their living on land held from the bishop or other ecclesiastical bodies and as tradesmen, many of whose customers would have been clerics. They paid tithes and made Easter offerings to their parish church and many gave voluntary sums to various religious devotions during life and at the time of their deaths. Clergy and laity were enmeshed in a complex web of mutual responsibilities, as landlords and tenants, patrons and clients, priests and parishioners.

The role of the bishop as lord of the manor has been discussed in chapters 5 and 6. The parish church and the hospital of St Katherine were also landowners and patrons, as well as having spiritual functions. They all had their part to play in shaping the medieval church, caring for and adding to the building, providing services and guiding the flock.

PORTIONARIES

The rectory of the church in Ledbury continued to be divided into two portions, in the gift of the bishop except when the see was vacant, when the king was able to appoint. The divisions were not in equal parts, the value of the Upper Hall being somewhat greater than the Lower Hall. By the time of Henry VIII's survey of the value of all ecclesiastical property in 1535, David Waller had an annual income from Upper Hall of £18 1s. 6½d., out of which he paid the bishop 8s. 10½d. John Parker, who held the Lower Hall, had just over half as much, £9 6s. 8d., but had to pay

Figure 72 The church of Sts Peter and Paul (now St Michael and All Angels) from the north-east, showing the chancel, north chapel and outer north chapel. Note the changing style of the windows, from left to right in the image. The great east window is a late 13th- or early 14th-century opening with 15th-century tracery, the small window in the north of the chancel is of the late 12th century. That further west is a 13th-century opening with 15th-century tracery. The east window of the north chapel is an elegant three-pointed light of the late 13th century. At the right is one of the ornate windows of the outer north chapel – see Fig. 73 for details.

the bishop 20s. and the precentor of the cathedral 10s. a year. Twenty years earlier the difference had been less. The value of the Upper Hall portion then was £17 and that of the Lower Hall £13. The income of the two portions in the preceding centuries is more difficult to ascertain, although some account rolls for the Lower Hall survive for the period 1485-1529, which give an indication of what land made up the Lower Hall portion. In 1535 the income of Lower Hall came mainly from the rent of land and from tithes on grain. This was also true of Upper Hall, though this benefited from miscellaneous payments from the burgesses and free tenants of Ledbury Foreign and from the parish of Coddington; the tithe of lambs, wool, piglets, ducks and fruit, valued at 2s. 8d.; an estimated 20d. for oblations in the chapel of St Blaise (unidentified) and mortuary fees in Ledbury Foreign and Eastnor, also estimated at 20d. It is likely that these incomes and dues were of ancient standing.[123]

Although there were a number of references to 'the collegiate church in Ledbury' in the mid-14th century, an inquest instituted by Bishop Gilbert in 1384 found that neither Bromyard nor Ledbury churches were collegiate, but portionary. The inquest confirmed that 'the vicars in them with cure of souls have neither common seals nor common chests, common bells, common houses nor chapter for transacting business.' Despite this, there were other later references to the 'collegiate church of Ledbury'. It seems that 'collegiate' was sometimes wrongly used as interchangeable with 'portionary'.[124]

Figure 73 Contrast the elegant simplicity of the 13th-century window in Fig. 72 with the windows of the outer north chapel, glorious early 14th-century openings with four trefoiled lights, each with quatrefoiled tracery (see also Fig. 79).

Figure 74 The tomb of John Swinfield (d.1311) in Hereford cathedral. He was a portionary of Ledbury, precentor of Hereford and nephew of Bishop Richard Swinfield. The tomb is surmounted by an arch carved with swine feeding on acorns, each carrying the arms of Swinfield. This device, a play on Swinefield's name, is known as a rebus.

As the portions in Ledbury were 'without cure of souls', not requiring the holder to reside and to minister to the people in person, they were ideal positions for bishops and kings to give to men who were engaged in business on their behalf. A number of bishops also seem to have favoured family members with portions at Ledbury. Records of their appointment survive in bishops' registers and royal letters, as do licences from the pope to allow them to hold more than one benefice at once or to exchange one benefice for another. Unfortunately, it is not always clear which portion a person held. Five of them were also masters of St Katherine's Hospital. Some held senior dignities at Hereford cathedral such as chancellor, treasurer or precentor (in charge of church music).

Figure 75 Illustration of John Prophete's memorial brass in the church of Ringwood, Hampshire. The embroidered panels (orphreys) on his vestments depict various saints.

Six portionaries between 1300 and 1558 were at some point dean of Hereford. John de Aigueblanche was presented to a portion in Ledbury in 1307, which had been held by his cousin James 20 years earlier and was later held by his brother Aymo. John was the most notable of the nephews of the even more notable, or notorious, bishop of Hereford, the Savoyard Peter de Aigueblanche (d.1268). John was appointed dean by his uncle and then, following a legal dispute with Giles de Avenbury over the post, was confirmed in position by the pope in 1282. John remained dean and portionary of Ledbury until his death in 1320. A hundred years later another very able administrator, John Prophete, dean from 1393 to 1404, held the Upper Hall in 1390-4 and again between 1402-6. Hugh Coren was presented to the Upper Hall in 1547, six years after he became dean. In 1558 he was promoted to be archbishop of Dublin by Queen Mary. Others had a far less glorious career, like poor John ap Richard, who was elected dean in 1462 but the election was overturned by Bishop Stanbury, who appointed Richard Pede in his stead. The bishop seems to have effected an exchange whereby John ap Richard was presented to the Upper Hall, previously held by Pede, in recompense for losing the dignity of dean.[125]

Particularly in the early 14th century a number of these men played a part on a far wider stage than the diocese of Hereford and it seems unlikely that they were ever frequent visitors to Ledbury. Some were often abroad on business of church or state. Dean John de Aigueblanche was a papal chaplain, frequently in Rome, and also in the service of Amedus, count of Savoy. Master Gilbert de Middleton, collated to Ledbury in 1318, was also archdeacon of Northampton and held prebends in London, Salisbury, Chichester, Wells, Hereford and Romsey. The income from all of these positions would have enabled him to act as the king's clerk without being a drain on the king's own resources. When Middleton died in 1331 his portion went to Master Itherius de Concoreto, a Frenchman who held prebends in London, Salisbury and Hereford. Itherius was a papal collector but his career ended in ignominy in 1343 when he took a wife. By 1355 he was said to have become a soldier. He had been replaced in 1343 by Bernard de Ortolis, a bachelor of canon and civil law who worked at the court of Rome and then as papal nuncio in Norway and Sweden. From the second half of the 14th century the portionaries seem to have been more local men, although some continued to use their Ledbury portions to support wider careers. John Prophete served Richard II efficiently and was clerk to the royal council in 1392, the year before he became dean of Hereford. He continued in royal service, becoming keeper of the Privy Seal in 1406, yet still found the time and energy to effect reforms to the administration of St Katherine's Hospital.[126]

Figure 76 Illustration of the memorial brass of Robert Preece, portionary, from Dingley's *History from Marble*. Dingley recorded the inscription as 'Here lyeth Magister Roberde Preece/who in life time was counted wise/For the love of Peter and St Paul/Sey a pater noster and ave for Magister Roberde Preece soul'.

The portionaries had to provide a vicar for the parish, taking it in turns to present a suitable person. They were also responsible for the upkeep of the chancel, upon pain of a fine of 40s. When the bishop visited the parish in 1397 as part of his inspection of the diocese, he was told by the parishioners that this was neglected by the portionaries Robert Preece and Hugh Carwy. At the same time it was reported that Robert Preece, who held the Upper Hall, had inappropriate relations with his servant Alice Smith and also with Maiota Crompe. This implies that he must have been resident in Ledbury for at least some of the time! He is also the only portionary we know to be buried in Ledbury (about 1420). Although the memorial has since disappeared, two 17th-century observers recorded the stone with its inset brass, then under the communion table. They gave slightly different versions of the wording, which is one of the earliest known English inscriptions on a memorial tablet, although the kneeling figure of Preece also had a scroll issuing from his mouth with the Latin prayer '*miserere mei dominus*' (have pity on me Lord).[127]

John de Aigueblanche was buried in the north transept of Hereford cathedral, close to his uncle, Bishop Peter. In his will he left money to the church at Ledbury, amongst bequests to many other parishes where he had interests. As was right and fitting for a portionary, he left 6s. 8d. for the repair of the chancel at Ledbury and for work on St Radegund's chapel.[128]

PARISH CHURCH

By the end of the 14th century the church had achieved the distinctive plan and form that it still has. The rebuilding of the aisles and chancel chapels, begun in the mid-13th century

Figure 77 Ledbury church from the north-west as drawn by Thomas Dingley in the 1670s or 1680s. The 14th-century rebuilding is clearly visible, with the north porch and vestry adjoining the north aisle at its western end and the beautiful outer north chapel projecting from the north chancel chapel.

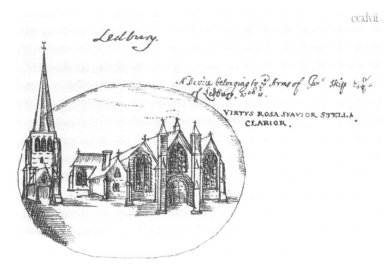

Katherine de Audley, the Recluse of Ledbury

According to legend, Katherine was a gentlewoman drawn to the religious life. She determined that she would become a recluse. (Not all recluses led strictly solitary lives but might keep a servant and even have lodgings in a religious house.) Katherine set out with her maid Mabel, following a dream that she would not settle until she came to a place where the bells rang of their own accord. Eventually they came to Ledbury. As they approached, they heard the church bells ringing, but when Mabel ran to the tower she found the door locked and the tower empty. The angels had rung the bells as a sign for Katherine to settle near Ledbury. There she led a blameless life, living on herbs and milk, fetched for her by her maid from the Hazle farm, according to a later elaboration of the legend.

In fact, in 1322 King Edward II granted the substantial pension of £30 a year out of land confiscated from Peter de Lymesey to Katherine de Audley, recluse of Ledbury. She would appear to have been established in Ledbury at least by 1313, when she granted to her daughter Ela and her son-in-law James de Perrers the castle and town of Llandovery and other land in Wales. The estate was to go to the king, should Ela and James die without issue. The grant was dated at Ledbury and witnessed not only by William the vicar, but also by the bishop of Hereford and other notables. Katherine's husband, Nicholas de Audley, had died in 1299 and it was not uncommon for widows to dispose of their worldly estate, often in return for an agreement for maintenance, and to turn to a religious life. Her pension from the king was to be paid in instalments of £10 at Easter, Michaelmas and Christmas, but was already in arrears by September 1323.

She probably died within the next few years as the last order to pay the arrears was in March 1325. Her memory was revered in the district although she was never canonised. In the Middle Ages the process of canonisation was quite fluid and reflected popular acclaim as well as pontifical approval. Local cult status was often an important part of the process. There was a very good example to hand at Hereford, where the tomb of bishop Thomas Cantilupe (d.1282) was already being turned into a shrine before his canonisation in 1320. His relics were first translated in 1287 by his protégé and successor as bishop, Richard Swinfield, who promoted his cause with diligence. However, there do not seem to be any records of a cause for canonisation for Katherine de Audley or any references to her cult in the Middle Ages.

Figure A   *This play bill was sent to John Biddulph, the owner of Ledbury Park, by J. Devereux. Devereux said that 'one of the players have got all the old account about her and they have been writing a play about it. They have been two or three days of painting fresh scenery all about Ledbury and the Church. I hope it will be a very full house.'*

Apart from these few contemporary references to Katharine de Audley, no early record of the legend has yet come to light. In the 1670s when Thomas Blount was assembling his notes towards a history of Herefordshire, he wrote under Ledbury:

Twill be expected I should say somewhat here of Katharine, or as she is commonly called St Catharine of Audley, of whose birth and history I confess I am much to seek – tho' I have consulted both Antiquaries and others of the most intelligent that live upon the place, nor can I find that anything has ever been delivered to us in print concerning her – I must therefore content myself with setting down the vulgar tradition which is thus ...

He then gave the story as in the opening paragraph here. The tale was circulating beyond the confines of Herefordshire in the 17th century. John Jenkins (1592-1678), a composer who seems to have spent most of his life in the eastern counties of England and in London, composed a piece called *The Lady Catherine Audley's Bells* for treble and bass viols. In 1835 a drama *Catherine Audley, the recluse of Ledbury* was performed at the Ledbury Theatre 'with the greatest approbation'. The text was subsequently published, anonymously, by J. Gibbs, junior, of the Homend, Ledbury. In that same year, William Wordsworth, whilst returning from a visit to friends at Brinsop, Herefordshire, wrote a sonnet about her.

WHEN human touch (as monkish books attest)
Nor was applied nor could be, Ledbury bells
Broke forth in concert flung adown the dells,
And upward, high as Malvern's cloudy crest;
Sweet tones, and caught by a noble Lady blest
To rapture! Mabel listened at the side
Of her loved mistress: soon the music died,
And Katherine said, 'Here I set up my rest.'
Warned in a dream, the Wanderer long had sought
A home that by such miracle of sound
Must be revealed: she heard it now, or felt
The deep, deep joy of a confiding thought;
And there, a saintly Anchoress, she dwelt
Till she exchanged for heaven that happy ground.

Figure B   *The cover of* The Travailes and cerches of saynte Kataryne the Recluse of Ledbury, *a booklet published in Ledbury in 1851, at the restoration of what was then called Saint Katherine's chapel, on the north of the parish church. The coloured frontispiece has a view of Ledbury church, tower, and the beautiful chapel of Saint Katherine.*

Sources: T. Blount, MS History of Herefordshire; *Cal. Close 1313-1318*, 75; *Cal. Fine, 1319-1327*, 99; *Cal. Close Roll 1318-1323*, 657; *Cal. Close Roll 1323-1327*, 19, 272. W. Wordsworth, 'Complete Poems'; Frank Parr's 'Historical Notes on Old Ledbury', *Hereford Times*, 17 May 1884.

Figure 78 A gilded angel boss on the roof of the outer north chapel.

(see chapter 3) had been completed. The south side followed the work on the north side, datable through the survival of a mid- to late 13th-century window in the east end of the north chancel chapel compared with one of early 14th-century date to the east end of the south chancel chapel. Although the external appearance of the church is dominated by the work of the later 13th and early 14th centuries, it incorporated much of the late 12th-century fabric, including the arcade arches. The north porch, which remains the principal entrance to the church, was constructed *c.*1300 (a window of this date survives in its west wall) and extended in the middle of the 14th century, with the outer archway of this later date. Adjoining the porch to the east, the two-storey vestry is also likely to be of 14th-century date. The most remarkable addition to have been made during the 14th century, however, is the beautiful outer north chapel, though its purpose remains a puzzle.[129]

The Outer North Chapel

From its architectural style, the chapel would appear to date to the first quarter of the 14th century, which fits with John de Aigueblanche's reference in his will to the roofing of St Radegund's

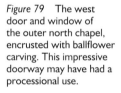

Figure 79 The west door and window of the outer north chapel, encrusted with ballflower carving. This impressive doorway may have had a processional use.

Figure 80 The entrance to the outer north chapel from the nave, inserted in the early 14th century. It cuts through the earlier window, the head of which can still be seen. Referred to in the early 19th century, if not before, as St Katherine's chapel, it was restored in the 1850s and was used as the baptistry. In the later 20th century a beautifully etched glass screen was inserted, which enclosed the chapel as a quiet place for meetings. It is now known as the chapter house, although the church was never collegiate.

chapel. It is entered from the north side of the north chancel chapel through a large specially created archway. The traceried windows which almost fill each wall and the panelled roof alive with flying angel bosses give the impression of a precious box or even a container of holy relics (a reliquary). The window jambs and the western external door surround are heavily encrusted with ballflowers, a form of decoration used by the masons of Hereford cathedral to enrich the central tower, which was begun between about 1310 and 1315. The use of ballflower decoration at Hereford cathedral, at nearby Tewkesbury abbey and the more distant Lichfield cathedral also influenced other work in the diocese, notably the nave of Weobley, the south aisle at Leominster, the north aisle of Ludlow and the chancel of Marden.[130]

Figure 81 Churchyard crosses such as this late medieval example, six miles from Ledbury at Putley, were important focal points for processional devotions.

Could the chapel have been the focus of some sort of cult activity? The very ornate external door, in the south-west angle, suggests the possibility of some processional function. Processions were an important part of the medieval liturgy. They were a regular part of the ceremonial on holy days, with priests, acolytes and servers following the thurifer (carrying the censer of burning incense) around the church. The procession might leave the church, visit churchyard crosses or other significant sites in the vicinity, and re-enter the church by a different route. Many pilgrimages also entailed a processional approach to a shrine. It may have been a Lady chapel, built to house the altar of the Virgin Mary. The first mention of the service of the altar of the blessed Mary was made in 1323, when John de Prato was presented as chaplain by the parishioners. It could have been intended as a mortuary or chantry chapel, but if it was built for John de Aigueblanche, he certainly was not buried there and left very clear instructions in his will for his burial at Hereford. There is no trace of an altar or *piscina* to show that mass was celebrated there, but perhaps these have been destroyed, either deliberately in the 16th or 17th centuries, or during later refurbishments.[131]

Another possibility is that the outer chapel may have been originally dedicated to St Radegund. John de Aigueblanche's will included a contribution towards the 'roofing [*cooperiandam*] of the chapel of St Radegund and decorating it with pictures'. This chapel must have been of some significance and perhaps held some important relic, because in 1369 Pope Urban V granted an indulgence of 100 days to penitents who visited and gave alms for its repair (during a 10-year period). Perhaps over the following centuries that dedication became eclipsed and conflated with the two important Katherines associated with Ledbury – Katherine de Audley the recluse and St Katherine of Alexandria, patron of the hospital. So far no later references to St Radegund's chapel at Ledbury have been found, unless Lewis Nash's will of 1543 contains a garbled version of her unusual name, when he stipulated that he wanted to be buried in 'Maid Bigod's chapel'.[132]

Memorials

Only the most prosperous would have had permanent memorials erected, be they in stone, brass or stained glass. Members of the aristocracy and upper gentry would have their tombs, resplendent with heraldry, but as time went on wealthy townsfolk, too, began to have simpler memorials made. Senior clergymen might have fine tombs in the cathedral but chaplains and parochial clergy might have their memorials in the parish church, as William Callewe and Robert Preece did in Ledbury.

Few medieval monuments remain in Ledbury church, two in stone and two in brass. There is only a very small collection of medieval glass fragments reset in a window of the outer north chapel and it is not possible to identify any of a memorial nature. (The window in the chapel of St Katherine's Hospital displays the arms of William de Grandison.) The fine monument to a lady now in the north chancel chapel at the church has caused some confusion. Popular thought has, as with the dedication of the outer chapel, sometimes wrongly identified her with Katherine de Audley. Examination of the heraldry on the tomb and canopy led St Clair Baddeley in 1927 to identify her with Lady Talbot, a great niece of the recluse. A more recent investigation by L. Gee has suggested that it is really the tomb of one of the sisters of

Figure 82 An unknown
13th-century priest
in massing robes. He
was clearly a man of
some status, perhaps
a portionary. His
monument now stands
upright in the outer north
chapel of Ledbury church.

Grimbauld Pauncefoot who married a Carew. As Lady Talbot's
connection with the church appears to be tenuous to say the least,
and the Pauncefoots held the manor of Hazle in the parish of
Ledbury, the latter identification seems more likely. Whoever she
was, it is a beautiful monument and shares stylistic details with
the even finer monument of Blanche Mortimer, Lady Grandison
(d.1347) at nearby Much Marcle.[133]

The only other medieval stone memorial in the church is
that of an unknown 13th-century priest. This fine carving was
probably once the top of a table tomb and may have been hidden
at the Reformation to preserve it from destruction. It was later

Figure 83 Monument of an unknown lady, now in the north chapel. It has obviously been moved from its original position and fitted somewhat awkwardly beneath the outer north window.

rediscovered and is now displayed propped upright in a niche in the outer north chapel.

Chantries

Figure 84 Memorial brass to Thomas Caple, esquire, d.1490. Members of this family are mentioned in various property deeds from the 14th to 16th centuries in Ledbury.

While few could afford elaborate tombs or brasses, many more would have paid for prayers to be said for the sake of their souls. Those who could afford it endowed chantries, with priests to say mass for the donor and, usually, for his immediate family for ever. Such chantries, where mass was sung, could be at existing altars within a church, or at specially constructed altars, forming little chapels within the church. Ledbury had three chantries, each with a single priest. The less wealthy might at least leave money for a funeral mass, and other masses to be said on the octave and trental (8th and 30th days) after their decease. Other people would join a fraternity or guild, whose collective finances would support a chaplain who said prayers for all the members entered onto the 'bede roll'. A simpler arrangement again was to give money to the support of a light (a lamp or candles before a particular shrine or effigy) in the church, such as the payment of 6d. to the light of St Peter recorded in a rental of St Katherine's Hospital, dating from around 1400. There are few surviving wills from medieval Ledbury to shed light on small pious bequests of this sort, although Richard Beneas left 1d. to 'each of the principal lights' in Ledbury church in 1504.[134]

The Chantry of St Mary   This chantry, founded during his lifetime by John Trefnant, bishop of Hereford, 1389-1404, was in addition to the 'service' of the altar of the Blessed Mary. In 1399 the king gave Trefnant licence to found a perpetual chantry at the altar of St Mary. John Thony was the first chaplain of this foundation, charged with saying mass for the spiritual and corporeal health of the king and the bishop. The bishop endowed the chantry with

Figure 85   Memorial brass of Sir William Callewe, the first priest of St Anne's chantry, appointed in 1384, died 1409. The inscription, another early example of the use of English, reads 'Sey þat nost [the Lord's Prayer] for sere William Calwe that loved wel god and alle hallwe [all saints]'.

four messuages, five shops, six tofts, 60 acres of arable land, three acres of meadow and 2s. 6d. rent, all in the parishes of Ledbury and Eastnor. That the altar of Mary was separate from the chantry is proved by Henry VIII's survey in 1535, when they were listed separately, with different chaplains.[135]

The Chantry of St Anne   This was founded at the request of John le Hop and Joan his wife, who had obtained a licence in 1354 to 'alienate in mortmain', that is give to the church for ever, property to support a chantry priest. Unfortunately, they both died before they were able to complete the arrangements, but in 1373 Robert Hunt and Alice Pauncefoot, the executors of Joan, who had outlived her husband, got the licence renewed. In 1384 all the arrangements were finally completed, and on 21 April William Callewe was inducted as chaplain. Three and a half years later, Henry, vicar of Ledbury, John Ewenet and John Birchore were allowed to alienate another messuage in Ledbury Denzein [Borough] for William Callewe and his successors to live in. The property was situated in Church End, 'between the land of Netherhall [Lower Hall] and the common way and extends from the way which leads from Mitchel towards Ledbury to the churchyard of Ledbury.' In return, the chaplain was to celebrate mass for the souls of the donor, William Bowyer and his family. Perhaps Bowyer felt particularly in need of intercession if he was the same William Bowyer, who had been pardoned 20 years earlier for the accidental death of John Hutchins. When William Callewe died in 1409 it was noted that the chaplain also held a piece of land conditional upon distributing one noble (6s. 8d.) to the poor on the anniversary of the death of William Bowyer.[136]

The Trinity Chantry   This chantry is less well documented. It is not clear when it was established, though in 1499 the feoffees of the service of the Holy Trinity held four acres of land in Longmore Field from the hospital of St Katherine, paying 16d. a year for it. It is not mentioned in the published version of the 1535 survey of church property, but may be missing because the original is defective. Judging by the income that was recorded in 1547 (below chapter 8), it was rather less well endowed than the other chantries.[137]

Priests and People

The portionaries regularly appointed vicars, taking turns alternately. The patronage involved in such a presentation was one of the benefits of holding a portion. Whilst the portionaries

Figure 86   A priest
celebrating mass, while a
clerk indicates to a layman
to observe the elevation
of the host, from a
13th-century manuscript
of the Decretals
of Gregory, in use
at Hereford cathedral.

were for the most part highly educated men with recognisable
careers, their vicars were more obscure. Not many of the Ledbury
vicars of the 14th and 15th centuries seem to have been university
educated. One of the first university men was Richard Smith, who
had been at Oxford. He was appointed to Ledbury in 1479, where
he remained until he became rector of Eastnor in 1511 and may
have died by 1516. He was followed by Edward Hill, not apparently
a university man, and then, in 1533, by William Musmare *alias*
Messenger, another Oxford graduate. His successor Hamnet
Malbon does not appear to have been a graduate. Many of the
earlier, non-graduates can be identified in the bishop's registers,
as well as in secular deeds to which they were often witnesses.

Figure 87   The remains
of a late medieval rood
screen now in the north
aisle of Ledbury church,
with vaulting and unusual
blind tracery heads.

While it is possible to produce lists of vicars and chaplains it is nigh impossible to ascertain anything of their character or the way in which they might have carried out their duties or related to their parishioners.[138]

Although many elements have been swept away by the work of time, 16th-century reform and 19th-century renovation, one may imagine the interior of the medieval church to have been a place of visual stimulation. Many of the windows had coloured glass, though now only a few fragments remain. The walls would have been plastered and painted, probably with figurative decoration depicting tales from scripture interspersed with patterned groundwork. The interior space itself would have been much more broken up than it is now. The chancel was separated from the nave by a carved screen, still partly in situ in 1805 when it was described as 'very beautiful', although half of it had been removed to make way for a seat for the portionaries. In the Middle Ages there seem to have been stone screens dividing the chancel from the north and south chapels. On the eastern respond of each arch one can see the rebates of doors through the screen. The mystery of the parish mass would be celebrated within the sacred enclosed space of the chancel, scarcely visible to the laity in the nave. In the side chapels private masses would be said by the chantry priests. The various altars would have had lights and candles burning and over all would have hung the scent of incense.[139]

The clergy tried to instil virtue into their flock. Example and exhortation in sermons was backed up by the discipline of confession, penance and absolution. In 1367 Henry, the vicar, was given power to hear parishioners' confessions and to give penance and absolution in cases normally reserved for the bishop. The teaching of the church and the leadership of the clergy was not always sufficient to produce good behaviour, and a system of church courts evolved to deal with a variety of cases, which included moral lapses and matrimonial disputes, failure to attend mass and the maintenance of churches and the regulation of parish boundaries, and oversaw the administration of wills. Bishops conducted regular visitations into the state of the parishes in their dioceses. The Hereford diocesan visitation conducted

Figure 89 The Master's House was built in 1487 to provide separate accommodation for the master, away from the communal living of the hospital. Although considerably extended in later years, it is at core a late medieval, timber-framed open-hall house with cross wings at each end. This reconstruction of the hall is based on surviving timbers, which include peg holes for a ridge louvre to let out the smoke. The chimney was inserted 25-50 years later. It was a little old-fashioned for such a high-status building at this time in still having a central hearth, but the reconstruction gives an idea of how impressive it would have been.

Figure 90 Decorative floor tiles in St Katherine's chapel. They date to around 1500 and were the work of the Malvern school of tilers. This floor, of about five hundred tiles, some set singly, others forming patterns of four or sixteen, is one of the finest collections of medieval tiles in the county. Even so, wear and tear took their toll, and the chapel floor was re-laid in the 19th century. Replica tiles by the firm of Godwin were laid on the altar platform and the salvaged medieval tiles were placed north and south in the body of the chapel. Whether they extend under the boarding in the centre of the chapel is unclear.

in 1397 recorded cases of fornication and adultery amongst the parishioners of Ledbury. The worst offender was Thomas Braban, who not only sinned with three separate women, but also had the temerity to take a testamentary case to a secular court. The sexual misconduct of Robert Preece has already been noted above, but the parishioners also complained that John Smythe, chaplain of Ledbury, was adulterous with Joan Tyler of their parish.[140]

The bishop might issue particular orders to his clergy in individual parishes to address failings in themselves or their parishioners. Such an order came from Bishop Gilbert in 1386, when he addressed the chaplains in the church at Ledbury. It had come to his notice that some parishioners were going to their parish church on Sunday and hearing the '*missam submissa voce*', the quietly said private masses in the chantries, not attending the

Figure 91 A re-construction based on the surviving roof timbers of the 15th-century hall in the master's house, which have been dated by dendrochronology to 1487.

parish high mass or other divine offices at their appointed times. Having hurriedly attended these chantry masses, they then went to taverns and eating houses (*commessaciones*) and consumed too much, or else went about their secular business. The chaplains were ordered not to celebrate mass on Sundays and holy days until after the parish high mass had begun and the gospel had been read.[141]

ST KATHERINE'S HOSPITAL

In common with a number of medieval hospitals, St Katherine's derived part of its income from donations that carried with them obligations to pray for the soul of the donors. This was true of the early gift of land of William of Ockeridge during the lifetime

of Bishop Foliot. In 1361 Thomas Eseger, a member of a Ledbury
family of wealth and influence, endowed the hospital with
480 acres of land at *la Hulle* and *Erlingham* (now Hill House and
Orlham farms). The bequest was conditional upon the payment
of a corrody, or pension, to Thomas' brother, William and his wife
Juliana Eseger and to their son Nicholas after their deaths. The
execution of the will was overseen by Thomas's son Adam, a canon
of Hereford cathedral. He added a gift of woodland in Little Marcle
to his father's bequest, with the stipulation that a chaplain was to
pray for his own wellbeing during life, for his soul after death and
for the souls of his parents and other family members.[142]

The services in the hospital chapel were evidently open to the
townspeople. In 1398 Pope Boniface IX acquiesced to a petition
from John Malvern, master of St Katherine's Hospital, to have a
bell to sound for the hours of the offices, even before those in the
parish church, and to celebrate mass solemnly and aloud in the
hospital chapel. In return, one quarter of the oblations collected
was to go to the parish church.[143]

It was not just through the religious services available in the
chapel that the hospital played a part in the spiritual life of the
town. The 10 alms people were also expected to pray regularly for
the donors to the hospital and their very existence in the town,
living right on the market place, was a constant reminder to the
townsfolk of the duty of the Christian to be charitable. One of the
duties of the hospital was to 'maintain hospitality' in the town. In
the early days this may well have meant providing accommodation
for ordinary travellers, although there is no clear evidence for
this. Certainly, the maintenance of hospitality was one of the rules
reiterated in the late 16th-century reordering of the hospital. It is
likely that important visitors were welcomed in the master's house
and it is possible that the bishop would have stayed there after the
abandonment of his manor house (see chapter 4).[144]

Tree-ring dating has shown that the master's house was built
from timber that was felled in 1487 and so it would have been
erected either in the same year or the following one. This date
means that the hall would have been built during the mastership
of Richard Wycherley (1483-1502). The wood for building it may
have come from the coppice at Dunbridge, still known as Hospital
Wood, which became part of the master's demesne during the
15th century. Wycherley was a doctor of theology and acted as
suffragan (assistant) bishop in both the dioceses of Hereford and
of Worcester, so a new house for him, offering greater privacy and
comfort, would have been appropriate. Such luxury might not
have sat so well with the fact that Wycherely was also a Dominican
friar. That did not prevent him from also holding the rectory

of Donnington and the control of Aylton and Pixley chapelries, attached to Ledbury. As suffragan, with the title of bishop of Olena, Wycherley performed many ordinations in Ledbury, 10 at the parish church and two in the chapel of St Katherine's, the latter in the winter of 1485/6. Wycherley may also be responsible for the beautification of the hospital chapel by the addition of the fine collection of late medieval tiles to the floor in there.[145]

Chapter 8

A Time of Change

LEDBURY IN THE EARLY 16TH CENTURY

Buildings

In the early years of the 16th century Ledbury was a small town, possibly with no more inhabitants than it had 200 years before, as recovery was generally slow after the collapse of population following the calamities of the 14th century. Other towns around the country were in a similar state, from tiny markets now dwindling to the status of villages to once prosperous cities like Coventry, a shrunken shadow of its former self. Yet a visitor to Ledbury from 1288, or even from 2008, would still recognise the shape of the town. The pattern of the streets discussed in chapter 3 had not altered or expanded. Indeed, in the late 15th century there was evidence of empty plots in the town as well as of a number of tenants who were defaulting on their rent to the bishop. In 1536-7 Thomas Lorymer's accounts for the bishop's manor showed a tenement lying vacant for lack of a tenant and a shop called 'Tylshope' empty for the same reason. Even worse, some shops 'lately being in the middle of the borough [paid no rent] because their buildings have fallen to the ground'.[146]

The majority of buildings in Ledbury would have been relatively small and timber-framed. These timber-framed buildings were probably thatched; broom, rushes and cereal straw were all used for thatching in Herefordshire. The parish church and St Katherine's chapel may well have been the only stone-built edifices in the town. No doubt many of the more substantial properties were already old and, like the smaller shops already mentioned, in need of repair or rebuilding. There are no surviving domestic buildings which

Figure 92 The so-called Bishop's Palace in Bye Street, photographed before its demolition sometime after 1945. This name seems only to have come into use in the 20th century. The suggestion that it was once part of St Katherine's Hospital, and may have been an occasional residence of the bishop, is not borne out by the records of the hospital.

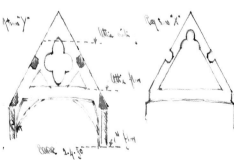

Figure 93 Nos 233 and 235 Homend. On the north gable end wall of this pair of tenements are two steeply pitched cruck blades that are probably of 15th-century date. It may be that they are either re-used material in a later building or relate to a lost building that stood to the north.

seem to date from before the third quarter of the 15th century and there are only six buildings that fall into the period 1475-1550. Not much is known about the early structure of the Upper and Lower Halls, although there is a piece of medieval stone carving embedded in the wall of Lower Hall and both, like the bishop's manor house at Bosbury, may well have been stone-built.[147]

Dendrochronology, or tree-ring dating, of roof timbers in the master's house of St Katherine's Hospital gives a felling date of 1487 (chapter 7). A similar analysis of timbers from the original vicarage next to the churchyard (now known as Abbot's Lodge) gives a date of 1480 for the first phase of building, with a second range added in 1519. Two other buildings in Church Lane, the western bay of what is now known as the town council buildings and the Old Grammar School may also date to this period, although not tested. Both of these buildings belonged to the parish in the early modern period. It is not clear whether they were parish property at the time of building, but if so it would mean that all the significant building of that period was done in connection with the church or other religious bodies.

We know little about the interior decoration of these buildings. No. 1 Church Lane (Fig. 94) contains a first-floor room with remarkable wall paintings imitating (at considerably less expense) the opulent wall hangings which might adorn the reception rooms of the rich. Although the paintings date from the 1560s and represent decoration appropriate to that period, they reflect a much older tradition which may well have been adopted by Ledbury's richest citizens. Painted wall papers were in existence by the end of the 15th century, although none survive. We do not know who commissioned the decoration at Ledbury, but he may have been a town official. The biblical texts in English which

Figure 94   The two westernmost bays of this substantial building overlooking the market place appear to have been built *c*.1500. The close-studding (close-set vertical timbers) is an indication of wealth. The overhanging jetty at the west has been underbuilt in brick at a later date.

Figure 95 One of the wall paintings recently discovered in an upper room of the building illustrated in Fig. 94. Although dating from the 1560s, this painting may well reflect the type of design that would have been used in the tapestry hangings or painted cloths favoured by the wealthier townsfolk throughout the later Middle Ages and Tudor period.

accompany the paintings lay emphasis on good citizenship and its duties.[148]

Local Government

The manor of Ledbury still belonged to the bishop and his steward would have been one of the most influential men in the area. He was assisted by a number of lesser officials including a bailiff of the Borough, a bailiff of the Foreign and a clerk to record the proceedings of the court of the hundred. This was a court leet or court with view of frankpledge, giving it jurisdiction over minor criminal offences (see also chapter 5). Such courts usually met monthly. In 1495 the salaries paid to these officers were: 33s. 4d. to the bailiff of the Borough and 20s. to the bailiff of the Foreign, while the clerk of the hundred received 6s. 8d. By 1537 the officers included a deputy to the bailiff and a sergeant. The bishop's three-weekly court still regulated the letting of land and the management of the market. The master of the hospital and the portionaries of Upper and Lower Halls also held courts for their estates and were influential people, both by virtue of their ecclesiastical dignity and the estates in their control. William Webbe, portionary of the

Upper Hall from 1515 until his death in 1523, was also archdeacon of Hereford. He seems to have been a particularly wealthy and well connected man, employing 15 servants and having in his household three young men of gentry family, including a relative of the bishop.[149]

WINDS OF CHANGE

Religious Reformation

For the first 30 years or so of the 16th century there was little change in religious practice or organisation in England and Wales. A few people were aware of new currents of thought on the Continent, but these were not countenanced by that 'defender of the faith', King Henry VIII. From about 1529, though, things began to change. There were increasing attacks on the income and the jurisdiction of papacy and in 1534, following the king's divorce and remarriage, the Act of Supremacy swept away papal authority in England and Wales. Reforming ideas were fostered by the introduction of vernacular bibles in parish churches from 1538 and a gradual attack began on a number of traditional beliefs. The efficacy of prayers for the dead was first questioned and then finally abolished as 'superstitious'. At the same time, the Crown cast an ever more beady eye on the wealth and power of the Church, instituting a detailed valuation of all church property and revenue in 1535 and a searching visitation of religious houses, ostensibly looking for abuses but really assessing wealth. In Ledbury the value of the bishop's holdings was assessed as was that of the portionaries' shares of the rectory, the vicarage, the hospital and the chantries. Unfortunately, the page containing the returns for the vicarage and for the hospital is badly damaged and scarcely legible. Over the next 25 years the Church swung from a zealously reforming Protestantism to communion with Rome, and back to a milder Protestantism under Queen Elizabeth.[150]

Little is known about how these religious changes were received in Ledbury. There are no surviving churchwardens' accounts from that period as at Morebath in Devon, from which Eamonn Duffy has woven such a revealing picture of those times. Nor have personal letters been found. The wording of the religious preambles to wills, where the testator piously commends his soul to God, can give an insight into the beliefs of the testator – or of the clerk who drew up the will (panel 7). There are a few glimpses of the changes that took place in the depositions (sworn statements) made during an investigation into the management and estates of St Katherine's Hospital in 1577-8. Many of the oldest men in the

Wills and their Spiritual Context

Figure A   *Legatees by a deathbed, while the scribe writes the will. An illustration from a book of canon law at Hereford cathedral.*

Wills were both legal and religious documents and had to be proved in the ecclesiastical courts. They followed a set formula. Beginning with the person's name and abode (and sometimes their occupation or status), there followed a commendation of the testator's soul to God and the body to burial, before the division of their worldly goods. The wording of the religious preamble, as it is termed, and the extent and nature of any pious or charitable bequests can tell us something of the religious tenor of the times and to a degree those of the individual, bearing in mind that the will was often drawn up by a lawyer or the parish priest when the testator was already seriously ill.

The will of Richard Beneas, drawn up in 1504, exemplifies pre-Reformation style. He gave his soul to 'Almighty God, the Blessed Mary and all his saints'

and left 6d. to Hereford cathedral, 6d. to the service of the altar of Ledbury church and 1d. to each of the principal lights in that church, as was usual. Similar bequests were made in 1522 by Giles Keyes, who also left money for the fabric of St Mary's chapel in Ledbury church and for masses for his soul to be said at the altar of St John. Of the eight testators in the final years under Henry's Church of England, seven simply gave their souls to the neutral-sounding 'Almighty God'. Only Lewis Nash retained the more elaborate 'Almighty God, Our Lady St Mary and the whole company of heaven'. Only Elizabeth Pycchyll, in 1544, made arrangements for the saying of a monthly mass and dirige (service for the dead, the first word of which is *dirige*) for a year after her death (see Fig. B).

During the time of Edward VI, when the Protestant cause was being driven forward apace, Ledbury testators used the plain formula 'Almighty God'. The four who made their wills in 1547 left money to the church of Ledbury and three of them left similar amounts to the cathedral, too. Only one of these, John Broke, made reference to any religious item, leaving two torches to burn during the sacring mass 'as long as they shall endure'. His continuing belief in the efficacy of post mortem acts, if not explicitly in prayers, was also shown by the fact that he left the residue of his worldly goods to the chantry chaplain John Potter and to William Sucley to 'bestow it at their discretion for the health of my soul'. After 1547 the four remaining wills in Edward's time left money to the poor instead of to the church. Three each left 4d. to the 'charity box' or 'poor men's box', referring to the collecting box which had been set up in accordance with the Injunctions of 1547 for the 'alms and devotions of the people', to be distributed to the poor of the parish. The fourth will was that of the vicar himself, William Musmare, who had been a curate at St Mary Magdalene, Oxford, before being appointed to Ledbury in 1533. The will was drawn up in February 1555, just after he had been appointed rector of St Mary Magdalene, Old Fish Street, London. He gave his soul to 'Almighty God' and 40s. 'to the poor'. He did not die until 1562, and was buried in Ledbury, having lived through all the religious changes of the English Reformation.

During the reign of Queen Mary a number of testators returned to the formula 'Almighty God, Our Lady St Mary and all the blessed company of heaven' and two of them left 4d., one to the cathedral and the other to the parish church. William Taylor remained neutral with 'Almighty God', but in the will of Edward Benyse, drawn up in 1556, there was the first overtly Protestant preamble, with its emphasis on the redeeming merits of Christ's passion: 'First and above

Figure B   *Will of Elizabeth Pycchyll, 1544. Lines 4-8 read 'First I bequeath my soul to Almighty God and my body to holy burial. Item I bequeath to the mother church of Hereford 2d. Item I bequeath to the high altar within the parish church of Ledbury for tithe forgotten, 8d., and I will that my executors shall cause Mass and dirige to be said every month in the first year for my soul and all Christian souls'.*

all other things I bequeath my soul to Almighty God trusting through his great mercy and by the merits of the passion and blood shedding of our Saviour Jesus Christ to have remission and forgiveness of all my sins.' Not until the 1570s were the majority of Ledbury wills prefaced by this stress on Christ's passion, suggesting that, while people were aware of changes and conformed their wills to the letter of the law, it was some time before they internalised this different emphasis of religious belief.

Sources: William Musmare: A.B. Emden, *A Biographical Register of the University of Oxford, AD1501-1540*; will: HRO X8/47/104. All surviving Ledbury wills 1500-1700 have been transcribed by the EPE volunteers and the transcripts are available at: www.englandspastforeveryone.org.uk/Counties/Herefordshire/ Projects/LedburyPre1558/Items/ Ledbury_Will_and_Inventories.

parish were asked a series of questions, a number of them touching on the manner and frequency of the services held in the chapel of the hospital.[151]

Thomas Gately, probably born around 1525, remembered that when John Elton alias Baker was master of the hospital he had seen Richard Baker, priest to John, and Richard Weler say mass. Gately himself had helped at the mass. John Elton alias Baker died in 1547, so Gately would have been a young altar boy. He went on to say that 'one, a priest of Coddington as he supposes, has said shrive [confession] in the said hospital in the queen's majesties time that now is', that is in the time of Elizabeth I. Although he was only 30, Thomas Baldwin, husbandman of Redmarley, Worcestershire, had heard that 'his cousin John Baldwin did serve there at two several times and the second time served there till his dying day.' He did not know much about what vestments or ornaments had been used then, but older deponents were able to give information. Christopher Meeke, aged 78, remembered that 'in the time mass was said there were ornaments such as were then used, as chalice, copes, vestments, and such like and one bell.' John Bradford (68) had also 'seen certain vestments used in the time of mass and a chalice and one bell and of late time has seen service said there the minister having on him a "surples" [surplice]'. This reflects the change from the elaborate vestments of the pre-Reformation church to the simpler surplice (white over-garment) worn by Protestant clergy. The bell, too, had been taken away, though Hugh Dunbridge (77) said that he did not know by whom.[152]

Dissolution of the Chantries

The chantries fell prey to the second wave of reform in the 1540s. The Chantry Acts of 1545 and 1547 first investigated and then entirely suppressed them as 'superstitious', only safeguarding those which had been associated with grammar schools (see below).[153]

Confiscated church and chantry properties were bought wholesale. Many London merchants, like Thomas Reve, gentleman, John Johnson of London, fishmonger, and Henry Herdson of London, skinner, invested in land around the country. In May 1549 they paid £1,572 for various chantry lands in London and the counties of Sussex, Shropshire, Buckingham, Warwick, Worcester and Lincoln. They also bought 'the [tithes] of hay, sheaves, corn, grain, lambs and wool and other tithes and all the oblations and obventions of the late free chapel of St James Apostle called le Chappell Parke [which served the detached part of the parish at Parkhold] in the parish of Ledbury' and others in Hereford, Woolhope and Stoke Edith. It is not clear whether these men had connections in any of the areas where they bought property. Two definitely Herefordshire men, John Harford of Bosbury and Richard Willison of Ledbury, bought the property of the chantries of the Trinity, St Mary and St Anne in Ledbury; they also invested in similar properties in many other counties, not only neighbouring Worcestershire but as far afield as Essex. (More will be said about Harford and Willison under 'New Men' below.) These sales stipulated that they did not include the bells and the lead roofs of the chantries. Nothing is known of what happened to the other ornaments and vestments of these chantries in Ledbury or what their devotees thought of the matter, though there is some information on what happened to the priests who had served them.[154]

When property of the chantry of the Blessed Mary was sold in 1549, it comprised an annual payment of 12d. from lands belonging to the hospital in Ledbury, and various 'messuages, burgages, cottages, shops, gardens, mills, barns and lands' in Ledbury and Eastnor. Valued at £8 18s. 8d. in 1548, it was then held by John Potter or Porter, aged 50 and 'of good conversation, able to keep a cure'. He may have been the John Porter who had been instituted as rector of Hope Bagot, Shropshire, in 1543, although it would have been an unusual move from a rectory to a chantry – unless Hope Bagot were particularly poor or Ledbury particularly attractive! With the abolition of the chantry he was awarded a pension of £6 p.a. and soon afterwards took up the benefice of Tedstone Wafer, near Bromyard; in 1554 he was also presented to the living of Lower Sapey. In the early years of Queen Elizabeth he was described as aged 60, unmarried and 'hospitable and resident' in Tedstone.[155]

Figure 96 Certificate signed by John Potter about 1554, regarding his pension of £6 a year as the former priest in the Chantry of Our Lady, Ledbury, and his current post as priest at Tedstone Wafer, Herefordshire, for which he received £1 10s. a year. It also states that he was never married.

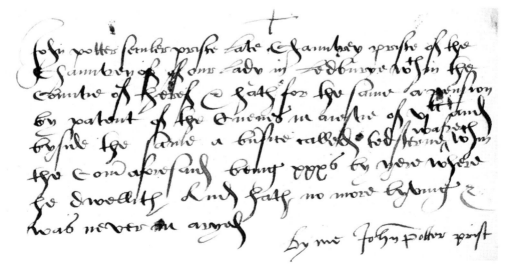

Figure 97 The Old Grammar School building in the churchyard at Bosbury, founded by Sir Rowland Morton in 1540, where Thomas Kylling taught after the dissolution of the Chantry of St Anne at Ledbury.

The chantry of St Anne was also well endowed, with property in the town and in the surrounding area. In 1548 it had produced a stipend of £5 10s. 10d. for the chaplain Griffith or Griffin Fowler. Described as 'a man able to keep a cure' and 'of honest conversation', Fowler was awarded a pension of £5 a year which he continued to receive at least until 1556. He seems originally to have been from Staffordshire and was ordained priest at Lichfield cathedral in 1528 and was presented to the Ledbury chantry in 1537 by John Blount of Grendon Warren. Unlike John Potter, he remained in Ledbury after the closure of the chantry and at some point became chaplain to the hospital until his death in 1559. The year before, 80-year-old Thomas Kylling had been buried. He had followed a similar path, being first chaplain in the chantry of St Anne and later at the hospital, although in 1548 it was said that he had been the schoolmaster of nearby Bosbury for four or five years; in 1554 he was receiving a pension £4 6s. 8d.[156]

The chantry of the Holy Trinity appears to have been the least well endowed of the three. In 1549 the property was described as various lands in Ledbury, Tybbynge Sparowhawke and Morefield (unidentified), also in Eastnor and Michelfelde (presumably the township of Mitchell in the north-east of the parish of Ledbury, immediately to the north of Eastnor). Richard Wheler the chaplain made ends meet by school teaching in 1548 and it was noted that he was 'of good conversation, daily occupied in teaching children grammar', and his stipend 'was £4.1.5. No other living except the little rewards of the friends of the scholars'. This may be why he was awarded a pension greater than his stipend, for he was receiving £5 a year at least until 1556.

He would appear not to have remained in Ledbury as the schoolmaster for very long, as in 1550 Bishop Hooper's examination of Gloucester clergy showed a Richard Wheler as vicar of Hartpury. There is an undated pension warrant (during Elizabeth's reign, probably the 1560s) for him saying that he then lived in Preston in Gloucestershire. Preston and Hartpury are not far from Ledbury, which perhaps increases the likelihood that they are the same man. Hooper's report noted that Richard Wheler, as vicar of Hartpury, had about 280 'houseling' people (those who took communion) in his care. He was satisfactory on all counts, that is, he could repeat the text, identify the authors and chapters of the Ten Commandments, Creed and Lord's Prayer. Compared with many others in the list, this made Richard Wheler well-educated, which reinforces the likelihood that he was the former schoolmaster of Ledbury. It is not clear where he had received his own education, but like John Potter he may have come from Staffordshire, as a Richard Wheler was ordained in Lichfield cathedral, as an acolyte on 21 May 1524 and as sub-deacon on 11 March 1525.[157]

Grammar School

Although it would appear from the above that Richard Wheler did not stay in Ledbury, it seems that the townsfolk of Ledbury had done their best to ensure that he should. The 1548 certificate recorded

> That the town of Ledbury is a poor town, and by the [...] of Richard Wheler stipendiary, have not only had profit and advantage by keeping of a grammar school there as in boarding & lodging of the scholars but also the country thereabouts, in uttering [selling] their victuals there by the means of the said scholars. In consideration there of the poor inhabitants of the said town humbly beseech that it may please the King's majesty, with the consent of his honourable council of their goodness to grant that the said stipendiary to remain for the maintaining thereof to the erudition of youth, & charitable deeds if it may please his highness.

The petition was accepted and the council ruled that 'the said grammar school in Ledbury aforesaid shall continue, and that Richard Wheler, schoolmaster there, shall have and enjoy the

Figure 98 This five-bay, timber-framed, two-storey range, laid out on an approximately east-west orientation, is probably of late 15th-century origin. The dates of 1480-1520 have been suggested, or possibly a little later. The building, which was restored in 1977/8 near to its original form, clearly had some public function rather than being purely domestic, and was certainly used as the Grammar School from the 17th to the 19th centuries.

room of Schoolmaster there, and shall have for his wages, yearly £3 – 11s – 3d.' This salary was secured out of the Royal Forests and continued to be paid until the mid-19th century. Of course, as it was set at the level paid in 1548, its real value declined considerably over the years. Thereafter the parish was responsible for the nomination of the schoolmaster, who had to be licensed by the bishop, and for maintenance of the school building.[158]

It is possible that the original school was kept in one of the two rooms above the 14th-century porch of the parish church, as was often the case in other parishes. Certainly one of the rooms has a fireplace (perhaps inserted after building) as well as a piscina and an aumbry (cupboard for sacramental vessels). At some stage the school was transferred to the large timber-framed building on the north-east corner of Church Lane, where it remained until the mid-19th century. It is not entirely clear when this transfer took place. In the late 17th century Thomas Blount said that 'on the north side of the church there is a certain building called the Deacon's lodgings now converted into a schoolhouse – I suppose John Stoke was the founder since upon a piece of wood there I found written in old Letters "and 6 marks were given by John Stoke. And two chambers were erected."' Some authors have interpreted this to mean a detached building, but Blount could have meant the porch, which is a two-storey, stone building on the north of the church. He went on to say that 'here is a free school partly maintained out of the chantry rents mentioned by order of Sir Walter Mildmay and Robert [blank] Esquire, commissioners appointed by K. Edw. 6 touching continuance of Schools and Preachers…'. It is not clear whether he meant that this was in a separate building or that it was held in the schoolhouse already mentioned. The churchwardens' accounts, which survive from a similar period to that in which Blount was writing, make regular references to repairs to the schoolhouse but again do not make it quite clear whether this was the church porch or the building in Church Lane.[159]

The Old Grammar School in Church Lane is of late 15th- to mid-16th-century date. Because of its layout it was obviously not originally a domestic building. It has sometimes been suggested that it was a guildhall, although no references to a guild in Ledbury have yet been found to support this theory. In 1976, just before the building was restored for use as a heritage centre, it was examined by English Heritage officers, who also entered into a long correspondence with Sylvia Robinson, then keeper of the church records and a keen local historian. They concluded that the building was of mid-16th-century date and could well have been erected as a school after the closure of the chantry school in 1547, although others date the west range to c.1500.[160]

Survival of the Hospital

The suppression of monasteries and later of chantries also posed a threat to almshouses and hospitals. Many, including St Katherine's, had accepted endowments from benefactors on the understanding that the donors would be included in the 'bede roll', the list of those for whom prayers would be said. Bishop Foliot's original foundation had established a chaplain to celebrate mass for ever, for the sake of his own soul and those of his predecessors and successors. In 1234 William of Ockeridge established a second chaplaincy, again stipulating prayers for himself and his wife; by the later 14th century there were supposed to be as many as five chaplains at the hospital. When the 1548 enquiry into 'all chantries and hospitals yet undissolved' took place, St Katherine's had an income of £22 5s. – more than twice that of St Ethelbert's in Hereford, which had been founded in 1225. At the time of the enquiry the master was that John Elton or Baker whom we have already met. He was a member of a rising local family from neighbouring Dymock in Gloucestershire. Having entered the church he soon rose under the patronage of Bishop Audley to be appointed master of St Katherine's in 1515, and then presented to the portion of Lower Hall in 1517. In 1544 he became chancellor of the diocese of Hereford. He would have been well placed, both at the centre of diocesan life and connected to a number of 'rising men' in the district, to defend the property of the hospital. However, his death in 1547 means that not all the glory for saving it can be laid at his feet. Perhaps as part of the campaign to protect the hospital's property, he began to copy and bring together in a single book the early charters and ordinances of the foundation. This book still exists in the archives of the dean and chapter of Hereford cathedral. The hospital survived this and a later attack in 1569 on its existence as a 'deserted or relinquished hospital'. In 1580 the court of the Exchequer confirmed its foundation and this was further strengthened by an act of parliament in 1581.[161]

Elton was followed by John Lord (1547-50), of whom little is known, and then by the energetic Edward Baskerville (1550-60). Baskerville was a Franciscan friar, who had been at the Oxford convent in 1513. He spent 13 years studying logic, philosophy and theology at the University of Oxford and became vice-commissary of the university in 1534 and 1535. Soon afterwards he was dispensed to hold a benefice and change his habit (that is, to leave the order). He became rector of Westcote, Gloucestershire and canon of Hereford; prebendary of Warham in 1540; rector of Staunton on Wye, Herefordshire, in 1541 and was appointed Master of St Katherine's Hospital in 1550. In 1555 he became chancellor of the diocese and died in 1567, five years after being replaced as master by Edward Cooper. In his will he bequeathed 'the works of St Jerome and Origene and all such other of my bookes as shall be thought good by mag. master Edw. Cooper to be placed in the library of the cathedral church'.[162]

Despite the energy of the masters in maintaining the existence of the hospital, it was in a poor way physically and spiritually in the middle years of the 16th century. The depositions given in the 1570s tell a sorry tale of buildings fallen into disrepair, old people neglected, and masters lining their pockets and those of their families by leases advantageous to the lessees but not to the hospital. As with all court papers, it must be borne in mind that these depositions only tell one side of the story, but there are many mutually corroborative statements. A number of men referred to a fencing school held there and that pigs were kept in the great hall and that sometimes bears were housed there before being baited in the street.

TOWNSFOLK

During the 1540s there were signs of economic recovery in Ledbury. In 1548, as part of the listing of the possessions of the chantries, estimates of the number of communicants, or 'houseling people', were given. The figure given for Ledbury was 640. The age of first communion was usually about twelve and it is probable that between 40-60 per cent of the population was under that age. This suggests a total population for the parish of Ledbury (town and country) of between 800 and 1,000 people. It is not possible to estimate what the population figures had been earlier in the century, for trying to make estimates of population based on the number of people assessed for tax in the Borough in 1524 and again in 1543 is fraught with problems. The 'tax bands' were not identical in both years, the starting rate being 40s. in 1524 and 20s. in 1543, so the overall number of people assessed was greater in 1543. It is also impossible to know how many evaded assessment and how many were too poor to be taxed. More significant was the increased value of their goods. Discounting the 26 people who were valued at £20 in 1543, leaves a comparison of 24 people with an assessed wealth of £89 in 1524 and 39 people with an assessed wealth of £292 in 1543. Six of the latter accounted for £128 of the wealth, whereas in 1524 no-one had been assessed on over £20. A study of 40 rural townships or parishes around the county also suggests an increase in persons taxed and a general increase in their wealth. Ledbury compares favourably in this respect with Leominster, where the population increased but the value fell slightly, and with the city of Hereford, where, despite increasing population, the average valuation went down from £9 to £8. Although the tax lists very rarely give occupations nor do the wills of the early 16th century, no doubt most people earned their livings in much the same way as their forebears, described in chapters 5 and 6.[163]

Figure 99   The tomb of Richard Willison and his wife Ann Elton at Madley, near Hereford. The monument proclaims their family connections through heraldry and also displays naïve kneeling figures of Richard and Ann on the opposite side to that illustrated.

Figure 100 John
Harford's tomb at
Bosbury, near Ledbury.

New Men

A group of families were emerging as the leaders of local society,
acquiring land and positions of authority, solidifying their
positions by intermarriage. The Skyppes came to Herefordshire
following the appointment of John Skyppe as bishop of Hereford
in 1539, a post he held until 1552. He helped a number of members
of his family with appointments and property. His sister Alice
married John Willison of Ledbury. It was their son Richard who,
with John Harford, purchased so much of the chantry lands in the
county. In 1542 Bishop Skyppe had already leased the Upper Hall,
Ledbury, to his nephew Richard on very favourable terms.

Richard Willison married Ann, daughter of William Elton of
Ledbury. William Elton was a wealthy man in the town and in
1524 had been assessed on goods valued at £16, the highest value
in Ledbury borough, and in 1545 again contributed the largest
amount to the 'benevolence' (a forced loan to the Crown). He

leased the demesne of St Katherine's Hospital from his brother John Elton alias Baker, master of the hospital and portionary of the Lower Hall. As portionary, John Baker presented his nephew Edward Elton to the vicarage in 1520, further tightening the web.[164]

John Harford of Worcester married Anne, daughter of Sir John Scrope of Castle Combe, Wiltshire. At some time he settled in Bosbury in the house now the *Crown Inn*, on the Ledbury road entering the village. He died in 1559 at the age of 57 and his tomb is in the church there. John and Anne's son Richard acted as steward of the manor of Bosbury until his death in 1578.[165]

AFTERWORD

This book has explored the history of a quiet corner of Herefordshire from the earliest days when hunter-gatherers wandered the land. Indeed, it began with the land itself, for the influence of geology, topography and climate upon human settlement is as important as the impact of man upon the landscape. The two are inescapably intertwined. Faint traces of the passing of wandering groups of hunter-gatherers have been garnered from scattered finds of stone tools. Enigmatic structures like Wall Hills and British Camp were the product of much labour by considerable numbers of people over long periods of time, although their precise purpose can only be guessed at. The daily efforts of countless generations went to shape the landscape in more subtle ways. From Iron-Age or Romano-British farmers to medieval foresters, the woods and fields, hedgerows and lanes bear the imprint of their daily round.

Millennia passed leaving no other record than what can be read from the palimpsest of the landscape or from occasional finds of artefacts or human remains. Only since the coming of the Normans do documents survive for Ledbury to give names to people or to illuminate events in their lives. As with many other places, Domesday Book provides the first surviving record, though it is obvious that Ledbury existed as a settlement before it had a name we can recognise. The form of the name Ledbury and the early history of the church in Herefordshire point to there having been a settlement here in Anglo-Saxon times, though no clear physical trace has been found. The Norman church had obliterated all trace of any earlier building. The development of the church, its size and ornamentation, the obvious wealth and money lavished on it over the centuries is in itself a significant clue to understanding the history of the town. Even by the standards of the Middle Ages, Ledbury was much under the influence of the church. The manor belonged to the bishop of Hereford who, certainly in earlier centuries, was a reasonably regular visitor. The rectory was well-endowed from an early date, making the two portionaries who shared it significant landowners as well as important ecclesiastics. Ledbury was also unusual in having a hospital for the care of a few old people at the very centre of its market place, which also owned a significant acreage in the surrounding countryside.

Apart from any spiritual or temporal effects this ecclesiastical presence had on the inhabitants of medieval Ledbury, it has helped succeeding generations of historians: many documents survive in the muniments of the diocese and of the hospital, especially those which deal with land transactions. By a careful study of the physical layout of the town, surviving buildings, archaeological finds and old documents, it has been possible to piece together the history of this little market town and the surrounding countryside over some five hundred years. It was not a history full of incident that made a mark upon the wider world. Its people were born and married and died, they worked and prayed, laughed and cried as people do the world over. But they did it in this corner of Herefordshire, under these hills, beside this river, on this soil. Although the laying out of the town in the 12th century reflected optimism about its prospect, Ledbury never really recovered from the long period of stagnation which followed the disasters of the 14th century, yet it did not dwindle into a mere village market. It benefited from a number of factors: its favourable position, between good arable land and meadow, with rough grazing, wood and stone on the hills behind; relatively easy access to Hereford and Gloucester and a number of lesser market towns within a day's travel; patronage by the bishop and other wealthy and influential ecclesiastics and, after the Reformation, support from a closely-knit local oligarchy of local families.

We leave Ledbury in 1558, a Catholic queen on the throne, but changes already afoot in the nation at large and in Ledbury. There were new people, new ideas and the glimmerings of a new wealth which would flourish at the end of the century. That development and its legacy of fine timber-framed buildings and the story of Ledbury through the next 500 years is the subject of a separate volume, *Ledbury: A Market Town and its Tudor Heritage*.

Endnotes

The following abbreviations are used throughout the endnotes:

BL	British Library
DCA	Dean and Chapter Archive, Hereford Cathedral Library
EPE	England's Past for Everyone
HRO	Herefordshire Record Office
HSMR	Herefordshire Sites and Monuments Record (http://www.herefordshire.gov.uk/htt/)
NMR	National Monuments Record
RCHM	Royal Commission on the Historical Monuments of England
Red Book	Bishop's rental for the manor of Ledbury *c.*1288, HRO AA59/1/1. Partly transcribed with introductory essay by A.T. Bannister, 'A Transcript of the "Red Book", A detailed account of Hereford Bishopric Estates in the thirteenth century', *Camden Miscellany*, vol. XV (1929); the Ledbury entries transcribed and translated by EPE volunteers in 2008-9.
TNA	The National Archives, Kew, formerly the Public Record Office
TS	In references to deeds at DCA, those listed in A.T. Bannister, 'Catalogue of MSS dealing with St Katherine's', *TWNFC* (1923), 231-53
TWNFC	*Transactions of the Woolhope Naturalists' Field Club*
Valor Eccl.	Valor Ecclesiasticus, 6 vols (1810-34)
VCH	*Victoria History of the Counties of England: Herefordshire*, vol. 1, 1908

CHAPTER 1 Introducing Leadon Land, pp.1-4

1 J. Masefield, 'London Town', in *Salt Water Ballads* (1902).

2 **Pre-glacial landscape**: G.R. Coope *et al.*, *Proceedings of the Geologists' Association*, 113 (2002), 237-58. **Earliest traces of human activity in southern Britain**: Worked flint flakes were retrieved in 2005 from a deposit exposed within a cliff at Pakefield on the Suffolk coast, dating from the Middle Pleistocene at around 750,000BP; S. Parfitt *et al.*, 'The earliest record of human activity in northern Europe', *Nature*, 438 (2005), 1,008-12. Meanwhile, the bones of proto-humans have been found at Boxgrove, Sussex, dating

to 500,000BP: M.B. Roberts and S.A. Parfit, *Boxgrove: A middle Pleistocene hominid site at Eartham Quarry, Boxgrove. West Sussex* (1999).

3   **Early agricultural character**: John Duncumb's *Agriculture of the County of Hereford* (1805) expressed this clearly in a frontispiece map. 'The heaviest crops of wheat are produced in a clayey tract extending from Hereford towards Ledbury' (*ibid.*, 10).

4   S. Pinches, *Ledbury: A Market Town and its Tudor Heritage* (2009).

CHAPTER 2 The Origins of Settlement to AD600, pp.5-28

5   J. Masefield, 'The Morris Dancers', in *The Country Scene* (1937).

6   **Early course of rivers**: S.G. Lewis and D. Maddy (eds), *The Pleistocene of the South Midlands and West Marches (Field Guide)*, Quaternary Research Association (1999); N. Barton, *Ice Age Britain* (2003).

7   **Mesolithic flints from the Ledbury area**: The 115 worked flint artefacts from Frith farm are now in Hereford Museum. They were collected by A.E. Brown in the 1950s. SMR, 8389. The Wall Hills flints are also in Hereford Museum. **Grovesend finds**: NMR 111995 [Accessed through Pastscape (http://www.pastscape.org.uk)].

8   **Neolithic activity at Midsummer Hill**: S. Stanford, *Midsummer Hill: An Iron Age Hillfort on the Malverns* (1981). For recent survey results, D. Field, *Midsummer Hill Camp: A survey of earthworks on Midsummer and Hollybush Hills, Eastnor*, English Heritage Archaeological Investigation Report AI/16/2000. The Neolithic axe fragment is of stone belonging to 'Group VII' petrology, from Graig Llwyd near Conwy.

9   **Earlier Neolithic enclosure at Bodenham**: In the Lugg valley. For details of the investigations at Hill Croft Field in 2006, see P. Dorling, *The Lugg Valley, Herefordshire: Archaeology, Landscape Change and Conservation* (*c.*2007), 20-5.

10   **Neolithic worked flint finds from the Ledbury area**: All information from Herefordshire SMR records.

11   **Exotic flint axe from Colwall**: S. Piggott, *Proc. Prehist. Soc.*, 4, 52-106; HSMR 3831; Hereford Museum Acc. 1306.

12   **Bradlow Knoll possible circular Bronze-Age burial mound**: T. Hoverd, 'Ledbury, woodland survey', *West Midlands Archaeology*, 43 (2000), 47-8. **Possible barrow at Glynch Brook, Eastnor**: Information from the Ledbury

Manpower Services Commission survey archive, 1983 (HSMR). **Hollybush Hill, Eastnor, Beaker pottery**: Stanford, *Midsummer Hill*, 137-8. **Arrowhead**: HSMR 3796.

13 **Mathon Bronze-Age cemeteries**: J.E.H. Blake, *Trans. Birmingham Archaeol. Soc*, 39 (1913), 90-3 and W.G. Hamilton, *TWNFC* 29 (1940), 120-7.

14 **Early fields in the area south of Ledbury**: M.C.B. Bowden, *Malvern Hills: an ancient landscape* (2005), 15-16 and Fig. 2.8.

15 **The late Iron-Age farmstead enclosure and open settlement at the Ridgeway, Cradley**: T. Hoverd, *West Midlands Archaeology*, 43 (2000), 45-6; Bowden, *Malvern Hills*, 25 and Fig. 2.14.

16 **Frith Wood survey**: C. Atkinson, 'Frith Wood, Ledbury, Herefordshire: An archaeological investigation', Herefordshire Archaeology Report 245 (2008). A booklet was also produced, containing information on the geology and natural history as well as the archaeology of Frith Wood. This is available for download at: http://www. englandspastforeveryone.org.uk/Counties/Herefordshire/ Projects/Ledburypre1558/Items/Frith_Wood.

17 **Midsummer Hill Camp**: Stanford, *Midsummer Hill.*

18 **The archaeology of Wall Hills Camp**: I am grateful to Mr John Tinson for facilitating access to the site to make first-hand observations. For information provided to members of the Woolhope Club visiting in the late 19th century, see H.G. Bull, 'Wall Hills, Ledbury', *TWNFC* (1883), 20-8.

19 **Kilbury no longer regarded as an Iron-Age camp**: Bowden, *Malvern Hills*, 18. The entry intended for Backbury/ St Ethelbert's Camp, **Dormington**, erroneously appears within the gazetteer entry for **Donnington**, in N. Pevsner's *Buildings of England: Herefordshire* (1963). (I am grateful to my colleagues Neil Rimmington and Melissa Seddon for detecting this error, which has caused considerable confusion since it was published.)

20 **Dobunni**: B. Cunliffe, *Iron Age Communities in Britain* (5th edn, 2005) and T. Moore and R. Reece, 'The Dobunni' among the papers of the Gloucester and District Archaeological Research Group (http://www.gadarg.org.uk/essays/e004. htm). **Dobunnic coinage**: R. van Arsdell, *Coinage of the Dobunni* (1997). **Local Iron-Age coin finds**: Information courtesy of the Portable Antiquities Scheme and Peter Reavill, Finds Liaison Officer.

21 **Dobunnic/Roman treaty relations**: M. Millett, *The Romanisation of Britain* (1990). **Discovery of bones**: Bull,

'Wall Hills'. **Sutton Walls**: K. Kenyon, 'Excavations at Sutton Walls Camp, Herefordshire, 1948-1951', *Archaeological Journal*, 110 (1954), 1-87.

22 **Pottery from Wall Hills**: HSMR 7123. **Croft Ambrey**: S.C. Stanford, *Croft Ambrey* (1974).

23 **Romano-British farms**: Identified from scatters of pottery sherds. Study of the Ledbury Manpower Services Commission survey archive (1983) suggests at least two concentrations of activity between Ledbury and Colwall, another in the south of Eastnor parish, and further sites south and west of Ledbury (archive held in SMR).

24 **Marley Hall**: A. Watkins, 'A Romano-British pottery in Herefordshire', *TWNFC* (1930), 110-12. A. Watkins, 'The Romano-British Pottery at Marley Hall', in Report of Sectional Editors, *TWNFC* 1930 (1932), 188-91.

25 **Late- and sub-Roman Herefordshire**: R. White, *Britannia Prima: Britain's Last Roman Province* (2007). **Stretton Grandison cemetery**: Border Archaeology, *Ledbury Trunk Main Archaeological Programme of Works, May-November 2007* (2009, CD-rom). **Dubricius**: W. Davies, *Wales in the Early Middle Ages* (1989).

26 **All place-name information**: Apart from the derivation of Dymock is from B. Coplestone-Crow, *Herefordshire Place-Names* (1989), but note that the inferences made concerning the light potentially thrown on British survival are those of the present author. **Sutton St Michael and the pagan Saxon circular ditch**: T. Hoverd, *Uncovering the Early Medieval Royal Manor of Marden: Investigations at Sutton St Michael, Herefordshire, 1999-2002* (Herefordshire Studies in Archaeology, 7 (forthcoming).

27 **Honey**: *Red Book*, 136-7.

28 **Dymock** and **Din Mocros**: A. Breeze, 'Dymock, Gloucestershire' in R. Coates and A. Breeze, *Celtic Voices, English Places: Studies of the Celtic Impact on Place-Names in England* (2000), 180-1. **Bank at Dingwood Park Farm**: NMR 1330802; http://www.pastscape.org.uk/hob.aspx?hob_id=1330802.

29 **British community at Canon Pyon**: Coplestone-Crow, *Herefordshire Place Names*, 172.

CHAPTER 3 Church and Parish to 1300, pp.29-48

30 F.M. Stenton, 'Pre-Conquest Herefordshire', in D.M. Stenton (ed.), *Preparatory to Anglo-Saxon England* (1970), 193; S. Keynes, 'Diocese and Cathedral before 1056', in G. Aylmer

and J. Tiller (eds), *Hereford Cathedral* (2000), 3-21. The map in K. Pretty, 'Defining the Magonsæte', in S. Bassett (ed.), *The Origins of Anglo-Saxon Kingdoms* (1989), 180, shows clearly the total lack of documentary evidence for the Ledbury region.

31 **Anglo-Saxon Herefordshire**: Pretty, 'Defining the Magonsæte', 171-83; Coplestone-Crow, *Herefordshire Place-Names*, 2-5; J. Blair, 'The Anglo-Saxon Church in Herefordshire', in A. Malpas *et al.* (eds), *The Early Church in Herefordshire* (2001), 3-13; K. Ray, 'Archaeology and the Three Early Churches of Herefordshire', in A. Malpas *et al.* (eds), *The Early Church in Herefordshire* (2001), 109-25. **Hereford Diocese**: Keynes, 'Diocese and Cathedral before 1056', 3-20.

32 **Ledbury as see**: Z.N. Brooke with Dom Adrian Morey and C.N.L. Brooke (eds), *Letters and Charters of Gilbert Foliot* (1967), no. 227, 300; *Reg. Swinfield*, II, 465. **Diocese**: Keynes, 'Diocese and Cathedral before 1056'; J. Hillaby, 'The Origins of the Diocese of Hereford', *TWNFC*, 42 (1976), 16-52; C.N.L. Brooke, 'The Diocese of Hereford 676-1200', *TWNFC*, 48 (1994), 23-36; Cf. the early history of the Mercian see: S. Bassett, 'Church and diocese in the West Midlands', in J. Blair and R. Sharpe (eds), *Pastoral Care before the Parish* (1992), 15. **Wulfgeat will**: D. Whitelock (ed.), *Anglo-Saxon Wills* (1930), 54-5, 165-6.

33 F. and C. Thorn (eds), *Domesday Book: Herefordshire* (1983); J.W. King, 'Two Herefordshire Minsters', *TWNFC*, 48 (1995), 282-90; Coplestone-Crow, *Herefordshire Place-Names*, 121, 188. **Nunnery**: J. and C. Hillaby, *Leominster Minster, Priory and Borough c.660-1539* (2006), 42-4.

34 **Bromyard minster**: H.P.R. Finberg, *Early Charters of the West Midlands* (1972), 141.

35 **Market**: S. Letters, *Gazetteer of Markets and Fairs in England* (List and Index Society special series 32), I, 163. **Hospital**: J. Hillaby, *St Katherine's Hospital, Ledbury, c.1230-1547* (2003), 1-7.

36 **Stream as boundary**: DCA 3692.

37 **'Bury'**: F.M. Stenton, 'The Historical Bearing of Place-Name Studies: the place of women in Anglo-Saxon Society', in D.M. Stenton (ed.), *Preparatory to Anglo-Saxon England* (1970), 320-1; S. Draper, 'The Significance of OE Burh in Anglo-Saxon England', *Anglo-Saxon Studies in Archaeology and History*, 15 (2008), 233-4; Blair, 'Anglo-Saxon Church in Herefordshire', 5-7; *VCH Worcestershire*, IV, 224-7.

38 *Domesday Book, Herefordshire*, no.2.26 (f. 182a); DCA 3692, 3705.

39 **Vicars**: Bodl. MS Rawl B329, f. 121, printed in J. Barrow, *English Episcopal Acta*, VII, Hereford, 1079-234, no.116, 75-6 (the MS reads '*vicar*' which might be either singular or plural); *Reg. Lewis Charlton*, 5. **Portionaries**: DCA, 3696, 7018/1/1, 41; *Reg. Swinfield*, II, 464.

40 King, 'Two Herefordshire Minsters', 283-7; BL Add MS 15555, f. 6v.; DCA, 3717; *Reg. Thomas Charlton*, 81; *Reg. Trillek*, ii, 374; *Reg. Lewis Charlton*, 68; *The registers of Ledbury, Co. Hereford. Baptisms, marriages and burials, 1556-1576*, transcribed G.H. Piper (ed.), C.H. Mayo (1899); Reg. Stanbury, 192.

41 RCHM, Herefordshire, II, East (1932), 100-4.

42 HSMR 5704, 32484; RCHM, *Herefordshire*, II, 100; **Bishops**: J.S. Barrow, *Fasti Ecclesiae Anglicanae 1066-1300*, vol. 8, Hereford (2002), 1-7, http://www.british-history.ac.uk/ report.aspx?compid=34422 [Accessed: 9 August 2008]; J. Barrow, 'A 12th-century bishop and literary patron: William de Vere', *Viator*, 18 (1987), 175-87, 179; J. Blair, 'Clerical Communities and Parochial Space: the Planning of Urban Mother Churches in the Twelfth and Thirteenth Centuries', in T.R. Slater and G. Rosser (eds), *The Church in the Medieval Town* (1998), 285.

43 **Dedication**: The dedication to St Peter was first recorded in the mid-13th century: DCA 1728, 2180; that to St Peter and St Paul in 1384: *Reg. Gilbert*, 60-1. The two saints shared a feast day on 29 June, which was presumably the church's patronal festival. **Tower**: Pevsner, *Herefordshire* (1963), 30-1, 215. **Bells**: DCA 3696, 7018/1/1, 41-2. **Hereford cathedral**: R. Morris, 'The Remodelling of the Hereford Aisles', *Journal of the British Archaeological Association*, vol. xxxvii (1974), 22.

44 *Reg. Cantilupe*, 63, 125-6, 141, 254; DCA, 3686, 3696; *Fasti Ecclesiae Anglicanae 1066-1300*, 8, Hereford, 26-9, http://www. british-history.ac.uk/report.aspx?compid=34428 [Accessed: 18 September 2008]; A.B. Emden, *Biographical Dictionary of the University of Oxford to 1500*, sv Anne.

45 HRO AA/59/A/1, 122; *Reg. Lewis Charlton*, 5; *Reg. Swinfield*, II, 464.

46 DCA, 7018/1/3, 57-8; *ibid.* 1728, 1741, 1801, 1802, 3260, 3681.

47 *Oxford Dictionary of Saints*, http://www.jesus.cam.ac.uk/ college/history/radegund.html [Accessed: 18 September 2008]; A. Binns, *Dedications of Monastic Houses in England and Wales 1066-1216*, 153, 167; *Cal. Papal Regs*, vi. 65.

48 **Walerand**: TNA, JUST 1/300C, rot. 1d.; DCA, 2180; HRO, AA/59/A/1, 125, 127. **Hospital's relics**: Hillaby, *St Katherine's Hospital*, 75-6, 136. **Chaplains**: DCA, 1727, 1801, 2462, 3675,

3693; W.W. Capes (ed.), *Charters and Records of Hereford Cathedral* (1908), 73; *Reg. Cantilupe*, 308; HRO, AH82/18, 21. **Simon the clerk**: *Cal. Inq. Misc.* I, no. 1459, 414.

49 *Fasti Ecclesiae Anglicanae 1066-1300, 8, Hereford*, 26-9, http://www.british-history.ac.uk/report.aspx?compid=34428 [Accessed: 18 September 2008]; *Reg. Cantilupe*, 28-9, 31, 163, 191, 309; *Reg. Swinfield*, 2.

50 Barrow, *English Episcopal Acta*, VII, *Hereford 1079-1234*, no. 348, 278-80; A.T. Bannister, 'Catalogue of MSS dealing with St Katherine's', *TWNFC* (1923), 232, 245; DCA (1643), 1727, 1741, 1888, 2184, 3665-6, 3673, 3679, 3683, 3699, 3701, 3722, 3724; *ibid.* 7018/1/3, 69; HRO AA/59/A/1, 133; For the foundation and early history of the hospital see Hillaby, *St Katherine's Hospital*, 1-36.

51 Bodl. MS Rawl B329, ff. 2v.-3, 153.

CHAPTER 4 The Development of the Borough, pp.49-72

52 **Foundation of Ledbury**: Capes, *Charters and Records*, 8; J. Hillaby, *Ledbury a Medieval Borough* (2005), 11-13.

53 The boundary of the Borough is clearly marked on the Tithe map (1841) and persisted until the formation of the Ledbury Urban District and the Ledbury Rural District Councils in 1894.

54 **Medieval town planning**: M.W. Beresford, *New Towns of the Middle Ages* (1969), 96; T.R. Slater, 'The analysis of burgages in medieval towns: three case studies from the West Midlands', *West Midlands Archaeology*, 23 (1981), 53-66; A. Catchpole, D. Clark and R. Peberdy, *Burford: Buildings and People in a Cotswold Town* (2008), 20-1; DCA 7018, 3.

55 HSMR references: **Church**: 5704. **Priory**: 41529. **West of Cattle Market**: 35367. **Ledbury Park**: 44996. *Feathers*: 25994. **St Katherine's**: 48626.

56 **The churchyard stream**: C.B. Andrews (ed.), *The Torrington Diaries: Tours through England and Wales of the Hon. John Byng* (1934), I, 43.

57 **Fish-ponds**: J. Webb (ed.), *A roll of the household expenses of Richard de Swinfield, Bishop of Hereford, during part of the years 1289 and 1290*, Camden Society (1854), 2 vols, II, 57-8.

58 **The site of the bishop's hall**: N.C. Reeves (ed.), *The 1675 Thomas Blount manuscript history of Herefordshire* (n.d.), 10; HRO AF4/11 f.9; HRO AM/33/13; TNA SC6/Hen VIII/1511; D. Rouse, 'Land adjacent to Eastnor House, Worcester Road, Ledbury, Herefordshire' (2005), *Hereford Archaeological Series*, 663.

59 **Alternative sites of the bishop's hall**: Hillaby, *Medieval Borough*, 14-15; J.W. King, 'Edward Skynner of Ledbury, clothier, and the New House', *TWNFC*, 49 (1997), 101-10.

60 **Church Street/Church Lane**: Hillaby, *Medieval Borough*, 14. **Market infill characteristics**: M.R.G. Conzen, 'Alnwick, Northumberland: a study in town-plan analysis', *Institute of British Geographers Special Publication*, 27 (1990) (revised from 1960 edn).

61 **Grammar School**: RCHM, *Herefordshire* II, 100; James, 'An analysis of the historic fabric', 10. **Council Offices**: RCHM, *Herefordshire* II, 100; D. James, 'An analysis of the historic fabric of late 16th century and early 17th century buildings in Ledbury, Herefordshire'. Unpublished Report for EPE (2007), 11.

62 **Shop Row**: DCA 3300, 5203.

63 **Fair booths**: *Cal. Close 1247-1251*, 277; *Cal. Close 1251-1253*, 80; *Cal. Close 1253-1254*, 53-4; *1254-1256*, 64. **Chester Rows**: VCH *Ches.*, V, part 2 (2005), 225-39 at http://www.british-history.ac.uk/report.aspx?compid=57327&strquery=seld [Accessed: 24 October 2008].

64 *Red Book*, 122-32, **1314 rental**: DCA 7018/1/2, 83.

65 **Homend plots**: Hillaby, *Medieval Borough*, 29.

66 **New House**: King, 'Edward Skynner of Ledbury'. **Tithe Map**: HRO diocesan ref. L265.

67 **New Street, Birmingham**: G. Demidowicz, *Medieval Birmingham: the Borough Rentals of 1296 and 1344-5*, Dugdale Society Occasional Papers, 48 (2008).

68 **Bye Street**: T. Wellicome, 'Archaeological evaluation, Rai Fashions, Bye Street, Ledbury' (2007), Border Archaeology.

69 **Bye Street cattle market**: N. Appleton-Fox, 'The Cattle Market, Ledbury, Herefordshire, a report on an evaluation excavation' (1999), *Marches Archaeology series*, 100; A. Nash and J. Wainwright, 'The former Cattle Market, Ledbury, Herefordshire, a report on an archaeological watching-brief' (2002), *Marches Archaeology series*, 254. **The 'Bishop's Palace', Bye Street**: James, 'An analysis', 8; RCHM *Herefordshire*, II, East (1932), 113.

70 **The 'town ditch', Bye Street**: HRO CJ75; A. Nash and J. Wainwright, 'The former Cattle Market, Ledbury, Herefordshire, a report on an archaeological watching-brief' (2002), *Marches Archaeology series*, 254.

71 **New Street**: Barrow, *English Episcopal Acta, VII, Hereford, 1079-1234*, 98; DCA 3709; Cat. Ant. DVI C4612, 107; *Red Book*, 120-1.

72 **New Street excavations**: M. Napthan, S. Ratkai and E. Pearson, 'Salvage recording at land to the rear of 26 New

Street, Ledbury', *Hereford & Worcester County Council report*, 455 (1996); N. Appleton-Fox, 'Linden House, New Street, Ledbury, Herefordshire, a report on an archaeological evaluation', *Marches Archaeology series*, 73 (1999).

CHAPTER 5 Town Life, 1200-1500, pp.73-92

73 **Hazle**: Thorn, *Domesday Book, Herefordshire*, 2.25. **Massington and Wellington**: TNA C 143/43/13. **Rights of manor of Ledbury**: *Reg. Cantilupe*, 163; TNA JUST 1/302 rot. 62.

74 **Upper Hall**: DCA 7018/1, 1. **St Katherine's**: Hillaby, *St Katherine's Hospital*, 53-62, passim; TNA E133/3/425 m1d. **Blount**: *Reg. Rob. Mascall*, 69; Collyer, *Cal. Pat. 1389-92*, 379. **Lorymer**: *Valor Eccl. III*, 3; *Letters & Papers, Foreign and Domestic, Henry VIII: August-December 1535*, vol. 9 (1886), 96-114, available online at http://www.british-history.ac.uk/report.aspx?compid=75667&strquery=ledbury [Accessed: 30 August 2008].

75 DCA A327; *Reg. Trefnant*, 163.

76 HRO 043; TNA LR10/7; HRO G2/988 f 6, BO92/60. **Land Tax**: HRO Q/REL/6/15/1-33; James, 'An analysis', 31-3.

77 C. Hopkinson, *Herefordshire under Arms* (1985), 39-40, 59-68. **Mortimer**: G.O. Sayles (ed.), *Select Cases in Court of King's Bench under Edw. II* (Selden Soc. lxxiv), no. 50. **Lawlessness**: *Cal. Papal Regs*, XI, 648-9.

78 TNA JUST 1/300C, rot. 1d (1255); JUST 1/302 rot. 60d-61d (1292). **Lyngyn**: STAC 3/10/24.

79 *Red Book*, Ledbury borough, 119-33. **Population**: Hillaby, *Medieval Borough*, 41, 85; Pinches, *Ledbury: A Market Town*, 26.

80 **Richard Unet**: *Cal. Pat. 1416-22*, 103. **Edmund Ekeney**: *Cal. Pat. 1446-52*, 19. **Thomas Bracy**: TNA C1/751/29. **Fulling**: *Red Book*, 130, 132; Hillaby, *Medieval Borough*, 38.

81 **John Cissor**: *Red Book*, 121. **Wm. Berde**: HRO AH82/29; *Swinfield Household Expenses*, II, 140.

82 *Swinfield Household Expenses*, II, 140. **Tanneries**: deeds for various properties; Tithe Survey 1839, HRO AF 4/26.

83 *Red Book*, 121, 132; *Swinfield Household Expenses*, II, 140-1.

84 **Butchers' Row**: in *Red Book*, 132; demolition of, HRO K13/17. **Fishmonger**: HRO 6/3/41.

85 **Mills**: *Red Book*, 133, 138; *Reg. Swinfield*, 283. **Wygmund's tree**: Hillaby, *Medieval Borough*, 7-8. **Ovens**: *Swinfield Household Expenses*, II, 29-30. **Cook shop**: HRO AH82/36. **Cook shops generally**: http://www.buildinghistory.org/bristol/cookshops.shtml [Accessed: 7 September 2009].

86 **Robert the vine dresser**: *The Letters and Charters of Gilbert*

Foliot, A. Morley and C.N.L. Brooke (eds), Cambridge (1967), 372. **Vineyard**: *Reg. Cantilupe*, 110; HRO AA59/A/1, 138; *Red Book*, 16, 24; *Swinfield Household Expenses*, II, 59; Cal. Inq. Misc., vii, no. 281, 152; HRO AM33/13; TNA SC 6/HenVIII/1511. **Bromsberrow**: VCH *Gloucestershire* XII, forthcoming. **George Skippe vineyard, Stony Hill**: HSMR 20097; *The Diary of George Skippe,* Hereford Central Library, W920.

87   **Wine**: TNA, JUST 1/302, rot. 62; *Swinfield Household Expenses*, II, 59. **Regulation**: *Reg. Spufford*, 245.

88   S. Letters, *Online Gazetteer of Markets and Fairs in England and Wales to 1516*, available online at http://www.history.ac.uk/cmh/gaz/gazweb2.html [Accessed: 13 February 2008]; J.E O'Donnell, 'Market Centres in Herefordshire, 1200-1400: some factors influencing their development', *TWNFC* (1971), 186-94.

89   **Duke of York**: Northants. RO, Westmorland (Apethorpe), 4xx4, ff 5v-6. Thanks are due to Dr J.P. Toomey for permission to quote from his translation, shortly to be published as J.P. Toomey (ed.), *A Household account of Edward duke of York, at Hanley Castle, Worcestershire, 1409-10* (Worcestershire Historical Society, forthcoming). **Bishop of Hereford**: *Swinfield Household Expenses*, II, 56-7. **Abbot of Reading**: *Swinfield Household Expenses*, II, 164. **Royal visits**: *Cal. Close 1231-4*, 175, 249, 329, 352; *Cal. Close 1237-42*, 271; *Cal. Close Roll Ed. II, 1323-7*, 622-3, 626, 654.

90   **Wye navigation**: I. Cohen, 'The non-tidal Wye and its navigation', *TWNFC*, 36 (1955), 83-10. **Eggs**: Northants. RO, Westmorland (Apethorpe), 4xx4, f.35r.

91   **Ledbury market and fair charters**: *Reg. Regum Anglo-Norm*, III, 148; Capes, *Charters and Records*, 8; *CR* 1247-5, 156; *Reg. Swinfield*, I, 18. **Market tolls**: TNA E372/80/m2 and E372/120 m22. **Hereford and Leominster markets**: *Cal. Close 1237-42*, 2.

92   **Market Cross**: HRO G2 MSS 85.

93   **Movement of Sheep**: *Swinfield Household Expenses*, II, 176. **Wool**: *Cal. Close 1337-9*, 148-9, 269, 499; T.H. Lloyd, *The English Wool Trade in the Middle Ages* (1977), 52, 132; T.H. Lloyd, 'The Movement of Wool Prices in Medieval England', *Econ. Hist. Soc. Rev. Supplement*, 6 (1973). **William Eseger**: DCA 3256, 3257 (from TS). **Eseger family**: Hillaby, *St Katherine's Hospital*, 102, 104, 131.

94   **Fish**: *Swinfield Household Expenses*, II, 56, 58. **Wheat and oats**: information from Dr J.P. Toomey. **Spices**: Northants

RO, Westmorland (Apethorpe), 4xx4, ff 11v, 16v. **London purchases**: *Swinfield Household Expenses*, II, 133. **Impact of aristocratic households' purchasing**: B.F. Harvey, 'The aristocratic consumer in England in the long thirteenth century', in M. Prestwich, R.H. Britnell and R. Frame (eds), *Thirteenth Century England VI: proceedings of the Durham conference 1995* (1997), 17-38.

95   **1288 rental**: *Red Book*; HRO AM/ 33/13. **1537 account**: TNA SC 6 Hen VIII/1511. **Plague**: A.W. Langford, 'The plague in Herefordshire', *TWNFC* 35 (1955-7), 46-53; W.J. Dohar, *The Black Death and Pastoral Leadership. The diocese of Hereford in the fourteenth century* (1995). **Bosbury**: Dohar, *Black Death*, 54.

96   DCA 7018/1, p.1; TNA SC 6 Hen VIII/1511.

CHAPTER 6 Woods and Fields, pp.93-114

97   For the paragraphs which follow see *VCH* 1, 263-345: text, with introductory essay by J.H. Round; C.P. Lewis, 'An Introduction to the Herefordshire Domesday', *The Herefordshire Domesday* (Alecto Historical Edns., 1988); C.W. Atkin, 'Herefordshire', in H.C. Darby and I. Terrett, *Domesday Geography of Midland England* (1971), 57-114.

98   *VCH* 1, 321-3.

99   **Manor of Hazle**: *Red Book*, 134; DCA 7018/1, 2, 3. **Grimbald Pauncefoot**: J. O'Donnell, 'A Border Knight', *TWNFC*, 197, 39-47. **Acreage**: Hillaby, *St Katherine's Hospital*, 23; J. Bartholomew, *Gazetteer of Great Britain* (1887) at http://www.visionofbritain.org.uk/place_page.jsp?p_id=530&st=ledbury [Accessed: 5 May 2009].

100   **Court of Park**: HRO G87/32/1-29. **Wellington and Massington**: *Red Book*, 133; TNA C143/431/3, CP 25/1/83/54, CP 25/1/83/56. **Pesebrugge**: *Reg. Rob. Mascall*, 190. **St Katherine's**: Records are kept at the Dean and Chapter Archive, Hereford. For a detailed study of these, Hillaby, *St Katherine's Hospital*, 45-52 (Ledbury and Eastnor estate) and 53-62 (estate administration and economy).

101   **New bailiffs**: DCA, 7018/1, f. 3. **Manor of Ledbury**: Rentals 1288 HRO AA59/A/1 ff 118-42, court roll 1475-6, AM33/1 1154-5 AM33/4, accounts 1496-7 AM33/13 accounts 1506 BL Add Roll 27311, view of frankpledge 1535 HRO; B38/18, accounts 1537 TNA SC 6/HenVIII/1511. **Lower Hall**: court rolls and accounts 1485, 1499, 1529 BL Add MS 15555. **Upper Hall**: Rental *c.*1400 DCA 7018/1/2.

102   Bannister, *Transcript of the 'Red Book'*, 18, 20, 22, 24. **Lugg Fishery**: *ibid.*, 7.

103   **Le Rede**: Bannister, *Transcript of the 'Red Book'*, 139. **Rede**: *OED*. **Whitbourne**: Bannister, *Transcript of the 'Red Book'*, 14.

104   *Red Book*, 139-42.

105   *Red Book*, 141. **Elured reeve**: DCA 3663.

106   **1495 account**: HRO AM33/13. **1537 account**: TNA, SC 6/Hen VIII/1511. **Butterfield survey**: HRO AA/59/A/2, 239-239v.

107   **Field boundary patterns and early landscape history**: A whole category of 'retentive character types' was defined for areas where the dominant pattern of boundaries reflects the enclosure of formerly open fields. K. Ray and P. White, 'Herefordshire's Historic Landscape: A Characterisation', *Herefordshire Studies in Archaeology*, 1 (forthcoming).

108   **Land in Eastnor**: DCA 3260. **Metes and bounds**: HRO AA26/II/29. **Field names**: All the Herefordshire field names recorded in the late 1830s by the Tithe Commissioners have been collated by members of the Woolhope Naturalists Field Club and are available in the County Record Office and on-line: http://www.smr.herefordshire.gov.uk/hfn/db.php.

109   **Assart**: DCA 3665. **Lynchets**: HSMR 3767-70, 48812.

110   **Wellecroft**: DCA 3669 and 3689. **Wetecroft**: DCA 3666. **Calves parroc**: DCA 3703.

111   **Enclosed land**: HRO G37/11/60; TNA SC/Hen VIII/1511; W.E. Tate, *A handlist of English enclosure, acts and awards.* Part 15: Herefordshire TWNFC (1941), 183-94. **Wall Hills**: HSMR 6077.

112   **Peas**: *Swinfield Household Expenses*, II, 30; Capes, *Charters and Records*, 186-90. **St Katherine's and Leominster Priory**: Hillaby, *St Katherine's Hospital*, 51-2.

113   **Gardens and orchards**: C. Dyer, *Everyday Life in Medieval England* (1994), 113-31, especially 121-4, 'urban gardens'. **Church Lane**: DCA 3692. **New Street**: DCA 7018/1, p.2. **Ympey**: BL Add MS 15555 ff 1v, 2v.

114   **Upper Hall Meadow**: BL Add MS 15555 f. 1. **Lonecotes**: DCA 3710, 7018/1; HRO AH 82/30, 31; TNA C 143/342/6.

115   **Horse feed**: *Swinfield Household Expenses*, II, 30. **Ox**: BL Add MS 15555, f. 2. **Cheese**: *Swinfield Household Expenses*, II, 24. **Cows**: 1354 *Reg. Trillek*, 231;*Cal. Pat. 1389-92*, 379.

116   **Pasture and pannage**: *Red Book*, 138; *Reg. Swinfield*, 283; AM33/13 etc. **Le Parc**: *Cal. Inq. Misc.*, vii, no. 281, 149.

117   **Booth Hall**: *Reg. Trefnant*, 163.

118   **Hurdles**: *Cal. Close Hen. III 1251-1263*, 80. **Brushwood**: *Swinfield Household Expenses*, II, 58.

119   *Swinfield Household Expenses*, II, 30, 59, 140.

120   **Malvern Chace**: P. Hurle, *Malvern Chace* (1982); *VCH Worcs.*, II, 206. **Does**: *Swinfield Household Expenses*, II, 19-20.

121   **Rabbits**: J. Sheil, *Rabbits and their History*, Newton Abbot (1971). **Warren**: *Reg. Rob. Mascall*, 73; *Reg. Trillek*, 201-2. **Pillow mounds**: HSMR 3795, 3797.

CHAPTER 7 Spiritual Life, pp.115-36

122   W. Langland, *Piers the Ploughman*, Prologue.

123   **Valuation**: *Valor Eccl.*, III, 47; *Reg. Mayew*, 61, 235. **Lower Hall account rolls**: BL Add. MS 15555.

124   **Collegiate church**: *Cal. Pat. 1343-5*, 209; *Cal. Pat. 1358-61*, 537; *Cal. Pat. 1377-81*, 329, 330; *Cal. Pat. 1388-92*, 107; *Reg. Trefnant, 138*; *Reg. Gilbert*, 60-1.

125   **John de Aigueblanche**: *Cal. Papal Regs*. II, 23; G. Aylmer and J. Tiller, *Hereford Cathedral: A History* (2000), 325-6, 501, 633, 637; J. Barrow, *English Episcopal Acta*, 35 (2009), Hereford, 1234-75. **John Prophete**: *Reg. Lacy*, 2; *Cal. Pat. 1389-93*; 308; *Reg. Trefnant*, 138; *Cal. Papal Regs*, IV, 354; Aylmer and Tiller, *Hereford Cathedral*, 610, 620, 623, 627, 637. **Hugh Coren**: A.T. Bannister, *Institutions of the Diocese of Hereford 1539-1900* (1923), 5; Aylmer and Tiller, *Hereford Cathedral*, 91, 637. **Promotion**: *Cal. Pat. Phil & Mary, 1555-7*, III, 1,117. **John ap Richard**: *Reg. Stanbury*, 178; Hillaby, *St Katherine's Hospital*, 118; Aylmer and Tiller, *Hereford Cathedral*, 637.

126   **Gilbert de Middleton**: *Reg. Orleton*, 85; *Cal. Papal Regs.*, LI, 327; *HDCA 3293*; *Reg. Trillek*, 505; *Cal. Pat. 1321-4*, 43. **Itherius de Concoreto**: *Cal. Papal Regs*. II, 327; *Cal. Pat. 1334-8*, 487; *Cal. Close roll 1337-1339*, 167. **Bernard de Ortolis**: *Cal. Papal Pets.*, I, 57. **John Prophete**: Emden, *Oxford to 1500*, sv Prophete; Hillaby, *St Katherine's Hospital*, 107.

127   **Visitation**: DCA 1779 published in A.T. Bannister, 'Visitation Returns of the Diocese of Hereford, 1397', *EHR*, 44 (1929), 279-89, 445-53, 45 (1930), 92-101, 444-64, *Ledbury*, 45 (1930), 93. **Preece memorial**: T. Dingley, *History from Marble*, 2 vols, Camden Soc. (1867-8), II, ccxlvii; Reeves, *Thomas Blount Manuscript*, 12.

128   **Will of John de Aigueblanche [Aquablanca]**: Capes, *Charters and Records*, 186-90.

129   RCHM, *Herefordshire*, II, 100.

130   R.K. Morris, 'The Local influence of Hereford Cathedral in the Decorated Period', *TWNFC*, 41 (1973), 48-67, 49, 61-5; RCHM *Herefordshire*, II, 1, 103; HRO, BO92/56 f. 213; H.C.A. 5832.

131   **Shrine of 'Blessed Katherine'**: Hillaby, *Medieval Borough*, 55. **Service of Blessed Mary**: *Reg. Orleton*, 388.

132   **Indulgence**: *Cal. Papal Regs*, IV, 67. **Maid Bigod**: HRO

        32/1/2. **Aigueblanche will**: Capes, *Charters and Records*, 186-90.

133   **William de Grandison**: Hillabyr, *St Katherine's Hospital*, 89. **Female tomb**: St Clair Baddeley, 'The 15th century effigy of an unknown lady at Ledbury', *TWNFC* (1927), 214-17; L. Gee, 'Fourteenth-century tombs for women in Herefordshire', in D. Whitehead (ed.), *Medieval Art, Architecture and Archaeology at Hereford*, 132-7.

134   **Light of St Peter**: DCA 7018/1. **Beneas will**: HRO 1/1/1.

135   *Cal. Pat. 1399-1401*, 62, 489, 509; TNA C143/431/3; *Val. Eccl.* III, 47.

136   **Foundation**: *Cal. Pat. 1370-4*, 372; *Reg. Gilbert*, 48-50. **Chaplain's house**: *Cal. Pat. 1385-9*, 376; *Reg. Rob. Mascall*, 175; BL Add. MS 15555 f. 5. **William Bowyer**: *Cal. Pat. 1364-1367*, 426; TNA C143/406/4.

137   BL Add MSS 15555 f. 3; *Cal. Pat. 1549-1551*, 27-30.

138   **Smith**: Emden, *Oxford to 1500*. **Hill**: *Reg. Mayhew*, 115. **Musmare**: A.B. Emden, A biographical Register of the University of *Oxford, AD 1501-1540* (1974). **Malbon**: Piper and Mayo, *The registers of Ledbury*; *Cal. Pat. 1550-1553*, 74, has a Stephen Malbon being inducted to 'Lydbyrie' vicarage in 1551, perhaps a mistake for Hamnet.

139   **Screen**: W. Brayley and J. Britton, *The Beauties of England and Wales* (1805), VI, 594; R. Wheeler, *The Medieval Church Screens of the Southern Marches* (2006), 233-4.

140   *Reg. Lewis Charlton*, 37; Bannister, 'Visitation Returns', 93.

141   *Reg. Gilbert*, 90-1.

142   **William of Ockeridge**: Hillaby, *St Katherine's Hospital*, 28. **Eseger family**: Hillaby, *St Katherine's*, 101-5. **Gift of land**: *Cal. Pat. 1361-1364*, 403; *Cal. Close 1364-1368*, 13; TNA C143/342/6.

143   *Cal. Papal Regs*, V, 263; 90-1 DCA 3696; *ibid.* 7018/1/1, 41.

144   Capes, *Charters and Records*, 68-71; DCA 2175, 3564, 3575, 3576, 7018/5/1.

145   **Wycherley**: Emden, *Oxford*, iii, 2,102-3. **Ordinations**: *Reg. Myllyng*, 162-83. **At Hospital chapel**: *Reg. Myllyng*, 171, 172. **Tiles**: Hillaby, *St Katherine's Hospital*, 121-8.

CHAPTER 8 A Time of Change, pp.137-54

146   **Accounts of the bishop's estates 1495 and 1537**: HRO AM 33/13 and TNA, SC 6/HenVIII/1511. **Nether Hall court roll 1499**: BL Add. MSS.15555. **Coventry**: C. Phythian-Adams, *Desolation of a City* (1979). **Ruined buildings**: TNA, SC 6/HenVIII/1511.

147	James, 'An analysis of the historic fabric', 9. **Thatch**: T. Overbury, 'The domestic architecture of Herefordshire', in *Herefordshire: its natural history, archaeology and history*, *TWNFC* (1951); 233. **Bosbury**: RCHM, II Herefordshire East, 20.

148	**Wall Paintings**: K. Davies, *Artisan Art: Vernacular wall paintings in the Welsh Marches*, 1550-1650 (2008), 5-7, 12-123, 14, 16, 89-90, 99, 140.

149	**Hundred court**: First recorded in 1404 *Cal. Inq. Misc.*, vii, no. 281, 149; TNA SC 6/HenVIII/1511. **Perquisites of bishop's court**: *Valor Eccl.*, III, 2. **Lower Hall Court**: BL Add. MS 1555 f1. **William Webbe**: *Reg. Mayew*, 283; Aylmer & Tiller, *Hereford Cathedral*: 64, 640.

150	**Ledbury in 1535**: *Valor Eccl.*, III, 2, 3, 4, 46-8.

151	E. Duffy, *The Voices of Morebath: Reformation and Rebellion in an English Village* (2001).

152	TNA E133/3/425 m 1d; TNA E 134/20 20 & 21 Eliz. Mich. [1578].

153	**Herefordshire chantry certificates**: TNA E 101/24, /84.

154	**London merchants**: *Cal. Pat. Edw. VI, 1549-51*, 376. **John Harford and Richard Willison**: *Cal. Pat. Edw. VI, 1547-1553*, 128, *Cal. Pat. Edw. VI, 1549-51*, 27-30. **Chantry priests**: I am grateful to Sylvia Gill for providing much of the following information on the Ledbury chantry priests.

155	*Valor Eccl.*, III, 47. **John Potter**: TNA E334/2; DCA 5602; F.C. Morgan and P.E. Morgan, 'Some nuns ex-religious and former chantry priests living in the diocese of Hereford (*c.*1554)', *TWNFC* XXXVII (1962), 135-48, 143; Bannister, *Institutions*; A.J. Knapton, 'Another Elizabethan Clergy List', *Trans Shrops Arch. Soc.*, 44 and 45 (1931), 31-50. **Chantry lands**: *Cal. Pat. Edw. VI, 1549-1551*, 28.

156	**Chantry lands**: *Cal. Pat. Edw. VI, 1549-1551*, 28. **Griffith Fowler**: Morgan and Morgan, 'Some Nuns', 141; HRO 92/1; TNA E310/24. **Thomas Kylling**: Morgan and Morgan, 'Some Nuns', 142; TNA E301/25.

157	**Chantry lands**: *Cal. Pat. Edw. VI, 1549-1551*, 28. **Richard Wheler**: Information from Sylvia Gill; Hillaby, *Medieval Borough*, 77, 83, 84.

158	The survey of Holy Trinity Chantry, petition and school continuance warrant are all printed in A.F. Leach, *English Schools at the Reformation* (1896), 92-3, 106-7. *See also* the Charity Commissioners' Reports Herefordshire (1819-37), 122; Hillaby, *Medieval Borough*, 83-4; N. Orme, 'The medieval schools of Herefordshire', *Nottingham Medieval Studies*, XL (1996), 47-62, 60.

159   **Porch: Churchwardens' accounts**: HRO BO92/55. **Blount**: Reeves, *The 1675 Thomas Blount Manuscript*, 11.

160   RCHM, *Herefordshire*, II, 67; NMR BF 039043 Addendum May 1976. See also James, 'An analysis of the historic fabric', 10-11.

161   **Elton's Book**: DCA 7018/1-3. **St Ethelbert's Hospital**: D. Whitehead, 'St Ethelbert's Hospital, Hereford', in G. Aylmer and J. Tiller, *Hereford Cathedral* (2000), 34-609. **Refoundation of St Katherine's**: *An Act Concerning the Hospital of Ledbury*, 23, Eliz. I. For the later history of the hospital, J. Hillaby, 'St Katherine's Hospital Ledbury' in G. Aylmer and J. Tiller, *Hereford Cathedral* (2000), 624-7.

162   **John Lorde**: Hillaby, *St Katherine's Hospital*, 133. **Edward Baskerville**: Emden, *Oxford, 1501-40*; TNA PROB 11/49.

163   **Chantry certificate**: TNA E301/24. **Taxation**: M. Faraday, *Herefordshire Taxes in the Reign of Henry VIII* (2005), 15-17, 34.

164   **Skyppe: William Elton**: Faraday, *Herefordshire Taxes*, 67, 246-7. **Lease of hospital demesne**: TNA E133/3/425 mm 1-4.

165   S. Bentley, *History and Description of the Parish of Bosbury* (1891), 40-1.

Bibliography

Place of publication is London unless otherwise stated.

PRINTED PRIMARY SOURCES

Andrews, C.B. (ed.), *The Torrington Diaries: Tours through England and Wales of the Hon. John Byng* (4 vols, 1934-8, London)

Bannister, A.T., 'Catalogue of MSS dealing with St Katherine's', *TWNFC* (1923), 231-3

Bannister, A.T. (ed.), 'A transcript of "The Red Book", A detailed account of the Hereford Bishopric Estates in the thirteenth century', *Camden Miscellany*, vol. XV (1929)

Barrow, J., *English Episcopal Acta*, VII, *Hereford 1079-1234* (Oxford, 1993)

Barrow, J.S., *Fasti Ecclesiae Anglicanae 1066-1300*: vol. 8: Hereford (2002), available online at http://www.british-history.ac.uk/report.aspx?compid=34422

Brooke, Z.N., Morey, A. and Brooke, C.N.L. (eds), *Letters and Charters of Gilbert Foliot* (Cambridge, 1967)

W.W. Capes (ed.), *Charters and Records of Hereford Cathedral* (Hereford, 1908)

Duncumb, J., *General View of the Agriculture of the County of Hereford; drawn up for the consideration of the Board of Agriculture and Internal Improvement* (East Ardsley, 1805)

Finberg, H.P.R., *Early Charters of the West Midlands* (Leicester, 1972)

Morley, A. and Brooke, C.N.L. (eds), *The Letters and Charters of Gilbert Foliot* (Cambridge, 1967)

Piper, G.H. (trans.), May, C.H. (ed.), *The registers of Ledbury, Co. Hereford. Baptisms, marriages and burials, 1556-1576* (London, 1899)

Reeves, N.C. (ed.), *The 1675 Thomas Blount manuscript history of Herefordshire* (Hereford, n.d.)

Thorn, F. and C. (eds), *Domesday Book: Herefordshire* (Chichester, 1983)

Toomey, J.P. (ed.), *A Household account of Edward duke of York, at Hanley Castle, Worcestershire, 1409-10* (Worcestershire Historical Society, forthcoming)

Webb, J. (ed.), *A roll of the household expenses of Richard de Swinfield, Bishop of Hereford, during part of the years 1289 and 1290*, Camden Society (1854), 2 vols, II, 57, 58

Whitelock, D. (ed.), *Anglo-Saxon Wills* (Cambridge, 1930)

Registers of the bishops of Hereford, variously published by the
   Cantilupe Society and by the Canterbury and York Society

FURTHER READING

Buildings

James, D., 'An analysis of the historic fabric of late 16th-century
   and early 17th-century buildings in Ledbury, Herefordshire'
   (unpub. report for EPE Herefordshire, 2007)
Pevsner, N., *The Buildings of England: Herefordshire*
   (Harmondsworth, 1963)

Church Life

Barrow, J., 'A 12th-century bishop and literary patron: William de
   Vere', *Viator*, 18 (1987), 175-87
Bassett, S., 'Church and diocese in the West Midlands', in J. Blair and
   R. Sharpe (eds), *Pastoral Care before the Parish* (Leicester, 1992)
Binns, A., *Dedications of Monastic Houses in England and Wales
   1066-1216* (Woodbridge, 1989)
Blair, J., 'The Anglo-Saxon Church in Herefordshire', in A. Malpas *et. al.*
   (eds), *The Early Church in Herefordshire* (Leominster, 2001), 3-13
Blair, J., 'Clerical Communities and Parochial Space: the Planning
   of Urban Mother Churches in the Twelfth and Thirteenth
   Centuries', in T.R. Slater and G. Rosser (eds), *The Church in the
   Medieval Town* (Aldershot, 1998)
Brooke, C.N.L., 'The Diocese of Hereford 676-1200', *TWNFC* 48
   (1994), 23-36
Dohar, W.J., *The Black Death and Pastoral Leadership. The diocese of
   Hereford in the fourteenth century* (Philadelphia, 1995)
Hillaby, J., 'The Origins of the Diocese of Hereford', *TWNFC* 42
   (1976), 16-52
Hillaby, J., *St Katherine's Hospital, Ledbury, c.1230-1547* (Almeley,
   2003)
Keynes, S., 'Diocese and Cathedral before 1056', in G. Aylmer and
   J. Tiller (eds), *Hereford Cathedral* (2000), 3-21
King, J.W., 'Two Herefordshire Minsters', *TWNFC 48* (1995), 282-90
Morris, R., 'The Remodelling of the Hereford Aisles', *Journal of the
   British Archaeological Association*, vol. xxxvii (1974), 22
Pretty, K., 'Defining the Magonsæte', in S. Basset (ed.), *The Origins
   of Anglo-Saxon Kingdoms* (Leicester, 1989)

Farming

Rackham, O., *The History of the Countryside* (1986 and 2000)
Postan, M.M., *Essays on Medieval Agriculture and General Problems
   of the Medieval Economy* (Cambridge, 1973)

Campbell, B.M.S., *The Medieval Antecedents of English Agricultural Progress* (Aldershot, 2007)

Campbell, B.M.S., 'Land, labour and productivity trends in English seigniorial agriculture, 1208-1450', in B.M.S. Campbell and M. Overton, *Land, Labour and Livestock: historical studies in European agricultural productivity* (Manchester, 1991), 144-82

Forests, Woods and Hunting

Dyer, C., 'Woodlands and Wood Pasture in Western England', in J. Thirsk (ed.), *The English Rural Landscape* (Oxford, 2000), 97-149

Rackham, O., *Trees and Woodland in the British Landscape* (London, 1996 edn)

Cox, J. Charles, *The Royal Forests of England* (London, 1905)

Langton, J. and Jones, G., *Forests and Chases of England and Wales c.1500-c.1850* (Oxford, 2005)

J. Sheil, *Rabbits and their History* (Newton Abbot, 1971)

Landscape and Geology

Barton, N., *Ice Age Britain* (London, 2003)

Bowden, M.C.B., *The Malvern Hills: An ancient landscape* (London, 2005)

Lewis, S.G. and Maddy, D. (eds), *The Quaternary of the South Midlands and the Welsh Marches: A Field Guide* (London, 1997)

Place Names

Coates, A. and Breeze, A., *Celtic Voices, English Places: Studies of the Celtic Impact on Place-Names in England* (Stamford, 2000)

Coplestone-Crow, B., *Herefordshire Place-Names* (Oxford, 1989)

Field, J., *English Field-Names: A Dictionary* (Newton Abbott, 1972)

Gelling, M. and Cole, A., *The Landscape of Place-Names* (Stamford, 2007)

Stenton, F.M., 'The Historical Bearing of Place-Name Studies: the place of women in Anglo-Saxon Society', in D.M. Stenton (ed.), *Preparatory to Anglo-Saxon England* (Oxford, 1970), 320-1

Prehistory

Cunliffe, B., *Iron Age Communities in Britain* (5th edn, 2005)

Darvill, T., *Prehistoric Gloucestershire* (Gloucester, 1987)

Dorling, P., *The Lugg Valley, Herefordshire: Archaeology, Landscape Change and Conservation* (Hereford, 2007)

Garwood, P., *The Undiscovered Country: The Earlier Prehistory of the West Midlands* (Oxford, 2007)

Fleming, A. and Hingley, R. (eds), *Prehistoric and Roman Landscapes* (Macclesfield, 2007)

Parfitt, S.A. *et al.*, 'The earliest record of human activity in northern Europe', *Nature*, 438 (2005)

Robert, M. and Parfitt, S.A., Boxgrove: *A middle Pleistocene hominid site at Eartham Quarry, Boxgrove. West Sussex* (London, 1999)

Pollard, J. (ed.), *Prehistoric Britain* (Oxford, 2008)

Stanford, S., *Midsummer Hill: an Iron Age Hillfort on the Malverns* (Leominster, 1981)

Roman History

Frere, S.S., *Britannia* (London, 1968 edn)

McWhirr, A., *Roman Gloucestershire* (Gloucester, 1986)

Millett, M., *The Romanization of Britain: An Essay in Archaeological Interpretation* (Cambridge, 1990)

Webster, G., *Rome Against Caratacus: the Roman campaigns in Britain, AD 48-58* (London, 1987)

White, R., *Britannia Prima: Britain's Last Roman Province* (Stroud, 2007)

Trade and Town Life

Dyer, C., *Everyday Life in Medieval England* (London, 2000, edn)

Harvey, B.F., 'The aristocratic consumer in England in the long thirteenth century', in M. Prestwich, R.H. Britnell and R. Frame (eds), *Thirteenth Century England VI: proceedings of the Durham conference 1995* (Woodbridge, 1997), 17-38

Letters, S., *Online Gazetteer of Markets and Fairs in England and Wales to 1516*, available online at http://www.history.ac.uk/cmh/gaz/gazweb2.html

Lloyd, T.H., T*he English Wool Trade in the Middle Ages* (Cambridge, 1977)

Woolgar, C.M., *The Great Household in Late Medieval England* (New Haven, 1999)

Urban Topography

Beresford, M.W., *New Towns of the Middle Ages* (London, 1969)

Demidowicz, G., *Medieval Birmingham: the Borough Rentals of 1296 and 1344-5*, Dugdale Society Occasional Papers, 48 (Stratford-upon-Avon, 2008)

Slater, T.R., 'The analysis of burgages in medieval towns: three case studies from the West Midlands', *West Midlands Archaeology*, 23 (1981), 53-66

Index

All places are in Herefordshire unless otherwise stated. All buildings, institutions, streets, fields etc. are in Ledbury unless otherwise stated. References to illustrations are in italics.

Abbot's Lodge, formerly vicarage, 52-4, Panel 4, 138
Acres, Jean de, m. Gilbert de Clare, 113
Acton Beauchamp (Worcs.), 33-4
Adam the goldsmith, 83
agriculture, 3, 8, 99, 102-9
Aigueblanche: Aymo de, portionary of Ledbury,
    118; James de, portionary of Ledbury, 43, 118;
    John de, portionary of Ledbury, 42, 107, 118-20,
    122, 125; Peter de, bishop of Hereford, 42, 44,
    118, 119
Alderton, Hugh of, Panel 5
Alfred, vicar of Ledbury, 33
Aluric, chaplain, 44
Aluric, reeve of Ledbury, 44
Aluric, son of Aluric the chaplain, 47
Amedus, count of Savoy, 118
Anne, Nicholas de, portionary of Ledbury, 43
arable, 99, 101, 104, 106-8
archaeology, 5-11, 15, 19, 22, 51-2, 55, 62, 68, Panel 4
Archenfield, 29
Ariconium, 29
Ashperton, 2, 19-20, 21, 44; Walsopthorne in, 22
assize of bread and ale, 73, 85-6
Athelstan, bishop of Hereford, 30, 31
Audley, Edmund, bishop of Hereford, 149; Ela de,
    m. James de Perrers, Panel 6; Katherine de,
    Panel 6, 125; Nicholas de, Panel 6
Avenbury, Giles de, 118
Aylton, 2, 31, 34, 35, 136

Bagburrow, probably in Mathon, 31, 34, 94, 97
bailiffs, 73-4, 78, 101
Baker, Richard, 144; see also Elton, John
Baldwin, John, 144; Thomas, 144
Barret, Edward, 83
barrows (burial mounds), 1, 7-9, 21-2
Baskerville, Edward, 150
Basset, Hugh, 76
Baynham, John, 114
beans, 108
Beccles (Suffolk), 65
Becket, Thomas, archbishop of Canterbury, 45

Belgium, 7
Beneas, Richard, 128, Panel 7
Benyse (Bennys), Edward (d. c.1556), Panel 7;
    Edward (fl. 1584), 90
Berde, Richard, 92; William, 82; family, 108
Bethune, Robert de, bishop of Hereford, 50, 88
Beyvin, Adam, 47
Bicknor, Welsh, 30
Biddulph, John, 75, Panel 6
Birchore, John, 129
Birmingham, 65
Bishop Street, see Bye Street
Bishops Castle (Salop.), 85
bishop's manor house, hall or palace, 32, 45, 49,
    53-5, 69
'Bishop's Palace', Bye Street, 67, 137
Black Death, 72, 92, 104
Black Mountains, 7
Blount, James, bailiff of Ledbury, 74; John, 146;
    Thomas, 54, Panel 6, 148
Bodenham, 7
Bonde, James, 74-5
Boniface VIII, pope, 42
Boniface IX, pope, 135
Booth Hall or Bothall, 59, 74-5
Bosbury, 2, 31, 34, 42, 84, 91-2, 94, 96, 102, 138,
    145-6, 146, 152
Bowyer, William, 129
Braban, Thomas, 133
Bracy, Edmund, 109; John, 79; Martin, 108; Thomas
    (d. 1485), 109; Thomas (fl. 1535), 79
Bradford, John, 144
Bradlow Knoll, 1, 8, 10, 18, 21, 49
Bradsole (Kent), 44
Braose, Giles de, bishop of Hereford, 43; Philip de,
    portionary of Ledbury, 42
Bristol, 88
British Camp (Herefordshire Beacon), in Colwall, 2,
    3, 5, Panel 1, 14, 15, 18, 114, 153
Broke, John, Panel 7
Bromsberrow (Glos.), 11
Bromyard, 29-32, 49, 54, 61, 86, 116, 145

Buckinghamshire, 144

Burford (Oxon.), 51

Butcher Row or Middle Row, *52*, 60, 83, 90, *see also* Shop Row

Butterfield, Swithun, Panel 5, 104

Bye Street, formerly Bishop Street, 32, 52, 58, *59*, 60-1, 65, *66*, 67, 82

Bytham river, 2

Calhulle, John de, 107

Callewe, William, 125, *128*, 129

Calverparruc (Calves Close), 107

Cambridge, 44

Cantilupe, Thomas, bishop of Hereford, 42-3, *45*, 45, 84, 113, Panel 6

Capella, Richard de, bishop of Hereford, 45

Caperun or Capron, Alice, 82; Walter, 85; William, 82

Cardiff, 86

Carew, 126

Carewe, Hugh, 107

Carwy, Hugh, portionary of Ledbury, 119

Castle Combe (Wilts.), 153

cattle market, 66-8

Chaloner, Warin le, 82

charcoal, 111

Chester, 60

Chichester (Sussex), 118

church (St Peter or St Peter and St Paul, later St Michael), 1, 4, 29-46, *36*, *37*, *39*, 49, 52, *53*, 76-7, 115-32, *116*, *119*, *122*, *123*, 134, 136, Panel 7, 148; altars, 123-4, 127, Panel 7; architecture, 35-8, 119, 122, 124-5, 129-30; chantries, 127-9, 144-6; chapels, 122-5, Panel 7; chaplains, 43-4, 131-2; lights, 43, 127; memorials in, 125-8; rectors or portionaries of, 33-5, 38, 42, 44, 73, 115-19, 129, 139; vicars of, 33-5, 38, 43-4, 116, 118, 129

Church End, 129

Church Lane, *56*, 57-8, 67, 79, 82, 108, 138-9, 148

Church Street, formerly Back Lane, *56*, 57-8, *59*, 65, 79

churchyard, 32, 53-5, 57-8

Cirencester (Glos.), 21

Clare, Gilbert de, earl of Gloucester, 113

clothing trade, 79, 82, *see also* weavers

Cobbler, Hugh the, 76

Cobet, John, Panel 5

Coddington, 2, 34, 84, *85*, 94, 97, 116, 144; Oyster Hill, 1

Colemer, Richard de, 76

Collyer, William, 74

Colwall, 1, *2*, *34*, 35, 94, 96-7, 99, 102, 113; Colwall

Stone, *8*

Concoreto, Itherius, portionary of Ledbury, 118

Conygree Wood, 49, 53, 114

Cooper, Edward, 150

Coren, Hugh, portionary of Ledbury, 118

Cornwall, 39

Cotswolds, 7

courts, 73-5, 99-100, 103, 140

Court-y-Park or Parkhold, 34, 100; chapel of St James, 144

Coventry (Warws.), 76, 137

Cradley, 1, 31, 34, 94-9; Ridgeway, 10

Cradley Brook, 1

Credenhill, *45*

Credenhill fort, Panel 1

crime, 76-8

Croft Ambrey, 19

Crompe, Maiota, 119

crops, *see* beans, flax, hemp, oats, peas, rye, wheat

Dean, Forest of (Glos.), 21, 87-8, 111-12

deer, 112-13

Dingwood park, 113

Dingwood Park Farm, 23-4

Dobunni, Iron-Age kingdom, 19

Dog Hill, 49, 53, *57*

Dog Hill wood, *50*

Domesday Book, 29-30, 49, 93-9, 109-10

domestic architecture, 75, *132*, *133*, *134*, 136, *138*, 148

Donnington, Peter of, 47

Donnington, 2, 10, *11*, 17-19, *20*, 34-5, 94-5, 98, 136; Great Heath, 9-10

Dore Abbey, *79*, *84*

Dorset, *7*

Dorstone Hill, 6

Droitwich (Worcs.), 16, 95, 99

Dublin (Ireland), 118

Dubricius, bishop, 21

Dunbridge, Gilbert of, 103; Hugh, 144

Duncomb, John, 4

Durham, 91

dykes, *22*, *23*, 24

Dymock (Glos.), 2, *18*, 19, 22-3, 24, 149; Callow Farm, 24

earthworks, 10-11, *see also* hill forts, Shire Ditch

Eastnor, 2, *18*, 34, 43, 46, 76, 94-5, 98, 99-100, 102, 105, 109, 112-13, *116*, 129, 145-6; Bronsil, 22, 112; Dead Woman's Thorn, 8; Eastnor Park, 6, *112*; Glynch Brook, 3, 8, 109; Hollybush Hill, 9, 15, 113; Howlers' Heath, 18; Sheep Hill, 9; *see also* Midsummer Hill fort

Edward I, 113

Edward II, 87, Panel 6

Edward III, 91

Edward, duke of York (d. 1415), 82, 87, 91

Ekeney, Edmund, 79

Elton, Anne, m. Richard Willison, *151*, 152; Edward,
vicar of Ledbury, 153; John (*alias* Baker), 144,
149, 153; William, 152

Elured (Alured) the reeve, 104

enclosure (of common fields), 104, *106*, 107

England, king of, 50, 59, 86, 91, 118; *see also* Edward
I, Edward II, Harold, Henry III, Henry VIII,
Stephen, William I

Erdesley, Philip de, 60

Ergyng, British kingdom, 29-30

Eseger, Adam, canon of Hereford, 135; Gilbert, 101;
Nicholas, 135; Thomas, 135; William (fl. 1312,
1337), 48, 90-2; William (fl. 1361) and Juliana
his wife, 135

Essex, 145

Ewenet, John, 129

Exeter (Devon), 44

fairs, 75, 88-90, 92

Fairtree, 105

Falconer (Fauconer), Richard le, 78, 101

Feathers Hotel, 52, 60, 74, *75*

Fetberton, Henry son of Hugh, 77

fields, 10, 14, 20-1, 24, 67

Filaby, Adam de, portionary of Ledbury, 42

flax, 108

Foliot, Gilbert, bishop of Hereford and London, 30,
84; Hugh, bishop of Hereford, 32, 39, 42, 45, *47*,
135, 149; Robert, bishop of Hereford, 30, 68;
Thomas, portionary of Ledbury, 42

Folur, William le, 79

food and drink trades, 83-6

Foreign of Ledbury, 51, 54, 63, 73, 76, 105, 109, 116;
Wymondestr, 83

Forester, Gilbert le, and Agnes his wife, 78

Fortrich, Roger, 76

Fowler, Griffith or Griffin, 146

Fox, Edward, bishop of Hereford, 74

Frith, Alured of the, 103

Frith Farm, 6, 106

Frith Wood, 8, 10-11, 49, *105*, 106, 109, *110*,
112

Frome Valley, 2, 19, 21-2

Frome, Bishops, 31, *34*, 84, 102

Frome, Canon, 19, *34*

Frome, Castle, *34*

fullers, 79

Furches, Robert, bailiff of Ledbury, 73

gallows, 73

Gately, Thomas, 144

Geldepirye, Robert de la, 105

Geoffrey the reeve, 73

geology, 2, 5

Gersant, John, 43, 46

Gibbs, J., Panel 6

Gilbert, chaplain, 44

Gilbert, John, bishop of Hereford, 116, 133

Gloucester, 29, 44, 49, 63, 86, 88, 91, 154

Gloucester, earl of, *see* Clare

Gloucestershire, 19, 91

Glover, Alditha, 82; Richard, 74-5, 110

Glyndwr, Owain, 76

Goldhull, Robert de, 109; William de, 109

Goldsmith, Geoffrey, 82

Grandison, Blanche, *see* Mortimer; John, bishop of
Exeter, 44; William, 125

Green Lane, *50*, 63

Grendon Warren, 146

Grinall, Richard, 75

Groves End, 6

Gruffyyd ap Maredudd, 24

Gruys, Alice, 83-4

Haffield (Donnington, formerly Ledbury), 1, *7*,
8, 10, 23, 34, 84, 108, 110; Haffield House, 17;
Haffield Park, *22*

Haffield Camp, 17, *18*, *22*, 24

Hampton Bishop, 102

Hampton Shelwyk, 74

Hanley Castle (Worcs.) 87-8, 91

Hanwell (Mdx.), 35

Harford, John, 145, *152*; Richard, 152

Harold, earl and later king, 31, 94, 97

Hartpury (Glos.), 147

Hasele, John de la, 90

Hazle, 73, 90, 94-5, 97-9, 100, 109, 126, Panel 6

Hellpitt Lane, 54

hemp, 108

Henry III, 87-9

Henry VIII, 141

Henry, master of St Katherine's hospital, 48

Henry, vicar of Ledbury, 129, 132

Herdson, Henry, 144

Hereford, 7, 29, 49, 59, 76, *84*, *86*, 88-9, 91, 99,
111, 135, 149-50, 144, 149, 154; Drybridge
House, *82*; Hay of, 112; St Ethelbert's fair, 88; St
Ethelbert's hospital, 149; St Guthlac's, 30

Hereford, bishops of, 30-2, 35, 38, 42, 46, 59,
73-4, 76, Panel 5, 83, 85-6, 90, 91, 93, 97-9,
108, 111, 113, 115-19, 132, 140, 148; *see
also* Aigueblanche, Peter; Audley, Edmund;
Bethune; Braose, Giles; Cantilupe; Foliot, Hugh;

Maidstone; Swinfield, Richard; Trefnant
Hereford cathedral, 30, *38*, 42, 43, *77*, *91*, 93, *113*, 116, *117*, 119, 123, 125, *130*, *131*, Panel 7
Hereford Museum, *8*
Hereford, Roger earl of, 88
Herefordshire Beacon, *see* British Camp
High Cross *see* Upper Cross
High Street, formerly Middle Town, 25, 43, 53, 56, 58, *59*, 60-1, 64-6, 68-9, 74
Highbridge Farm, 8
Highwood (Glos.), *18*
Hill, Edward, vicar of Ledbury (fl. 1516), 130; Edward (fl. 1616), 55
Hill Farm, 135
hill forts, 1, 3, 6, 7, 11-18, Panel 1; *see also* British Camp, Croft Ambrey, Haffield Camp, Kilbury Camp, Midsummer Hill, Wall Hills
Hole meadow, 46
Homend, 60-1, *62*, 63-7, 69, 82, *138*
Homme, John de, 60
Hooper, John, bishop of Gloucester, 147
Hop, John le and Joan his wife, 129
Hope Bagot (Salop.), 145
Horse Lane *see* Worcester Road
Hospital Wood, Dunbridge, 135
Hunt, Robert, 129
Hutchins, John, 129

industry, 21, 67, 79-85
Ivington Camp, Leominster, Panel 1

Jenkins, John, composer, Panel 6
Joce, Margery daughter of Osbert, 45
Johnson, John, 144

Katherine of Alexandria, saint, 44, 125
Kempley (Glos.), 32
Kenchester, 21
Keyes, Giles, Panel 7
Kilbury Camp, *1*, *2*, 18
Kilpeck, *38*
King, John, 74; William, 83
Kingsholm (Glos.), 19
Kington, 86
Kintbury (Berks.), 33
Knapp Lane, 63-4
Knight, John, bailiff of Ledbury, 78
Knottsford, Mr, 74
Kylling, Thomas, 146

Lacy, Walter de, 32
Leadon, Matilda de, 103
Leadon river, 1-3, 9, 20-2, 24-5, 32, 49, 58, 67, 91, 94

Leadon valley, 1, 6-7, 17, 21, 24, Panel 2, 49, 98, 104, 109
leather working, 82
Ledbury Park, 52, 55, 64
Ledon, 73
Leominster, 7, 30-1, 65, 72, 86-7, 89, 108, 123, 151; *see also* Ivington Camp
Lichfield (Staffs.), 44, 76, 123, 146
Lincoln, 91
Lincolnshire, 144
Linden House, 69
Little Harlot, William le, 76
Llandaff (Cardiff), 29
Llandovery (Carmarthen), Panel 6
local government, 140-1; *see also* bailiffs, reeves
London, 44, 79, 86, 91, 112, 118, Panel 7, 144; bishop of, *see* Foliot, Gilbert
Long, Richard le, 108
Longchamp, Geoffrey de and Isabel his wife, 32
Longmore Field, 129
Lorde, John, 150
Lorymer, Thomas, bailiff of Ledbury, 59, 74, 92, 104, 137
Lower Cross, 32, 53, 58, 63, 67
Lower Hall, 30, *32*, 33, 52, 54, *57*, 73, 100, 108, 115-16, 129, 138, 149, 153
Ludlow, 63, 72, 123
Lugg, river, 7, 22, 102, 106
Lydbury North (Salop.), 30
Lymesey, Peter de, Panel 6
Lyngyn, John, 78

Mabel, maid to Katherine Audley, Panel 6
Mabel's Furlong, 109
Madley, *151*
Magonsæte, 30-1
Maiden Castle (Dorchester, Dorset), Panel 1
Maidstone, Ralph of, bishop of Hereford, 39
Mainstone, *34*
Malbon, Hamnet, vicar of Ledbury, 130
Malvern, John, 135
Malvern (Worcs.), 29, 77
Malvern Chace, 113
Malvern Hills, 1-3, 5-7, 10, 14-15, 17, 24, 28-9, 31, 49, 68, 86, 94, 106, 113
Malvern, Little (Worcs.), 49
Marcle, Little, 31, *34*, 135; Laddin Farm, 8
Marcle, Much, 2, *18*, 31, *34*; Huntley's Farm, 21-2; *see also* Oldbury Camp
Marcle Ridge, 1-2, 6
Marden, 22, 93, 123
Mareschal, William, 77
Market House or Hall, *52*, *56*, 58, *89*

market place, 55, 57-8, *59*, 60-2, 65, 82-3
markets, 21, 32, 50, 75, 86, 88-91; *see also* cattle market
Marley Hall, 21
Mary, queen of England, 118
Mary Magdalene, saint, 44
Mary the Virgin, saint, 44
Mascall, Robert, bishop of Hereford, 74
Masefield, John, poet, 1, 5, 112
Massington, 73, 100, 105, 114
Massington Farm, 8
Mathon, 1, 2, 9, 31, *34*; Hoe Farm, 5; South End Farm, 9
Mathon basin, 104
Mathon river (prehistoric), 2-3
Maund, district, 30
meadow, 98-9, 101, 107, 109
Meeke, Christopher, 144
Melksop, Walter, 76
Mercer, Oldred le, 79
mercers, 79
Mercia, Anglo-Saxon kingdom, 22, 30, 31
Merewalh, king, 30
Messenger, *see* Musmare
metal working, 82-3
Middle Row, *see* Butcher Row, Shop Row
Middle Town, *see* High Street
Middleton, Gilbert, portionary of Ledbury, 118
Midsummer Hill fort (Eastnor), 6, 10-11, Panel 1, 14-16, *17*, 17
mills, 47, 49, 83, 96, 98
Mitchell, 105, 129, 146
Monmouth (Gwent), 86
Monnow, river, 30
Montgomery (Powys), 90
More, Hugh de la, 103
Moreb, Robert, 83
Morebath (Devon), 141
Morefield, 146
Mortimer, Blanche, Lady Grandison, 126; Roger, of Wigmore, 76; Roger (nephew of last), 76
Morton, Walter, 114
Munsley, 2, 31, *34*, 35
Musmare or Messenger, William, vicar of Ledbury, 29, Panel 7

Nantwich (Cheshire), 16
Napper, Nicholas, 79
Nash, John atte and Emma his wife, 107; Lewis, 125, Panel 7
Netherton, 47, 105
New House, 52, 55
New Mills, *9*
New Street, 45, 58, 60-1, 64-6, *68*, 69, 82, 83, 108-9

Newent (Glos.), 44, 86
Northampton, 118
Northinton (Netherton), Roger of, and Alice his wife, 46
Northleach (Glos.), 90
Norton, William de and Alice his wife, 108
Norway, 118

oats, 91, 107-9
Ockeridge, William of, 46, 106, 134, 149
Ockeridge, 46, 105
Old Grammar School, 57, 58, 139, 147, *148*
Oldbury Camp (Much Marcle), 18
Orleton, Adam de, bishop of Hereford, 76
Orlham Farm, 135
Ortolis, Bernard de, portionary of Ledbury, 118
Owen, Humphrey, 75
Oxford, John of, 76
Oxford, Panel 7
Oxford University, 43, 130, 150
Oxfordshire, 19, 43

Pantall, Thomas, 75
Parc, le, 110
parish (or *parochia*), 31, 34
Parker, John, portionary of Ledbury, 115
Parkhold *see* Court-y-Park
Parminter, Geoffrey, 82
pasture, 99, 101, 108-9
Pauncefoot, Alice, 129; Grimbald, 100; Grimbauld, 126
peas, 107-8
Pede, Richard, portionary of Ledbury, 118-19
Pembridge, 87
Pembroke, earl of, 88
Perrers, James de, Panel 6
Peruzzi (Italian financiers), 91
Pesebrugge, 100
Piers Ploughman, 114
Pixley, 2, 31, 34, *35*, 136
place-name, 29, 33
Playstow, 105
Polter, Geoffrey le, 83
population, 31, 150
Porter, John, 145
Potter, John, Panel 7, 145
pottery, *9*, 15, *17*, 19-21, 22, 25, 52, 55, 69, Panel 4
Prato, John de, 124
Preece (Prys), Robert, portionary of Ledbury, 119, *119*, 125, 133
Prestbury (Glos.), 86, 87
Preston, John de, 45
Preston (Glos.), 147

Priory, The, 52, 55

prison, 73

Prophete, John, portionary of Ledbury, 118, *118*

Putley, 2, 10, *18*, 19, *124*

Pycchyll, Elizabeth, Panel 7

Pyon, Canon, 24

rabbits, 113-14

Radegund, saint, *44*

Radlow hundred, 31, 35, 73, 96

Reading (Berks.), 86-7, 89

Red Book, The, Panel 5

Redmarley (Worcs.), 144

reeves, 73, 101, 104; *see also* Aluric

Reformation, the, 141-7

rents: fish, 101-2; honey, 23-4, 101-2

Reve, Thomas, 144

Richard II, 118

Richard the deacon, 43

Richard, John ap, portionary of Ledbury, 118-19

Ringwood (Hants.), *118*

roads, 19-21, 29, 49

Robert, vicar of Ledbury, 33

Robert the vine dresser, 84

Robinson, Sylvia, 149

Roger, chaplain, 44

Roger, vicar of Ledbury, 43

Rome (Italy), 118

Romsey (Hants.), 118

Ross-on-Wye, 7, 19, 54, 65, 68, 83, 86, 88, 114

Rotarius, Robert, 82

Royal Oak Hotel, 64

Ruddoc, Philip, 46

Ryan, Robert, 74

rye, 107

St Blaise's chapel, 116

St Briavels (Glos.), 88

St Katherine's Hospital, 4, 32, 39, 42, 44, *46*, *48*, 55, 64, 66, 68, 100, 104, 106, 108, 115, 117-18, 125, 127, 129, 134-6, 138, 140, 149-50; chapel, 74, 99, *133*, 135, 136, 140; lights in, 43, 47, 52; master of, 73, 138; Master's House, *52*, *132*, *134*

St Peter, *38*

Salisbury (Wilts.), 118

salt trade, 16, 95

Sapey, Lower (Worcs.), 145

Scandinavia, *7*, 8

school, 147-9

Scrope, Anne, m. John Harford, 153; John, 153

settlement, early, 6-11, Panel 1, 15, 17, Panel 2, 19-22, 24-5, 29, 31, 54

Severn, river, 7, 88, 91

Severn river valley, 17-19

sheep, 8, *90*, 109

Shire Ditch, 113

Shop Row or Middle Row, 58-60

Shropshire, 30, 76, 112, 144

Siddington, formerly Suthinton, 105

Simon the clerk, 45

Skinner, Edward, 90

Skyppe, Alice, m. John Willison, 152; John, bishop of Hereford, 152; family, 152

Smith, Alice, 119; Richard, vicar of Ledbury, 130; Vincent son of Thomas, 76

Smythe, John, chaplain, 133

Soller, John, 100

Somerset, 19

Southend (street), 55, 60-1, 63, 64, 68-9, Panel 5, 82

Sparcheford, Richard, 74

Staffordshire, 146

Stanbury, John, bishop of Hereford, 118

Staniale, Walter le, 77

Staplow, 10, 21

Staunton-on-Wye, 150

Stephen, king of England, 88

Stephen (fl. 1086), 93

Stoke, John, 148

Stoke Edith, 31, 34, 144

Stores Brook, Panel 2

Stourbridge (Cambs.), 91

Stratford-upon-Avon (Warws.), 51

Street, Adam de, 47; Street, John de la, 77

street plan, 53-69, 137

Stretton Grandison, 19, 21

Sucley, William, Panel 7

Sussex, 111, 144

Suthinton, Osbert de, 109

Sutton St Michael, 22

Sutton Walls (Sutton), 19

Sweden, 118

Swinfield, John, portionary of Ledbury, *117*; Richard, bishop of Hereford, 45, Panel 5, 82, 84, 86, 91, 109, 111-13, *117*, Panel 6

Syrecock, John, 77; William, 77

Tailor, John, 82

tailors, 82

Talbot, Lady, 125

Tarrington, 31, 34

Taskere, Adam le, 76

Taylor, Giles, 75; William, Panel 7

Tedstone Wafer, 145

Teme river, 1

Tewkesbury (Glos.), 86, 88, 91, 123

Tharcenor, Richard, 82
Thelsford (Warws.), 44
Thomas the bailiff, 73
Thony, John, 128
timber, 110-11
tithe, 35, 115-16
Tosny, Ralph de, 93
town council buildings (No. 1 Church Lane), 138, *139*
travel and transport, 86-7
Trefnant, John, bishop of Hereford, 113, 128
Tretire, *83*
Tupsley, 74
Tybbynge Sparowhawke, 146
Tyler, Joan, 133
Tyrrell's Frith, 110

Unet, Richard, 79
Upper Cross, High Cross or Top Cross, 58, 63-4, 68
Upper Hall, 30, *32*, 33, 42, *52*, 54, 73, 100, 108-9, 115-18, 138
Upton Bishop, 114
Upton-on-Severn (Worcs.), 86, 88, 91
Urban V, pope, 125
Usk (Gwent), 44, 88

Vere, William de, bishop of Hereford, 38
vineyard, 84, 85, 99

Walerand the chaplain, 44
Wales, 6, 76, 87, 90, Panel 6
Walinter, Obayn de, Panel 5
Wall Hills fort, 2, 6, Panel 1, 14, *16*, *17*, *18*, 19, 21, 24, *25*, Panel 2, 29, 153
Wall Hills vill, 73, 105, 107, 110
wall paintings, 139, *140*
Waller, David, portionary of Ledbury, 115
Walsued, Matilda of, 103; Roger son of Alice of, 103
Waltham Abbey (Essex), 38
Walwyn, Richard, 78
Warham, 150
Warwickshire, 99, 144
water courses and streams, 25, 32, 49, 53-4, 57-8, 66, 67, 79, 82, 108
weavers, 68, 79, 82
Webb, Adam, 82
Webbe, Henry le, 79; John le, 79; William,

portionary of Ledbury, 140
Wellecroft, 107
Wellington, Juliana daughter of Alan of, 47
Wellington Heath, 2, 10, *18*
Wellington vill, 73, 76, 100, 105
Wells (Somerset), 118
Wenlock, Much (Salop.), 30
Weobley, 86, 123
Westcote (Glos.), 150
Weston Beggard, 32
Weston-under-Penyard, 29
Wetecroft, 107
wheat, 4, 91, 107-8
wheelwrights, 82
Wheler (Weler), Richard, 146, 147-8
Wheolare, Walter, 82
Whitbourne, 102-3
Wigmore, 76, 86, 91
William I, 31
William the chaplain, 76
William, vicar of Ledbury, Panel 6
Willison, John, 152; Richard, 145, 152
Wiltshire, 19
Winsters Elms Copse, 31
Winstree hundred, 31, 93-4, 96-8
Wolputtor, Matilda of, Panel 5
Wood, Reynold of the, Panel 5
wood working, 82-3
woodland, 99, 106, 109-14
wool, 79, 90-1
Woolhope, *111*, 144
Woolhope Dome hills, 19
Worcester, 29, 51, 57, 86, 88, 91, 97, 135, 153
Worcester Road, formerly Horse Lane, 54-6, 58, 64, 68
Worcester, Nicholas of, 60
Worcestershire, 19, 29, 49, 91, 99, 112, 144-5
Wordsworth, William, poet, Panel 6
works, agricultural, 102-4
Wulfgeat, landowner, 30
Wycherley, Richard, 135-7
Wye, river, 7, 21, 24, 88, 91, 106
Wynyard, William, 60
Wyte, Richard le, 107

Yarkhill, 32
York, duke of, *see* Edward
Yorkshire, *7*

Picture Credits

The authors and publishers wish to thank the following for permission to reproduce their material. Any infringement of copyright is entirely accidental: every care has been taken to contact or trace all copyright owners. We would be pleased to correct in future editions any errors or omissions brought to our attention. References are to page numbers except where stated.

E.T. Beaumant, 118
British Library, 78, 79, 83 (Fig. 50)
Butler and Hegarty Architects, 132, 134
Clwyd-Powys Archaeological Trust (Chris Musson), 20
T. Dingley, 119
English Heritage (NMR), 15, 16, 137, 122 (Fig. 79), 136 (Fig. 93); (Mike Hesketh-Roberts), 35, 37, 39, 41 (Fig. B), 45, 46, 48, 57, 68, 89, 122 (Fig. 78), 123, 124, 126, 127 (Fig. 84), 128, 130 (Fig. 87), 133; (Peter Williams), 50, 66
Hereford Cathedral Library; Dean and Chapter of Hereford and the Hereford Mappa Mundi Trust, 30, 38 (Fig. 27), 77, 91, 113, 117 (Fig. 74), 130 (Fig. 86), 131, 140, 143
Hereford Museum and Art Gallery, 6, 8 (Fig. 6), 9, 17 (Fig. 13), 82, 83 (Fig. 49), 84 (Fig. 52), 86; (Portable Antiquities Scheme), 7
Herefordshire Archaeology, x, 3, 8 (Fig. 7), 13, 14, 22, 25, 27, 53, 56, 59, 70 (Fig. B)
Herefordshire Archive Service, 32, 62, 80, 81, 98, 101, 103, 106, 111, 112, 120, 141, 143, 145
Duncan James, 75, 139, 148
Jesus College Cambridge, 44
Last Refuge Ltd (www.lastrefuge.co.uk), 12
Ledbury and District Civic Society: Butcher Row House Museum, 121
Malvern Hills Conservators, 26
Robin Mence (www.ryelandsheep.co.uk), 90
Denis Savage, 85
University of London, 36 (RCHME Herefordshire II – Ledbury Monument 1), 38 (Fig. 26), 47, 84 (Fig. 51), 94-5, 105, 115, 116, 117 (Fig. 73), 127 (Fig. 83), 135, 138, 146, 151, 152; (Ben Pardoe) 110, (Philip Weaver), 41 (Fig. C), 70 (Fig. A); (Rebecca Lane), 40
Kate Wilks, 64
Woolhope Naturalists Field Club (Chris Musson), 17 (Fig. 14)

The following maps were drawn by Cath D'Alton Figs 2, 15, 22, 35, Panel 4 (Fig. C), 55, 60 © University of London.
The following maps were redrawn by Cath D'Alton, based on maps supplied by Herefordshire Archaeology, Figs 9, 18 (based on OS 1st Edition).